SHAH
ABBAS

David Blow studied History at Cambridge and Persian at SOAS, was Assistant Director of the British Institute of Persian Studies in Tehran 1968–9 and worked for the BBC Persian Service 1969–71, broadcasting in Persian. He went on to work in publishing and for the BBC World Service, where he was correspondent in Berlin and Vienna. He is the Editor of *Persia: Through Writers' Eyes*, a collection of mainly European writings about Iran.

'This is a lively, well-written biography that is sure to keep the reader engaged . . . strikes the right balance between the anecdotal and the analytical'

Rudi Matthee, Professor of Middle Eastern History,
University of Delaware

'The subject of Shah Abbas is fascinating and important. Moreover the book will fill a very large gap, moving beyond an ordinary biography to reflect recent scholarship.'

Gene Garthwaite, Jane and Raphael Bernstein Professor,
Dartmouth College

Praise for *Persia: Through Writers' Eyes*:

'lucid and well-informed . . . This is a worthwhile, enjoyable and instructive book.'

David Morgan, *Times Literary Supplement*

SHAH ABBAS

The Ruthless King Who Became an Iranian Legend

DAVID BLOW

I.B. TAURIS

LONDON · NEW YORK

For my wife, Laurence,
and my children,
John and Lucy

Published in 2009 by I.B.Tauris & Co. Ltd; reprinted 2014
6 Salem Road, London W2 4BU
175 Fifth Avenue, New York NY 10010
www.ibtauris.com

ISBN: 978 1 84511 989 8

A full CIP record for this book is available from the British Library
A full CIP record is available from the Library of Congress

Library of Congress Catalog Card Number: available

Typeset in Sabon by Ellipsis Books Limited, Glasgow

Contents

List of Illustrations

Black and White Section (between pages 178 and 179)

1. Shah Abbas receiving the Moghul ambassador, Khan Alam. Painting by the Moghul artist Bishan Das, c.1619. Courtesy of Sotheby's Picture Library.

2. Fritware tile panel, which originally covered the lower part of a wall, probably in a palace in Isfahan. Period of Shah Abbas. © Victoria and Albert Museum, London.

3. Shah Abbas with a gun. Contemporary Safavid painting from an eighteenth-century Moghul Album. © Christie's Images Ltd, 1995

4. Drawing of a calligrapher by Riza Abbasi, Isfahan, c.1600. The shah's royal seal is at the bottom right-hand corner. © The Trustees of the British Museum.

5. Meidan-e Shah (the Royal Square) in Isfahan, now renamed Meidan-e Imam. The dome of the Sheikh Lutfallah Mosque is on the left and the portal and minarets of the Royal Mosque, the Masjid-e Shah, now renamed the Masjid-e Imam, can be seen at the far end of the square. Photograph taken by the author in 1964.

6. The interior of the Royal Mosque in Isfahan. Photograph taken by the author in 1964.

7. A sample of nastaliq script for collection in an album by the Iranian calligrapher, Abd al-Rashid Daylami (d.1670). He emigrated to India, where he held high office at the Moghul court, after his uncle, the calligrapher Mir Imad Qazvini, was murdered on the orders of Shah Abbas. © The Trustees of the British Museum.

8. Portrait of a European, probably by Riza Abbasi. Gouache heightened with gold on paper. © Christie's Images Ltd, 1995.

9. A falconer by Riza Abbasi, late sixteenth century. © The Trustees of the British Museum.

10. Sir Robert Sherley (1581–1628) in Persian costume by Sir Anthony van Dyck (1599–1641), Petworth House, The Egremont Collection (acquired in lieu of tax by H.M.Treasury in 1957 and subsequently transferred to The National Trust). © NTPL/Derrick E. Witty.

11. The Allahvirdi Khan Bridge over the Zayandeh River in Isfahan. The river is virtually dry in the summer. Photograph taken by the author in 1964.

12. One of the pigeon towers outside Isfahan. The pigeon dung was used as fertiliser. There were more than 3,500 such towers around the city in Safavid times. Photograph taken by the author in 1964.

13. Shah Abbas portrayed on a late nineteenth-century 'Mohtashem' rug from Kashan in central Iran. Courtesy of Sotheby's Picture Library.

Preface

My interest in Shah Abbas began over forty years ago when, as a young man just down from university, I spent the best part of a year in his capital of Isfahan. Its population at that time, in the early 1960s, was barely what it had been in Abbas's day and considerably less than it became later in the seventeenth century, when it is generally thought to have amounted to about 600,000, which made it one of the most populous cities in the world. It only reached this level again in the 1970s, although since then it has greatly surpassed it. But despite many changes, it is still possible to walk through the great central square Shah Abbas created and feel something of his presence and of the world he lived in.

This book addresses the general reader about a key figure and a crucial period in the history of Iran – a country of great importance in the world then as now. It owes much to an immense amount of scholarly work that has been done with increasing momentum over the past three or four decades. This has enormously enlarged our understanding not only of the reign of Shah Abbas, but of the whole Safavid period.

My main original Iranian source has been the *Tarikh-e Alam-Ara-ye Abbasi*, or 'The World-Adorning History of Shah Abbas', which was written by his official chronicler, Iskandar Beg Munshi (c.1560–c.1632), and covers the whole of Abbas's reign. Iskandar Beg was a chancery scribe, as the designation *munshi* indicates, was often with Abbas, including when the shah was on campaign, and was therefore an eyewitness of much that he recounts. Despite its 'official' nature, his very full chronicle remains by far the most important single Iranian source. Iskandar Beg also has one of the main qualities of a genuine historian, in that he attempts to understand the causes of events and why people acted as they did. Even those English-speakers who are able to read Persian must be grateful to Professor Roger Savory for making this great chronicle available in an English translation.

But it is the European sources that really make it possible to write a biography of Shah Abbas. Few Europeans visited Iran before his reign. But from then until the fall of the Safavid Empire in 1722, for reasons that will be explained, there was a steady stream of European visitors. A number of them, who had access to the court and to the shah himself, left valuable accounts of their experiences. But none of the Safavid rulers is more richly and intimately described, his actions and policies more thoroughly related and examined, than Shah Abbas. These European accounts make it possible to get a much fuller picture of Abbas than of any Iranian ruler before him. They reveal how he behaved and what he said in a whole variety of situations – whether at a banquet in one of his palaces, relaxing in an Isfahan coffee-house late at night, preparing a barbecue with Roman Catholic friars, or engaging in a public exchange of words with an envoy of the Ottoman sultan, to name just a few. They also provide a huge amount of information about almost every aspect of life in Safavid Iran that is not to be found in the contemporary Iranian chronicles. Although I have drawn mainly on the accounts of Europeans who visited Iran during the reign of Shah Abbas, I have also made use of accounts from the later Safavid period where they provide additional relevant information.

For help in writing this book I should like in particular to thank my editor at I.B.Tauris, Liz Friend-Smith, for her constant enthusiasm and encouragement, as well as for her helpful comments on the work in progress, John Gurney and Sandy Morton for their readiness in answering whatever questions I put to them, Antony Tyler for valuable criticism of early drafts of some of the chapters in the book, and the staff of the library of the School of Oriental and African Studies, the British Library and the London Library. But as it is always customary and correct to say, the responsibility for what I have written is mine alone.

David Blow

Introduction

Shah Abbas is the outstanding enlightened despot of Iran. He overcame divisive feudal forces that were tearing the country apart and imposed a strong centralised monarchy. He revived a collapsing economy by providing security, a stable currency and a hugely improved economic infrastructure. For strategic and commercial reasons, but also because he was outward-looking and free of religious bigotry, he encouraged extensive relations with Christian Europe. He promoted the visual arts and created a suitably grand setting for his rule in his magnificent new capital of Isfahan. He also took on the foremost military power of the time, the Ottoman Empire, and defeated it.

Abbas's achievements fully justify the epithet of 'the Great', which has been popularly attached to his name in Iran. He is indeed the only ruler from the Islamic period in Iran to have been so designated. It puts him in the company of Cyrus the Great, the founder of the first Iranian Empire in the sixth Century BCE,[1] which is a reminder that Iran existed as a major civilisation for some twelve hundred years before it was conquered and converted to Islam by the invading Arabs in the mid-seventh century AD. Other great rulers were Abbas's contemporaries: the Moghul Emperor Akbar, Queen Elizabeth I of England, Henry IV of France and Philip II of Spain. Abbas more than measures up to all of them.

Despite this, up till now there has been no biography in English of Shah Abbas.[2] This book sets out to show why this is a serious oversight and that Abbas is not only of great importance for Iran and the Muslim world, but is also part of the history of Europe and a fascinating personality in his own right. Furthermore, some of the events and developments that took place during the reign of Abbas have an obvious contemporary relevance. They throw light, for instance, on the rivalry and tensions between the two great branches of Islam, the Sunni and the Shi'a, as well as on the crucial relationship between the Iranian monarchy and the Shi'i clergy who eventually overthrew it in the Islamic Revolution of 1978–9.

Shah Abbas was the fifth ruler of the Safavid dynasty which came to power in 1501, reuniting Iran within its historic borders for the first time since the Arab conquest and imposing the Shi'i form of Islam which has defined the country ever since. It is not possible to understand the challenges which faced Abbas without an understanding of what happened between 1501 and 1587, when he was put on the throne at the age of seventeen in a *coup d'état*. This is covered in the first two chapters of the book, which also deal with Abbas's birth and upbringing.

This is a turbulent period of political and religious upheaval, of foreign and civil war, during which a new theocratic state took shape in Iran, legitimised through a mix of heterodox Shi'ism and mystic Sufism. The Safavid ruler – or shah – was regarded as divine by his followers, while the state was supported by the military power of Turkoman tribes – tribes that spoke a dialect of Turkish – and the age-old administrative skills of the indigenous Iranian population. This newly emergent and dynamic Shi'i Iran briefly threatened to dominate the Muslim world before being thrown onto the defensive by the hostile Sunni Muslim powers on its borders – the Ottoman Turkish Empire in the west and the Uzbek khanate of Central Asia in the east. Meanwhile, Iran began to be torn apart internally by the Turkoman tribes which fought for supremacy whenever the shah was weak or a minor. This provided the background to Abbas's youth, which is described in Chapter 2, when he saw many of his relatives killed on the orders of his half-crazed uncle, when he was ruling as shah, his mother and elder brother murdered by warring tribal chiefs and large swathes of the country occupied by Ottoman and Uzbek forces. The absence of any clear rule of succession enabled the tribal chiefs to use Safavid princes as pawns in their power struggle, and the chapter ends with one of these warlords placing the seventeen-year-old Abbas on the throne in a coup which ousted his father.

The following chapters show the extraordinary resolution – and ruthlessness – with which the young shah set about overcoming these severe challenges to the very existence of the state. They detail the summary executions, the determined suppression of rebellion and the military and administrative reforms which brought an end to the internal anarchy and created a strong centralised government. They also describe how Abbas freed the country from foreign occupation in a series of campaigns, first against the Uzbeks and then against the Ottomans.

The conflict with the Ottomans persuaded Abbas to open up relations with Europe, which is one of the main themes of the book. The initial aim was to bring about concerted military action against their common Ottoman enemy. This was never achieved and Abbas was to feel badly let down by the Austrian and Spanish Habsburgs on whom he had pinned most of his hopes. With Abbas's encouragement, contacts with Europe soon spread into the commercial and other fields. The long and controversial British involvement in Iran began during his reign when he granted trading privileges to the English East India Company and persuaded it, in return, to provide him with the warships which he lacked to seize the island of Hormuz, an important trading entrepôt at the mouth of the Persian Gulf, from the Portuguese. The company remained in Iran, with one brief interruption, until its effective demise in the mid-nineteenth century, although for most of the seventeenth century it was the Dutch East India Company, to which Abbas granted similar privileges, which became the dominant European trading partner. Meanwhile, the welcome Abbas extended to Europeans, the orderly and prosperous condition of the country, the lure of his court and his impressive new capital of Isfahan, attracted an increasing flow of merchants, missionaries, soldiers-of-fortune, artists, craftsmen and travellers from Europe. Of all these, it was the European artists who perhaps had the most lasting influence, gradually changing, as they did, the style of the great tradition of painting in Iran.

Shah Abbas made Europeans sit up and take notice of Iran and its ruler in a way they had not done since the days of ancient Iran. They continued, however, to call the country 'Persia', the name by which it had been known since the days of the ancient Greeks. Its ruler, on the other hand, came to be known as the Sophy, a corruption of Safavi - the name of the dynasty to which Abbas belonged. From Abbas's reign onwards, references to Persia and the Sophy become frequent in European literature. An early reference occurs in Shakespeare's play *Twelfth Night*, in which one of the characters, Fabian, exclaims, 'I will not give my part of this sport for a pension of thousands to be paid from the Sophy!' The play was first produced in 1602, a few years after Abbas gave a warm welcome to those two remarkable English adventurers, Anthony and Robert Sherley, who were certainly persuaded to go to Iran by reports of his generosity. In this they seem to have been disappointed, but it was probably widely believed that the riches of Persia had been showered on them.

Considerable space is devoted to the diplomatic exchanges between Shah Abbas and various European powers - Spain-Portugal, the papacy, Austria and England - not only because they are of great interest from a European perspective, but also because they show Abbas in action, promoting and defending his country's interests. Apart from his struggle with the Ottomans, which occupied so much of his time, they also relate to two other important concerns of his. One is the assertion of his authority over the littoral of the Persian Gulf, which most Muslim rulers of Iran before him had paid little attention to, focusing instead on the centre and north of the country. The other is Abbas's strong interest in expanding foreign trade and in extracting the maximum possible benefit from Iran's most valuable export item, which was raw silk.

I believe firmly in the value of narrative history both because a good story is worth telling and because actions of any kind can only be properly understood within a narrative framework. For these reasons I have preferred not to interrupt the narrative with discourses on important aspects and features of Abbas's reign, but to deal with these more fully in separate chapters at the end.

The story of how Abbas rescued Iran from internal disintegration and foreign occupation; gave it order, prosperity and good government, with firmer foundations for both the state and his own legitimacy as ruler; and how he established wide-ranging relations with Europe – all this is of the greatest importance and is more than enough to justify his status as a legendary figure. But what clothes the legend in flesh and blood and gives it a huge added interest is the complex and colourful personality of Abbas himself, with his excitable conversation, his endless curiosity, his sense of theatre and what one can only describe as his brilliant play-acting, which made it very difficult to know what was really going on in his mind. He was an engaging character and for the most part must have been thoroughly good company – so long, that is, as one could stand the pace, for he never seemed to tire or to want to go to bed. He was less fun, however, when he chose to slice off the head of a Turkish prisoner in the presence of a shocked and terrified European envoy. As the subtitle of this book makes clear, he was quite ruthless in achieving his ends and deliberately made himself feared in order to secure unquestioning obedience. He did not hesitate to eliminate people he considered a threat and often suppressed rebellions with extreme violence and savagery, notably in Georgia. He was also subject to paranoid suspicions, which led him to kill his eldest son and blind his other two. In the case of his eldest son, he was subsequently filled with deep remorse which brought on moods of profound melancholy. All in all he was, in the words of his chief court chronicler, Iskandar Beg Munshi, a man of contradictions. This is yet another reason for attempting the biography of him in English that is long overdue.

Chapter 1

Shah Abbas's Inheritance: The Birth of a Shi'i State

The future Shah Abbas belonged to a ruling dynasty in Iran, that of the Safavids, which had very unusual origins. The name Safavid comes from Abbas's distant ancestor, Sheikh Safi ud-Din (1252–1334), who was a Sufi or Islamic mystic and who founded his own Safavid Sufi order in 1301, when Iran was part of the vast Mongol Empire. The order was based in the town of Ardabil, in the north-western Iranian province of Azerbaijan. The Safavids are thought to have been Kurdish in origin, but by Sheikh Safi's day they were a Persian-speaking family of small landowners, living near Ardabil, which was a commercial centre in mountainous country, about 40 miles inland from the Caspian Sea. There was also a large Turkoman tribal population in Azerbaijan, who spoke a language closely related to Turkish, known today as Azeri. In time the province would become almost entirely Azeri-speaking.

As the head of a Sufi order, Sheikh Safi was known as 'the perfect guide' (*murshid-e kamil*) and his followers as 'disciples' (*muridan*), who owed him absolute obedience. This relationship was to be of great importance in the Safavid seizure of power and for most of the first century of Safavid rule. Like all Sufi masters, Safi guided his disciples along a path towards a mystical union with the Divine. He was a great believer in the ecstatic communal exercises of Sufism, especially the practice known as *zikr* or remembrance of God, when devotees worked themselves into a frenzy as they recited the divine name, *Allah*. Safi and his successors won great renown as Sufi sheikhs and with the help of missionaries they attracted large numbers of followers over a wide area. Prominent among these were the Turkoman tribes in

1

Azerbaijan itself, but also much further afield in Anatolia (the territory covered by modern Turkey) and northern Syria. They were also revered by the rich and powerful, whose generous donations helped to make the order extremely wealthy.

Up until the middle of the fifteenth century the Safavid sheikhs remained orthodox Sunni Muslims and purely religious leaders. After that, there was a fundamental change in their ideology and activity. As a hostile contemporary chronicler wrote of the chief instigator of this change, Sheikh Junaid (d.1460), 'the bird of anxiety laid an egg of longing for power in the nest of his imagination'.[1] Junaid and his successors adopted an extreme form of Shi'ism, which was current among their Turkoman followers in Anatolia,[2] and gathered these followers around them as a military force which they used to acquire temporal power.

Mainstream or 'orthodox' Shi'ism is known as Twelver or Imami Shi'ism. Its adherents believe that, after the death of the Prophet Muhammad in AD 632, God entrusted the guidance of mankind to a line of twelve divinely inspired Imams from the family of the Prophet. The line begins with Ali, the cousin and son-in-law of the Prophet, and passes through his son, Husain, who died what the Shi'a regard as a martyr's death at the hands of his enemies on the plain of Karbala, north of Baghdad, in October 680 – an event that is commemorated annually in passionate mourning ceremonies. Husain is the key figure in Shi'ism and the source of its powerful emotional appeal. Shi'i tradition associates him closely with Iran, as he is said to have married the daughter of the last king of ancient Iran, Yazdgird III, who was overthrown by the invading Arabs in the mid-seventh century AD. Husain's son, the Fourth Imam, known as Zain al-Abidin ('the ornament of the worshippers'), is said to have been born of this marriage. The line of Imams continues until the Eleventh Imam, Hasan al-Askari, who died in 874 – according to the Shi'a, poisoned on the orders of the Sunni Caliph,[3] like most of his predecessors. The Shi'a believe that his son, the Twelfth Imam, often referred to as the 'Hidden Imam', disappeared from sight in order to avoid a similar fate, but remains present in the world as its legitimate ruler and will reappear at the end of time as the Mahdi, 'to fill the world with justice'.[4]

Early Safavid Shi'ism was unorthodox in that it attributed a common divinity to the Shi'i Imams and regarded the Mahdi as a messiah or saviour who might assume different human forms and intervene in the world on many occasions to institute a reign of justice – not merely once at the end of time. More significantly, the Safavid sheikh was seen by his enthusiastic

2

Turkoman followers as sharing in the divinity of the Imams and as an incarnation of the Mahdi. A contributory factor that no doubt carried weight with the Turkomans was the Safavid claim to be descended from Ali, the First Shi'i Imam and the fourth Caliph of Islam. This claim was made before Junaid's time, when it did not necessarily imply Shi'i sympathies. It was common for Sufi sheikhs to reinforce their authority by claiming descent from the Prophet or from one of the first four 'rightly guided' Caliphs, as they are called by Sunnis.[5] Of these, Ali was the most popular and was venerated by Sunnis and Shi'a alike. The claim is now known to have been fabricated, as most such claims undoubtedly were, but there is no doubt that the Safavids and their followers believed it to be genuine.

The Safavid movement as it took shape under Junaid was only one of a number of extreme Sufi-Shi'i movements during the fourteenth and fifteenth centuries that attracted popular support by holding out the hope of an end to injustice and a more egalitarian society. Throughout the region, incessant warfare, insecurity, famine, plague and heavy financial exactions by those in power created a climate in which messianic and millenarian movements flourished.

The Safavid Turkoman tribesmen were known as *Qizilbash*, a Turkish word meaning 'red-head', because they wore a red bonnet with twelve folds, symbolizing the Twelve Shi'i Imams. It was with their fanatical support that Abbas's great-grandfather, Shah Ismail I (1501–24), was able to conquer Iran in the first decade of the sixteenth century.[6] By this time the Safavids themselves had become Turkoman in their language and their ways. Besides living among Turkomans, they had married princesses from the Turkoman dynasty which preceded them as rulers of western Iran.[7] But they continued to speak Persian as well as Azeri Turkish, and both Ismail and his father, Sheikh Haidar, identified strongly with the heroes of Iranian legend.

Ismail began his conquest of Iran in Azerbaijan, the home of the Safavid Sufi order. In the summer of 1501 he captured its principal city of Tabriz – a great commercial entrepôt on the Silk Road which became the first Safavid capital. There, at the age of fourteen, he crowned himself king of Iran (*padeshah-e Iran*) and took the momentous step of declaring the Shi'i form of Islam to be the official religion of his new kingdom. But it was mainstream Imami or Twelver Shi'ism that Ismail proclaimed as the state religion, and not the extremist Shi'ism of the Qizilbash which had brought him to power. Imami Shi'ism, which did not offer a heaven on earth, offered a more stable basis on which to build a state. It could also be expected to meet less opposition from Sunnis, who at that time constituted the

3

overwhelming majority of the population. However, there was to be continuing tension between these two forms of Shi'ism, the heterodox Shi'ism of the Qizilbash which was mixed up with their Sufi mysticism as followers of the Safavid Sufi order, and the orthodox Imami Shi'ism of a new clerical establishment. It was a tension that was to be finally resolved by Shah Abbas in favour of Imami Shi'ism.

Ismail was ruthless in suppressing rival messianic movements and most other Sufi orders[8] and was quite prepared to use violent methods to impose Shi'ism, especially in the early years of his reign. Untold numbers of recalcitrant Sunnis were either killed,[9] or fled to neighbouring Sunni lands. Most, however, remained and the conversion of even the majority of the population to Shi'ism would take many years. Ismail invited Arab Imami clerics to help him in the task, but met with little response. The only one known to have responded favourably during Ismail's reign was a senior Lebanese Shi'i cleric, Sheikh Ali al-Karaki al-Amili, who made the first of a number of visits to his court in 1504-5, eventually settling in Iran and spearheading a major conversion drive under Ismail's successor, Shah Tahmasp. The great majority of Arab Shi'i clerics held firm to the traditional Shi'i refusal to serve any government, even one that claimed to be Shi'i, in the absence of the Hidden Imam. Others were put off by the extremist manifestations of Safavid Shi'ism. They objected to the deification of Ismail, the practice of prostration before the king - a practice they believed should be reserved for prayer before God alone - the cavalier attitude towards the precepts of the Sharia (Islamic law), such as the prohibition on drinking wine, and the ritual cursing of the first three caliphs of Islam who, in the eyes of the Shi'a, had usurped the office that rightly belonged to the Imam Ali. Ismail had officials go through the streets carrying axes over their shoulders and crying out: 'Cursed be Abu Bakr! Cursed be Omar! Cursed be Uthman!' - the names of the first three caliphs. Anyone who heard this was obliged, on pain of death, to express their approval. Arab Shi'i clerics feared that this practice would provoke retaliation against Shi'a living under Sunni regimes. Ismail does seem to have made some attempt to distance himself from the extremism of his Qizilbash followers. Venetians who visited Tabriz during the early years of his reign reported that he was displeased with being called a god or a prophet.[10]

Nonetheless, Ismail was a theocratic and absolute ruler, as were all his successors. He claimed to be the divinely appointed representative of the Hidden Imam - a claim which in itself was not compatible with orthodox Imami Shi'ism, which regarded the most senior Shi'i clerics, the *mujtaheds*, as the vicegerents of the Imam during his absence. He also claimed to partake of the sinlessness and infallibility attributed to the Shi'i Imams. It was probably during Ismail's reign that the claim to descent from the Imam Ali was refined and traced back through the Seventh Shi'i Imam, Musa al-Kazim (AD 745/6-799). All this was combined with the ancient Iranian concept of the king as 'the shadow of God on earth'. Until the reign of Shah Abbas, however, the subjects who mattered most to the shah were the Qizilbash tribesmen on whom his power rested. In their eyes the shah's legitimacy resided quite as much in his position as their Sufi master. The word *sufigari*, which meant 'behaviour becoming a Sufi', was synonymous with 'loyalty to the shah'.

The early Safavid state was often referred to by contemporary Iranian chroniclers as 'the Qizilbash kingdom', because of the dominance of the Qizilbash tribes and their chiefs. The largest of these tribes were the Ustajlu, the Rumlu, the Shamlu, the Zul Qadr, the Tekkelu, the Türkman, the Afshar and the Qajar.[11] Together with a number of smaller Qizilbash tribes, they provided the military backbone of the state. Expert horsemen armed with bow and arrow, sword, dagger and battle-axe, they were a fearsome fighting force. When not fighting, they were nomadic pastoralists who occupied a particular area of the country within which they migrated with their livestock between summer uplands and winter lowlands, while also practising a certain amount of settled agriculture. There was, in addition, a large tribal population that was not Qizilbash, but in the sixteenth century it did not play an important role in the Safavid state. This population included Iranian, Kurdish, Arab and Baluch tribes, as well as other Turkish-speaking tribes. In all, nomadic tribes accounted for a quarter to a third of the total population of Iran in Safavid times, a proportion that remained more or less constant until well into the twentieth century.[12]

Until the reign of Shah Abbas, most of the land was assigned to Qizilbash tribal chieftains as administrative fiefs.[13] They collected the taxes and used the revenue to maintain their households and their military forces. Their only obligations to the shah were to bring an agreed number of mounted troops to serve him when called upon to do so and to send him a rich present at the New Year. They bore the title of *amir* and the most important among them presided over a smaller version of the royal court and the central administration. These fiefs could be, and sometimes were, revoked by the shah, but there was an inevitable tendency for them to come to be regarded as the hereditary possession, if not of one family or clan, then of one tribe. Thus the south-western province of Fars, with its capital of Shiraz, was governed by Zul Qadr chiefs from 1503 until 1595, when the last of them was removed by Abbas as he set about breaking the power of the Qizilbash. Some lands were administered directly by the central government and others were governed by their hereditary rulers as vassals of the shah.

Since Ismail was not a Turkoman tribesman himself, he had no tribal force of his own. He had a personal bodyguard of two hundred of the most devoted Qizilbash Sufis, who were armed with sword and dagger and carried an axe. But he needed a larger body of regular troops he could rely on. So he created a kind of Praetorian Guard, paid for out of the royal treasury, available to serve the shah at all times, and taking its orders directly from him. This elite corps was made up mainly of Qizilbash horsemen chosen from all the tribes for their outstanding soldierly qualities. They were known as *qurchis* – a Mongol word meaning 'quiver-bearer' – and their Qizilbash commander was the *qurchi-bashi*. The Qurchis were 3,000-strong under Ismail and represented the beginnings of a standing army, which only came fully into existence under Shah Abbas.[14]

For the first seven years of Ismail's reign, Qizilbash domination was almost total. They held all the key civil and military positions. But when Ismail came of age he began to appoint members of the indigenous Persian-speaking population, known then as Tajiks, to some of these positions, using them as a counterweight to the Qizilbash.[15] A highly educated and generally well-to-do class of urban Tajiks had traditionally filled the ranks of the government bureaucracy and the religious institution, whatever regime was in power, and they now began to do so again. In particular, they took charge of the central administration. The head of this and the most senior government official was known to begin with as the *vakil* – the 'alter ego of the shah', according to one modern authority[16] – although later he bore the more traditional title of vizier. The Qizilbash disliked being subjected to the authority of these Tajik chief ministers and murdered two of them in the course of the sixteenth century. They particularly disliked it when a Tajik usurped the military role which the Qizilbash regarded as exclusively theirs. But otherwise Qizilbash provincial amirs were only too ready to employ Tajiks to run their administration.

The gradual normalisation of the Safavid state must have been a severe disappointment to many of the ordinary Qizilbash tribesmen, and to many among the poorer classes in general, who had hoped that Ismail would fulfil his messianic promise by bringing about a social and economic revolution. Safavid propaganda had encouraged these hopes before and during the conquest of Iran. As late as 1515 a Portuguese official on a visit to the

Persian Gulf, Duarte Barbosa, heard Ismail referred to as 'the leveller'.[17] But Ismail soon jettisoned any radical ideas in the interests of building a stable and powerful state, while the Qizilbash chieftains were too busy enjoying the fruits of conquest to have any interest in disturbing the status quo. This left the field open for other messianic and millenarian movements which would arise in the future and challenge the Safavids in their turn.

Safavid Iran was in conflict from the beginning with two principal external enemies – the Ottoman Turkish Empire in the west and the Uzbek Khanate in Transoxania in the east, with its capital in Bukhara. The conflict was sharpened by sectarian differences, since both the Ottoman Turks and the Uzbeks were Sunni Muslims. The Uzbeks, who were a confederation of Turkish and Mongol tribes, had a particular hatred of Shi'ism. Islam forbade the enslavement of fellow-Muslims, but the Uzbeks regarded it as legitimate to enslave Iranian Shi'a, on the grounds that they were not Muslims at all, but infidels. Shah Ismail succeeded in driving the Uzbeks out of the north-eastern Iranian province of Khurasan and restoring Iran's ancient frontier on the Oxus River. But Uzbek attacks on the province continued and were a major problem that Shah Abbas had to contend with.

In the early years of his reign, Shah Ismail posed a serious threat to the Ottomans.[18] Not only did he wield great power as ruler of a restored Iranian empire that included Baghdad and Mesopotamia and extended into eastern Anatolia, but he also had the support of large numbers of Turkoman tribesmen on Ottoman territory, who gave him their allegiance as their Sufi sheikh and 'perfect guide'. He maintained contact with them through an underground network of deputies. The Safavid threat hung over the Ottomans until August 1514, when they inflicted a crushing defeat on Ismail's army at Chaldiran in north-west Iran. The Ottoman army also suffered heavy losses in the battle and withdrew shortly afterwards, but Ismail lost eastern Anatolia and thereafter the Safavids were generally on the defensive against the Ottomans. The Ottoman victory had two other important consequences. It damaged Ismail's charisma in the eyes of the Turkoman tribesmen who up till then had believed him to be invincible, making them less manageable and more inclined to put their own interests first. It also encouraged Ismail to look for allies to Christian Europe, which, like Iran, was under attack by the Ottomans.

The first European power Ismail turned to was Portugal, which was establishing commercial and military bases in the East following Vasco da Gama's discovery of the sea route round Africa in 1497. Barely a year after Chaldiran, in 1515, Shah Ismail sought help from the Portuguese admiral

Albuquerque, who had just taken control of the island of Hormuz, a great trading entrepôt at the mouth of the Persian Gulf ruled by Arab kings who were nominally vassals of the shah. The move gave Portugal control of the Gulf for more than a century. Albuquerque responded enthusiastically to the idea of an Irano-European alliance against the Ottomans, urged Ismail to send ambassadors to Lisbon and pressed King Manuel of Portugal to lend his support. Other European potentates whom Ismail appealed to included Pope Leo X, King Ladislas II of Hungary and the Holy Roman Emperor, Charles V. But although he received envoys from the Vatican and Venice, no concrete help was forthcoming. Disappointed and frustrated, he wrote to the Emperor Charles V in 1523, expressing his astonishment that the Christian powers were fighting each other instead of combining against the Turks. These exchanges between Iran and Europe were to continue for the rest of the century and to reach a new intensity during the reign of Shah Abbas.

Shah Ismail I died in 1524 and was succeeded by his eldest son, Tahmasp, who was only ten years old. Without a strong ruler to hold them in check, the fractious Qizilbash tribes fought one another for supremacy and for the next nine years the Safavid state was wracked by civil war. During these years, the young Tahmasp also had to fend off a series of Uzbek attacks on Khurasan.[19] Fortunately the Ottomans were fully engaged in Europe, where they defeated the Hungarians and for a while laid siege to the Austrian Habsburg capital of Vienna. Habsburg envoys visited Shah Tahmasp to press for an anti-Ottoman alliance and were given a warm welcome. These contacts alarmed the Ottomans, who were fearful of having to fight a war on two fronts, and they did everything to prevent them. In 1531 the Ottoman authorities in Aleppo had the Venetian consul, Andrea Morosoni, dragged behind a horse and impaled for giving assistance to a Habsburg envoy who was trying to reach Iran.[20]

The Iranian civil war was finally brought to an end in 1533, when Tahmasp, now aged nineteen, managed to assert his authority by executing the most powerful of the Qizilbash amirs, who was suspected of plotting to put the shah's younger brother on the throne. Afterwards, Tahmasp used a variety of means to keep the Qizilbash in check. He kept a tighter control over the Qizilbash governors in the provinces through centrally appointed viziers who worked alongside them, running the administration. He used divide-and-rule tactics by encouraging rivalries between amirs of the same tribe. He also strengthened the existing military force under his direct control – the Qurchis, or household cavalry – and began to build a new one of captured Circassians, Georgians and Armenians and their descendants. But the Qizilbash still provided the main fighting force, governed most of the provinces and held most of the important offices at the court. Their potential for causing trouble remained undiminished and was to burst out into the open again after Tahmasp's death.

Tahmasp restored order just in time, for in the same year, 1533, the Ottoman sultan, Sulaiman the Magnificent, made peace with the Habsburgs and, encouraged by Iranian renegades, launched the first of four invasions of Iran. Sulaiman was angered by the activities of the Safavid Sufi missionaries in Ottoman Anatolia and by the Safavid persecution of Sunnis, which aroused strong feelings among his own Sunni clergy. In the course of these campaigns, Sulaiman captured Baghdad and drove the Iranians out of Mesopotamia, and on two occasions he briefly occupied the Safavid capital of Tabriz. However, Shah Tahmasp's scorched earth tactics, which included blocking the wells and underground water channels, prevented Sulaiman making any further lasting gains. The futility of continuing the war became apparent to Sulaiman after the failure of his fourth campaign in 1553, and two years later a peace treaty was signed which held for a quarter of a century. Known as the Treaty of Amasya, this broadly recognised the territorial status quo, leaving the Ottomans in possession of Baghdad and Mesopotamia. Shah Tahmasp promised to stop the Safavid agitation in the Ottoman lands and in return Sulaiman agreed to allow Iranian pilgrims to visit the Holy Cities of Mecca and Medina and the Shi'i shrines in Iraq – all places that were now under Ottoman rule.

The treaty also divided the Christian kingdom of Georgia into an Ottoman sphere of influence in the west and a Safavid one in the east. Shah Ismail I had begun the process of bringing eastern Georgia under Safavid control by ordering a number of attacks on the region after his defeat at Chaldiran, with the aim of exploiting its human and material resources and creating a compliant buffer state against the Ottomans. Following his father's example, Shah Tahmasp invaded eastern Georgia on four occasions between 1540 and 1554. Tens of thousands of Georgian boys, youths and young women were taken back to Iran as slaves.[21] The women were noted for their beauty and came to occupy a prominent position in the harems of the shah and other members of the Safavid elite. The boys and young men were made to convert to Islam and were trained for employment in various capacities at the court and in the households of the elite. They were known as *ghulams*. Some went to form the nucleus of a slave or *ghulam* military corps, which was later to be greatly expanded by Abbas and to be a major element in his reform of the Safavid state. By the end of Shah Tahmasp's reign, former

Christians from the Caucasus – not only Georgians, but also Armenians and Circassians – who had either been captured in war, bought or gifted as slaves, had come to constitute a 'third force' in the state, alongside the Persian-speaking Tajiks and the Turkish-speaking Qizilbash. Tahmasp followed up his campaigns in eastern Georgia with a policy of Iranianisation, placing on the throne a Georgian prince who had converted to Islam and promoting the use of Persian as the language of administration.

The Ottoman invasions had exposed the vulnerability of Tabriz, which was all too close to the Ottoman frontier. Shortly after the peace treaty was signed, Shah Tahmasp transferred the capital to Qazvin, 300 miles away to the south-east. This affected the nature of the Safavid state because it was a move away from an area of strong Turkoman influence into the Persian-speaking heartlands, and away too from the Sufi milieu of the Qizilbash into one governed by the Islamic law of the Shi'i clergy.[22]

Meanwhile, a third major Sunni Muslim power had emerged on Iran's south-eastern border. This was the Moghul Empire recently established in Afghanistan and northern India by Babur, a descendant of both Genghis Khan and Tamerlane, who had been an ally of Shah Ismail I in his struggle against the Uzbeks. Babur died in 1530 and was succeeded by his eldest son, Humayun, who in 1543 sought refuge in Iran from his enemies at home. He was given a lavish welcome by Shah Tahmasp, who provided him with troops to help him recover his throne, in return for converting to Shi'ism and promising to hand over Qandahar, a city of commercial and strategic importance on the frontier of their two empires. Once back in India, Humayun soon forgot about the Shi'ism. Although he did hand over Qandahar, he managed to take it back not long afterwards. But when Humayun died in 1556 and was succeeded by his fourteen-year-old son, Akbar, Tahmasp took advantage of the new Moghul emperor's temporary weakness to recapture the fortress. Qandahar was to remain a bone of contention between the Safavids and the Moghuls.

Another issue that caused friction was Safavid support for the principalities of Golconda, Bijapur and Ahmadnagar in the Deccan, which had adopted Shi'ism under Iranian influence. The rulers of Bijapur and Golconda even recognised the Safavid shah as co-sovereign of their kingdoms. All three rulers sent envoys to Tahmasp. The Moghuls resented what they saw as Iranian interference in Indian affairs. But they did not share the same degree of sectarian hostility towards the Safavids as the Uzbeks and the Ottomans.

Up till now Iranian contacts with Europe had been mostly confined to those European powers directly concerned by the Ottoman threat – the

10

Habsburgs, the Venetians and the papacy. The exception was Portugal, which controlled all the trade in the Persian Gulf from its base on the island of Hormuz and supplied the Iranian market with spices from southeast Asia. Any other European country wishing to trade directly with Iran had to find an alternative route. English merchants, who were looking for new markets for their cloth, opened up a trade route to Iran through Russia. This was first explored on behalf of the Muscovy Company in London by an intrepid Leicestershire merchant, Anthony Jenkinson, who travelled down the Volga River, crossed the Caspian Sea, and reached Qazvin early in November 1562. But he was not well received by Tahmasp, who told him Iran had 'no need to have friendship with the unbelievers'.[23] Although by this time Tahmasp had become obsessively pious, his reaction seems to have been influenced more by a fear of jeopardising the peace with the Ottomans.

The Muscovy Company persisted, however, and an expedition in 1565 finally succeeded in obtaining from Tahmasp the right to trade throughout Iran, without paying customs or tolls. The shah also gave the merchants a list of the goods he wanted from England. Apart from velvets, satins, damasks and all kinds of cloth, these included 'shirts of mail', twenty handguns and 'three or foure complete harnesses that will abide the shot of a handgunne', one hundred 'brushes for garments' which were not to be 'made of swines hair', and 'a mill to grinde corne in the field as they goe'.[24] The Company, for its part, imported raw silk and spices, mainly cinnamon and mace, from Iran. Two more expeditions were sent before the end of Shah Tahmasp's reign, both of which obtained further privileges.

As Tahmasp had feared, the news of his dealings with the Muscovy Company got back to Istanbul, where they aroused the suspicion that the shah was forming a European alliance. In the summer of 1571 a Venetian envoy, Vincenzo d'Alessandri, arrived in Iran with precisely this in mind, but the shah refused even to meet him, lest this fuel Ottoman suspicions. D'Alessandri eventually gave the letter he had brought from the Doge to Tahmasp's third and favourite son, Prince Haidar, who was now discharging many of his father's duties. The prince said he was personally sympathetic to the idea of an alliance, but doubted that his father would be. D'Alessandri was also told that the Iranian government wanted to see how the war with the Ottomans in Europe developed, before taking any decisions.

That war now produced the first great victory of the Christian powers when they annihilated the Ottoman fleet at the battle of Lepanto in October 1571. Pope Pius V immediately wrote to Shah Tahmasp urging him to take advantage of the victory to attack the Ottomans, but to no avail. Throughout the sixteenth century the papacy was tireless in its efforts to include Iran in a broad alliance against the Ottomans and dismissed objections, occasionally raised by Spain, that as a Muslim power, Iran was as much an enemy as Turkey.

Tahmasp was a more orthodox Shi'a than his father. He was anxious to observe Islamic law, which the Qizilbash paid little heed to, and issued two Edicts of Repentance in which he attempted to ban all practices considered sinful or contrary to Islamic law. These seem to have had little effect, and the Qizilbash amirs told him bluntly that drinking wine was a 'necessity' for them. Besides the pleasure it gave, wine had a ritual significance in their Turkoman culture. Tahmasp also abandoned any claim to divinity and had a group of his more extreme followers executed for heresy after they proclaimed him to be the Mahdi. On the other hand, he held firmly to the extremist Shi'i belief in the imminent coming of the Mahdi. He refused to allow his favourite sister, Shahzada Sultanim, to marry, on the grounds that he was keeping her as a bride for the Mahdi. He also kept a white horse with a cloth of crimson velvet and silver shoes in readiness for him.

Tahmasp's more orthodox outlook made it easier for Arab Shi'i clerics to respond favourably to the appeal for help in converting Iran to mainstream Twelver Shi'ism. Other Lebanese Shi'i clerics followed in the footsteps of al-Karaki, who organised and led a thoroughgoing campaign to win over to Twelver Shi'ism not just Sunnis but also those who espoused various heterodox beliefs, like the Qizilbash. Prayer-leaders were appointed in all the mosques to spread the teachings of Twelver Shi'ism. A stream of books on Shi'ism began to appear in Persian – some of them original works, but most of them translations from Arabic, which up till then had been considered the natural language of religious writing. All means of propaganda were mobilised for the cause. Poets, always hugely influential in Iran, were put under pressure to write poems in praise of the Shi'i Imams. Shi'i mourning ceremonies were promoted to encourage an emotional commitment to Shi'ism, especially the ceremonies to commemorate the 'martyrdom' of Husain, the Third Imam, at the battle of Karbala in AD 680.

Virtually all the Arab Shi'i clerics who came to Safavid Iran were from Lebanon. Unlike most Shi'i clerics from other parts of the Arab world, they saw merit in supporting the Safavid ruler on the grounds that he was making Shi'ism stronger and more self-confident. From the point of view of the Safavids, this support was particularly valuable for two reasons. Firstly, it strengthened their claim to Shi'i legitimacy. Secondly, it provided a legal basis for their government in the absence of the Hidden Imam, because the Lebanese clerics belonged to a school of Shi'i jurisprudence that allowed the most learned and pious among them, known as *mujtaheds*, to apply rationalist principles to Shi'i teachings in order to make new legal rulings. Lebanese *mujtaheds* like al-Karaki used this power to make Safavid rule legally possible in the absence of the Hidden Imam.[25]

Tahmasp was as ruthless as his father in suppressing messianic religious movements and Sufi orders. The most serious messianic movement to emerge, which was later to give trouble to Shah Abbas, was that of the Nuqtavis[26] – the name comes from the word *nuqta*, meaning 'point' or 'dot', but its precise significance is unclear. They were followers of a certain Mahmud Pasikhan from the Caspian region of Gilan who died about 1427–8, after proclaiming himself the Mahdi and announcing a new dispensation. His esoteric teachings were influenced by ancient Iranian religions, as well as by earlier messianic movements under Islam. They included the promise of a gnostic union with God through a life of celibacy and spiritual perfection, and a belief in reincarnation in which the merit of a person's previous life determined their present level of existence. The Nuqtavis also believed in a cyclical theory of time, which they interpreted as heralding an Iranian revival. They claimed that an Arab epoch in the history of the world had just ended and a new Iranian epoch was beginning, in which the Caspian regions of Gilan and Mazandaran would replace Mecca and Medina.

The Nuqtavis made little impact until the reign of Shah Ismail I, when they began to attract a large following among the literate urban professions of western Iran, such as craftsmen, artists and poets. They were detested by the new Shi'i clerical establishment, whose interests Shah Tahmasp was anxious to promote. In 1565 he blinded the Nuqtavi poet Abul-Qasim Amri, and several years later, towards the end of his reign, he massacred a Nuqtavi community near Kashan. But despite complaints from the Shi'i clergy, he took no action against a Nuqtavi community in Qazvin that was to constitute a serious challenge for Shah Abbas. The community was led by a wandering dervish from a humble peasant background who was known as Darvish Khusraw; the adoption of an ancient Iranian name like Khusraw underlined the Nuqtavi movement's pro-Iranian outlook. Tahmasp instituted an inquiry into Darvish Khusraw's beliefs and activities, but could find no evidence that he had done anything contrary to Islamic law.

Towards the end of his life, Shah Tahmasp became a religious obsessive and rarely left his palace in Qazvin. This caused much distress to his subjects, who valued the right to petition him directly about any injustice they might have suffered. The Venetian envoy, Vincenzo d'Alessandri, says hundreds of people gathered outside his palace day and night, crying out for justice.[27]

Tahmasp's neglect of the business of government contributed to growing insecurity and social unrest. The roads became unsafe, there was a peasant uprising in Gilan from 1568 to 1570, and in 1571 Tabriz was shaken by violent riots led by tradesmen and artisans who more or less took over the city. Shah Tahmasp was slow to take action and order was only finally restored two years later, when the ringleaders were arrested and executed. High-handed action by the Safavid governor sparked the revolt, but the underlying cause was almost certainly a severe economic recession. The price of silk, Iran's most valuable export commodity, had collapsed and commercial activity was much reduced.[28]

This was the deteriorating situation when the future Shah Abbas I was born, on 27 January 1571, in what was then the Iranian city of Herat. In the following years, the young prince was to live through tumultuous and terrifying events which left their mark upon him, both for good and ill.

Chapter 2

A Turbulent Childhood and the Seizure of Power

Herat, where Abbas was born and grew up, was a city full of reminders of past glory. During the fifteenth century, as the capital of the Timurid Empire, it had been a testimony to the proverb which describes the province of Khurasan as 'the oyster-shell of the world', and Herat as its 'pearl'. The Timurids, who were the descendants of the great conqueror Tamerlane, ruled over Transoxania and Khurasan, although in the latter part of the fifteenth century, the Timurid ruler in Herat lost control of the lands beyond the Oxus to rival princes of the dynasty. During this period, Herat became one of the most magnificent and delightful cities in the Islamic world. The Timurids embellished it with innumerable fine buildings, laid out enchanting gardens and promoted its commerce. They also made it a major centre of art and learning, famed for its poets, painters and scholars.

Early in the sixteenth century, Timurid rule was brought to an end by the Uzbeks, who overran Transoxania and swept on into Khurasan, capturing Herat in 1507. Three years later, however, Shah Ismail I crushed the Uzbeks at the battle of Marv and drove them back across the Oxus. In the following years, the Uzbeks returned repeatedly to the attack, but the Safavids managed to retain control of Herat and most of Khurasan. Herat suffered terribly from this continuous warfare until 1538, when Shah Tahmasp repelled the last of five Uzbek invasions. Two years later the Uzbek khanate was plunged into civil war, removing the threat to Khurasan for the rest of Shah Tahmasp's reign. The Safavids now set about repairing the damage to Herat and the surrounding region.

Although no longer an imperial capital, Herat was nonetheless of great importance to the Safavids. It was the capital of a province, Khurasan, noted for its wealthy cities and its fertile soil, which sustained large numbers of sheep and an extensive cotton cultivation, and where all sorts of fruit grew in abundance.[1] The best melons in all Iran came from a village in Khurasan and in the seventeenth century, if not before, were brought to the court for the shah's personal consumption.[2] All this was a valuable asset in a country where much of the land is desert or semi-desert. Herat itself, in normal times, was a thriving commercial centre on the trade route between Central Asia and India and was known, among other things, for its beautiful carpets, its fine silks and its well-tempered swords. It stood in the broad and fertile valley of the Herirud River and its surrounding region was dotted with prosperous villages. Herat was also a forward defence for Mashhad, the second city of Khurasan and the site of the holiest Shi'i shrine in Iran – the tomb of the Eighth Imam, Ali ar-Riza (d.818). Mashhad had its own governor who was responsible for an extensive territory in western Khurasan, but was subordinate to the governor in Herat. Rivalry between these two governorships would one day propel Abbas to the throne.

It is hardly surprising, therefore, that the Safavids attached a high priority to holding Herat against the Uzbeks. They made this clear for most of the sixteenth century by appointing a Safavid prince as titular governor of Herat, and designating it a 'royal city' (dar al-Saltana), a title otherwise enjoyed only by the capital, Qazvin, and the former capital, Tabriz.[3] The royal governor always had a Qizilbash amir at his side, who commanded the provincial forces. If the prince was a minor, the amir also carried out the actual business of government, and acted as guardian and tutor to the prince, while the amir's wife would act as his foster-mother.

When Abbas was born his father, Prince Muhammad Khodabanda ('Muhammad, the slave of God'), was the governor of Khurasan. He was forty years old and Shah Tahmasp's eldest son, but he was disqualified under Sharia (Islamic) law from succeeding him on the throne because an eye disease had left him almost completely blind.[4] The Safavid chronicler Iskandar Beg Munshi describes Muhammad Khodabanda as 'a pious, ascetic and gentle soul'. Abbas's mother, Khair al-Nisa Begum ('the best of women'), was much the stronger character of the two, as she was to demonstrate before long. She was a princess from the southern Caspian region of Mazandaran, from a family which, like the Safavids, claimed descent from the Shi'i Imams, in her case from the Fourth Imam, Zain al-Abidin. This meant she could also claim descent from the last dynasty of ancient Iran, the Sasanid dynasty, since the Fourth Imam's mother was said to have been

16

the daughter of the last of the Sasanids, Yazdgird III. Whatever the truth in that, Mazandaran and the neighbouring Caspian region of Gilan, with their mountains and dense forests, long resisted Arab Muslim penetration. They remained strongholds of ancient Iranian beliefs and customs, and Iranian families who had ruled there as Sasanid vassals continued to rule there long after the Arab conquest of Iran.

Half of Mazandaran had been ruled by Khair al-Nisa Begum's father as a vassal of the Safavids until 1562, when he was murdered and his kingdom seized by a cousin who was ruling the other half. Khair al-Nisa Begum fled to the Iranian court, where Shah Tahmasp gave her refuge and later married her to Muhammad Khodabanda. The cousin meanwhile died, whereupon, dividing the kingdom once again, Shah Tahmasp confirmed the cousin's son, Mirza Khan, as ruler of one half, while appointing Khodabanda's eldest son, Prince Hasan, to govern the rest. Khair al-Nisa Begum lived in the hope of one day exacting vengeance on Mirza Khan. She and Muhammad Khodabanda already had two sons when Abbas was born – Hasan and Hamza, and were to have two more later – Abu Taleb and Tahmasp. All except Abbas were to come to unhappy ends.

When Abbas was barely eighteen months old, Muhammad Khodabanda quarrelled with the Qizilbash military commander of Khurasan, causing Tahmasp to transfer him to Shiraz, the capital of the south-western province of Fars, at the other end of Iran. In his place, Tahmasp initially appointed Prince Hamza, then aged eight, as titular governor of Herat. But Khair al-Nisa Begum was unwilling to be separated from Hamza, who was her favourite son. So she persuaded Tahmasp to appoint Abbas instead. The fact that Abbas was still a baby was not considered an obstacle, as Tahmasp himself had been appointed titular governor of Khurasan at the age of two. An amir from the dominant Ustajlu tribe, Shah Quli Sultan Ustajlu, was appointed as the actual governor and as Abbas's guardian.

Abbas was to spend most of the next sixteen years in Herat, watching and reflecting as arbitrary killings became the order of the day and the quarrelsome Qizilbash tribes brought the country to the verge of collapse. He saw close family members murdered, while he himself narrowly escaped death only to become a pawn in the hands of ambitious Qizilbash amirs. It was the experiences of these years that determined his actions after he became king.

Abbas's Qizilbash guardians and their wives became substitute parents for Abbas. He never again saw his mother and only saw his father after he ousted him in a coup fifteen years later. He became particularly attached

17

to the second of his Qizilbash guardians, Ali Quli Khan Shamlu, and his wife, Jan Aqa Khanum, who had care of him for the greater part of his childhood and youth. After he became king, he gave official expression to the affection and esteem in which he held Jan Aqa Khanum. He honoured her with title of 'nana, or mother, and [she] became the doyenne of the royal harem and the object of the Shah's special favour'.[5]

From his Qizilbash guardians, he learnt the necessary skills of the soldier – riding, archery and swordsmanship. He also learnt to play polo and to hunt. Like most Iranian kings, he developed a passion for hunting, which was regarded as a form of military training. As he grew older he would also have been able to gain an increasing insight into the business of government.

A particularly interesting aspect of his education is the craft skills he acquired and which he often put to use in later life, when he sought relaxation. That he should have learnt a craft was not unusual. Islam holds craftsmen in high regard and learning a craft was considered meritorious by members of the elite.[6] What is perhaps surprising is the wide range of Abbas's craft skills. The Carmelite, Father John Thaddeus, who spent several years in Iran during the reign of Shah Abbas, wrote that, 'He enjoys making scimitars, arquebuses, bridles and saddles for horses, weaving cloth, distilling salts, orange-flower water and medicaments, and – in short – with all mechanical crafts, if not perfect, he is at least somewhat conversant.'[7]

Abbas would have acquired these skills from the craftsmen in the workshops that were part of the amir's establishment and that provided the amir and his household with virtually all they required in the way of necessities and luxuries.

The great Qizilbash amirs, as well as being soldiers and administrators, were also patrons of art and culture. This was particularly true of Abbas's second guardian, Ali Quli Khan Shamlu, who possessed an important library and employed talented poets, painters and calligraphers.[8] During his time in Herat, Abbas would have received instruction in painting and calligraphy, and although there is no evidence that he had any particular talent himself, he developed a sophisticated taste for both these art forms, which he indulged to the full once he was on the throne. Architecture, however, was to be his great passion, and undoubtedly had its origin in the strong impression made upon him by the Timurid architectural heritage which he saw all around him in Herat, and later in Mashhad too. The Timurid influence on Abbas was not to be confined to the arts. It was also to affect his view of the Safavid dynasty's legitimacy, which he was to seek to strengthen through association with Timur, or Tamerlane, himself.[9]

18

His intellectual education was entrusted to a learned cleric from Mashhad, Sheikh Hasan Davud,[10] and would have included instruction in the Koran, the Sharia and the principal teachings of Shi'ism, as well as the study of some of the masterpieces of Persian poetry, in particular the national epic, the *Shahnama* of Firdausi. Book learning, however, seems to have had little appeal to Abbas at this time, and he is said often to have skipped his studies in order to go hunting. His modern Iranian biographer, Nasrullah Falsafi, says that by the time he became king at the age of seventeen he could do little more than read and write, and that he acquired knowledge later from the company of learned and artistic people.

Abbas was educated alongside household 'slaves', or *ghulams*, who would have become his childhood companions. Some or perhaps most of them are likely to have been Georgians, Armenians or Circassians – the same people he would later place at the centre of his military and administrative reforms. Almost certainly it was in Herat that he first learnt to value their ability and loyalty. One of his closest friends was a Kurd, Ganj Ali Khan, who had been removed from his tribe to be brought up, like the *ghulams*, owing loyalty only to the shah. Such men from a tribal background were known as *shahsevans*, or 'lovers of the shah'. The friendship continued after Abbas became king, with Abbas calling Ganj Ali Khan affectionately *baba* ('papa'), and appointing him to important provincial governorships.

While Abbas was still in his infancy, a crisis was brewing at the Safavid court over the succession. Despite his advancing years, Tahmasp had failed to say which of his sons he wished to succeed him. This was the only hope of securing a smooth succession, as otherwise the Safavids were governed by the Turco-Mongol tribal tradition, according to which all the princes had an equal right to the throne. While Tahmasp remained silent, two rival factions emerged at the court, each with its own princely contender, and began jockeying for position.

One of the contenders was the shah's third son, Prince Haidar (b.1555), who regarded himself as the natural successor, since his father had already devolved many of his duties upon him. His supporters included the dominant Ustajlu tribe, who looked to Haidar to maintain their supremacy, and the Georgian *ghulams* at the court, since Haidar's mother was a Georgian. The other candidate was promoted *in absentia*. This was Tahmasp's second son, Prince Ismail (b. c.1533–4), who had fought with distinction against the Ottomans but had been imprisoned for nearly twenty years on suspicion of plotting to overthrow the shah. He was backed by most of the other Qizilbash tribes, who saw an opportunity to oust the Ustajlu from their position of dominance and the lucrative offices that went with it. They also preferred Ismail because his mother was a Turkoman, like themselves, and because he had shown the soldierly qualities they appreciated.

Two influential individuals who were soon to play an important role were also in the pro-Ismail camp. They were a senior Tajik official, Mirza Salman Jaberi Isfahani, who was later to become grand vizier, and Ismail's clever and ambitious half-sister, Pari Khan Khanum (1548–78). She had come to exercise a strong influence over Shah Tahmasp and clearly hoped to do the same with Ismail. As she was half-Circassian, she was able to rally the Circassian *ghulams* at the court behind Ismail. The involvement of the Georgians and Circassians in the succession crisis shows that these 'slave' elements were now a force to be reckoned with alongside the Qizilbash and the Tajiks.

Tensions between the two factions intensified when Tahmasp fell seriously ill for several months in 1574. At one point fighting nearly broke out when thousands of their followers carrying arms massed in front of the palace gate in Qazvin. The tensions subsided when the shah recovered, but in his two remaining years he still failed to name a successor. He died in the early hours of 14 May 1576, at the age of 62, after suffering severe burns from a depilatory that had been applied to his legs in the bath.

The following day Prince Haidar made a hasty and ill-prepared attempt to seize power, which was foiled largely due to the cunning and duplicity of Pari Khan Khanum. The attempt ended in farce, with Haidar taking refuge in the harem disguised as a woman, only to be dragged out by his opponents and executed. This was an extraordinary act of violence by the Qizilbash against a Safavid prince, the favourite son of their former Sufi 'guide', Shah Tahmasp, and a recognised descendant of the Shi'i Imams. It sparked a complete breakdown of law and order in Qazvin. Undisciplined bands of Qizilbash roamed the streets, killing and plundering, rioting broke out and barricades were set up as local toughs took control of the various quarters of the city. This marked the beginning of what is known as 'the second civil war', which was only ended after Abbas came to the throne and broke the power of the Qizilbash.

The slide into anarchy was arrested by Pari Khan Khanum who took a firm control of affairs, restoring order and securing the throne for her half-brother, Ismail. He was brought out of his prison and escorted to Qazvin, where he was crowned as Shah Ismail II on 22 August, 1576.

Pari Khan Khanum had expected Ismail to rule only in name, while she continued to hold the reins of power. The Qizilbash amirs made the same assumption and went out of their way to pay court to her. But Ismail had other ideas. He summoned the amirs and told them that 'interference in matters of state by women is demeaning to the King's honour, and for men to associate with women of the Safavid royal house is an abominable crime'.[11] That marked the end of the princess's bid for power, for the moment.

Ismail II's reign turned out to be short and murderous. The long years of imprisonment had left him suffering from acute paranoia, with the result that he saw enemies everywhere who had to be eliminated. He began with the vengeful killing of prominent members of the Ustajlu tribe, regardless of whether or not they had supported his rival, Prince Haidar. The young Abbas was directly affected when a body of horsemen galloped into Herat, burst into the home of his Ustajlu guardian, Shah Quli Sultan, and cut him down as he stood there unarmed. He was replaced with an amir from the Shamlu tribe, Ali Quli Khan Shamlu.

Ismail then turned on his own family to prevent any attempt to topple him from that quarter. He had two of his younger brothers murdered and a third blinded, thereby disqualifying him as a possible claimant to the throne. He also disposed of several of his cousins. But for the time being he left his elder brother, Muhammad Khodabanda, and his children unharmed – in part, no doubt, because Khodabanda was blind anyway, but also apparently out of a lingering respect for the mother he shared with him. He also ordered the massacre of several hundred followers of the Safavid Sufi order who arrived in Qazvin from Anatolia, fearing they might be used against him.

The growing disenchantment of the Qizilbash amirs was increased by Ismail's attempt to moderate the anti-Sunni rhetoric of Safavid Shi'ism. But they hesitated to move against the man they still regarded as their 'spiritual guide'. Ismail, however, heard rumours that they were plotting to replace him with Khodabanda's eldest son, Prince Hasan, whereupon he broke his self-imposed taboo on touching Khodabanda's family and had Hasan garrotted in Tehran by members of the royal bodyguard. In the autumn of 1577, after a son had been born to him, Ismail sent out orders for the elimination of the rest of the family. They were not carried out – for this Abbas would always be grateful to his guardian, Ali Quli Khan Shamlu – and on the morning of 25 November 1577 Ismail was found dead in his bed apparently from an overdose of opium and Indian hemp, although some suspected that he had been poisoned by Pari Khan Khanum.

The Tajik official, Mirza Salman Jaberi Isfahani, who had been appointed grand vizier by Ismail, moved swiftly to prevent Qizilbash rivalries from erupting into violence. He persuaded the amirs to swear an oath of friendship and to place on the throne Abbas's father, Muhammad Khodabanda. The fact that he had a Turkoman mother made him more acceptable to the Qizilbash, despite his virtual blindness, than his sons, twelve-year-old Hamza and seven-year-old Abbas, who were possible alternative candidates but whose mother was a Tajik.

Pari Khan Khanum was confident that she could manipulate the weak Khodabanda and again attempted to seize power. But she had reckoned without his wife and Abbas's mother, Khair al-Nisa Begum, now known by the title often accorded to royal wives of Mahd-e Oliya ('the lofty cradle'). This strong-willed woman was more than ready to compensate for her husband's deficiencies, and once this became clear the princess's support began to ebb away. One of the first to desert her was Mirza Salman, who had a keen sense of which way the wind was blowing. He joined Mahd-e Oliya and Sultan Muhammad Shah, as Muhammad Khodabanda was now known, in Shiraz and warned them they would be unable to rule as long as Pari Khan Khanum was alive. The Qizilbash amirs also began to leave Qazvin, ignoring frantic orders from the princess to stay. They went in increasing numbers to meet the new shah and Mahd-e Oliya as they made their way to the capital, which they entered on 11 February 1578. Mahd-e Oliya wasted no time in disposing of her rival, who was taken from the royal harem and strangled. A Qizilbash amir, who was present, later recalled that the princess's head was displayed at the gates of Qazvin, 'all bloody and dishevelled, stuck on a lance point, thus exposed to public view, a sight very sad and horrid'.[12] Shah Ismail II's infant son was also murdered.

The amirs had been prepared to see Mahd-e Oliya exercise considerable influence. They were not so happy to see her take complete charge of the administration and make all the decisions, even in military matters. She, in turn, had a low opinion of them, which she made no attempt to hide. All her efforts were centred on securing the succession for her eldest surviving son, Prince Hamza, who was now twelve or thirteen. She had him appointed vakil or vicegerent in charge of the entire administration. Hamza soon came to efface his father to such an extent that some foreign observers thought he was the shah.

The divisions and blood-letting at the Safavid court encouraged rebellions in various parts of the country and the old Qizilbash rivalries flared up again. Khurasan became a focus of unrest as fighting broke out between Ali Quli Khan Shamlu in Herat, the guardian of Prince Abbas, and his subordinate in Mashhad, Morteza Quli Khan Türkman. Mahd-e Oliya feared that Ali Quli Khan was preparing to use Prince Abbas in a bid for power and tried in vain to have the prince sent to Qazvin.

The weak state of the country offered an inviting prospect to those inveterate enemies of Shi'i Iran, the Uzbeks and the Ottomans. An Uzbek raid on Khurasan was repulsed, but the Ottomans, aided by their allies the Crimean Tartars, occupied a swathe of Iranian territory in the Caucasus, overrunning eastern Georgia and Shirvan – a province on the south-west corner of the Caspian, which is now the independent republic of Azerbaijan. A new phase of the Ottoman-Safavid wars had begun that was to continue for the next twelve years.

The Safavid armies suffered a number of defeats before Mahd-e Oliya mounted a counteroffensive. Together with Prince Hamza and the grand vizier, Mirza Salman, she led a Qizilbash army north to confront the Ottoman and Tartar forces in Shirvan. But her attempt to dictate the campaign strategy angered the Qizilbash amirs. Strong and determined character that she was, she wanted the Qizilbash forces to stay on the offensive. After winning a significant victory and taking prisoner the Tartar commander Adel Giray, who was the brother of the Tartar khan, she urged the amirs to pursue the Ottomans, who had taken refuge in the fortress of Darband on the Caspian. They refused and were supported by Mirza Salman, who seems to have sensed that Mahd-e Oliya was beginning to push her luck too far. After berating the amirs at a highly charged council of war, the campaign was broken off and an enraged Mahd-e Oliya returned to Qazvin, the army following behind.

Many of the Qizilbash amirs now began to regard the shah's wife as a direct threat to their interests. They also watched with growing resentment the favour she showed towards Tajiks in general, but particularly towards people from her home province of Mazandaran, many of whom were given profitable jobs in the administration.

Mahd-e Oliya further antagonised the Qizilbash by her treatment of the vassal ruler of half of Mazandaran, Mirza Khan, on whom she had longed to wreak vengeance for the murder of her father and for her own exile. She sent an army against Mirza Khan commanded by a senior Qizilbash amir, who persuaded him to surrender with a promise of safe conduct. But Mahd-e Oliya insisted on having him executed and his wives and children distributed like chattel among the amirs, thereby offending the Qizilbash sense of honour.

A number of prominent Qizilbash amirs at the court decided they had had enough and that Mahd-e Oliya had to go. They were joined by Mirza Salman, who displayed his usual opportunism. To rally their soldiers behind them, the amirs spread the message through the ranks that the shah should never have handed the reins of power to a woman. Mahd-e Oliya was aware of what was going on and tried to create divisions among the Qizilbash.

Towards the end of July 1579, a Qizilbash delegation delivered an ultimatum to Sultan Muhammad Shah in the presence of his wife. 'Your Majesty well knows', they said, 'that women are notoriously lacking in intelligence, weak in judgement, and extremely obstinate.'[13] They accused Mahd-e Oliya of seeking to humiliate and degrade the Qizilbash, and demanded her removal from power. Otherwise, they warned, there would be rebellions.

The shah gently rebuked the amirs, but was willing to listen to them. Mahd-e Oliya, however, was not. In a fury, she heaped words of contempt on them and said she had no intention of changing her ways.

That night the amirs decided to kill her. To justify this they made a fresh accusation – that she had been having an affair with Adel Giray, the captured brother of the Tartar khan. He had been well treated by Mahd-e Oliya and Prince Hamza, in the hope of weaning the Tartars away from their alliance with the Ottomans. There was even talk of him marrying one of the shah's daughters. A number of amirs accompanied by their soldiers burst in on him and ran him through with their swords, 'cutting off first his privy members, and slapping them upon his mouth after a most barbarous and filthy manner'.[14] They then went to the shah and demanded that Mahd-e Oliya be put to death. He pleaded with them in vain, offering to send her back to Mazandaran or to banish her to the Shi'i holy city of Qom, even to abdicate. But the amirs were implacable. They forced their way into the harem and strangled both Mahd-e Oliya and her mother, whom they blamed equally for violating the safe conduct given to Mirza Khan.

Although Prince Abbas was still only a boy and barely knew his mother, her brutal murder at the hands of the Qizilbash must have made a deep impression on him. From that time at least the conviction must have grown in him that the power of the Qizilbash had to be broken. Subsequent events can only have served to reinforce that conviction.

The next day anyone associated with Mahd-e Oliya became the target of Qizilbash mobs. Their homes were attacked and looted and some of them were killed. Mazandaranis and Tajik functionaries were particular objects of Qizilbash anger. The Tajik grand vizier, Mirza Salman, was not exempted, despite his opportunistic abandonment of Mahd-e Oliya. Like a number of other prominent figures, he was forced to take refuge with a friendly amir. The disturbances continued for the best part of a week, only dying down after a public reconciliation between the shah and the amirs. Sultan Muhammad

Shah, pious and weak as ever, announced that he accepted the murder of his wife as God's will. The amirs, for their part, reaffirmed their oath of loyalty and recognised Prince Hamza as the heir apparent. But the prince himself remained mistrustful and determined to punish his mother's murderers.

The growing instability and chaos created a favourable climate for messianic movements. There were four uprisings in the early 1580s, all led by wandering dervishes claiming to be Shah Ismail II, who, they insisted, had not really died. Three of the uprisings were in western Iran and one in the east, in Khurasan. These 'false Ismails' addressed the people as Sufis and called on them to rally round their true spiritual leader. They quickly attracted many followers, mainly among the Persian- and Kurdish-speaking tribes. The first of these pretenders is said to have raised an army of 20,000 from among the Lur tribesmen of the western Zagros Mountains and to have set up his own royal court, before he was finally defeated and beheaded. The second drew support from Kurds as well as Lurs. After he was captured, a gunpowder shirt was put on him and he was blown up in public in Qazvin, so that his followers should be in no doubt that nothing of him had survived.

Ottoman and Tartar forces remained in Shirvan where the Tartar khan, Muhammad Giray, angered by the killing of his brother, defeated the army of the Safavid governor and ravaged the province. Azerbaijan and its capital, Tabriz, were once again threatened. The grand vizier, Mirza Salman, led an army into eastern Georgia in an attempt to shore up the Safavid position there. But Sultan Muhammad Shah's ability to resist the Ottomans was undermined by the frequent refusal of many Qizilbash amirs to provide troops when called upon to do so. This represented a complete breakdown of the system whereby lands were assigned to the amirs in return for military service.

Sultan Muhammad Shah turned to Europe for help and received an encouraging response from the papacy and also from Spain, which had dropped its earlier reservations about giving assistance to Muslim Iran in its struggle with the Ottomans. Pope Sixtus V called the Ottoman-Safavid war a gift sent by God for the good of Christendom.[15] Once again, however, action did not match the talk, although Spain, which now ruled Portugal, is said to have supplied the shah with firearms from the Portuguese island of Hormuz in the Persian Gulf.

The Ottoman invasion and the disturbed state of the country put an end to English trade with Iran through Russia. After a last expedition in 1579, the Muscovy Company decided that the trade was too risky to be worth continuing.

The Qizilbash amirs now ruled the roost as they had done in the early years of Shah Tahmasp's reign, and they showed they had lost none of their capacity for debilitating rivalry. The amirs from the Türkman and Tekkelu tribes engaged in a struggle for supremacy with their Shamlu and Ustajlu rivals. The conflict was most intense at the court in Qazvin and in Khurasan, where the governor in Herat, Ali Quli Khan Shamlu, and his principal ally, Murshid Quli Khan Ustajlu, had for some time been at war with the Türkman governor of Mashhad, Morteza Quli Khan Pornak.

The Türkman and Tekkelu finally got the upper hand at the court, and in the process a number of prominent Shamlu were killed, among them the mother and father of Ali Quli Khan Shamlu. The latter reacted just as Mahd-e Oliya had feared he would. He made his ward, Prince Abbas, who was then ten years old, the figurehead of a rebellion in Khurasan by proclaiming him shah.

The grand vizier, Mirza Salman, persuaded Sultan Muhammad Shah to mount a punitive expedition to crush the rebellion. He had a personal interest in this, since he had now tied his fortunes to Abbas's elder brother, Prince Hamza. He had had his own son appointed as Hamza's vizier, and in his biggest coup of all, he had arranged for his daughter to marry the prince.

The campaign went ahead despite opposition from many of the amirs, who resented Mirza Salman's growing influence and the authority he exercised over military as well as administrative affairs. The amirs also attached much importance to the symbols of their superior status, and their resentment was fuelled when the shah absolved his Tajik grand vizier from standing in their presence and gave him a rank equivalent to a Qizilbash provincial governor. For his part, Mirza Salman regarded the amirs as a threat to the state, and told the shah as much.

The course of the campaign in Khurasan further exacerbated these tensions. It resolved itself into sieges which the amirs pursued half-heartedly. After suffering an initial defeat, Ali Quli Khan Shamlu shut himself up in the citadel of Herat with Prince Abbas, while his ally, Murshid Quli Khan Ustajlu, suffered a light siege of six months at Torbat-e Heydariya, south of Mashhad, before negotiating terms of surrender under which he was pardoned.

Mirza Salman accused the amirs of trying to sabotage the campaign. They, for their part, were furious when he insisted on executing a number of amirs' sons who had been taken prisoner. They decided to get rid of him and went to see the shah and Prince Hamza to demand that he be handed over. They said Mirza Salman's hostility towards the Qizilbash was destroying the state, and they complained bitterly that a Tajik, a 'man of the pen', should dare to put himself on a level with the Qizilbash. As a Tajik, they said, Mirza Salman 'was only expected to look after the accounts and divan business. It did not fall within his province to have an army at his disposal and to interfere in state affairs on his own behalf.'[16]

The grand vizier's reliance on his close ties to the Safavid royal house now proved to be vain. Although Mirza Salman had defended the interests of the crown against the centrifugal tendencies of the Qizilbash, the shah and Prince Hamza were much too afraid of the amirs to attempt to stand up for him. After receiving renewed pledges of loyalty from the amirs, they abandoned him to his fate. He was detained while all his possessions were seized, and he was then put to death. To complete the grand vizier's disgrace, Prince Hamza divorced his daughter.

With Mirza Salman out of the way, the attempt to assert royal authority in Khurasan lost all impetus. The situation in north-west Iran, where the Ottomans were again threatening Tabriz, also demanded immediate attention. So an agreement was hurriedly reached with Ali Quli Khan Shamlu and the campaign was wound up. Nothing more was demanded of the former rebel than another pledge of loyalty and the recognition of Prince Hamza as the heir apparent. In return for this, he retained his former offices of governor of Khurasan and guardian of Prince Abbas. He even received a reward from the shah, whom he succeeded in persuading to remove his old enemy, Morteza Quli Khan Türkman, from his position as governor of Mashhad and replace him with a friendly Ustajlu amir. Iskandar Beg Munshi says many concluded that the future lay with Prince Abbas.

The Ottomans had meanwhile rejected an Iranian peace overture and a large Ottoman army was poised to capture Tabriz. Prince Hamza, who was now shah in all but name, completely effacing his ineffectual father, hurried west in a desperate attempt to save the former Safavid capital. But his efforts were frustrated by the disobedience and disunity of the Qizilbash tribes. In vain he appealed to the amirs to rally around him as 'faithful Sufis of the Safavid house'. The Shamlu and Ustajlu amirs were among those who supported the prince, but for that very reason their Türkman and Tekkelu rivals refused to give any assistance. Tabriz fell to the Ottomans and although they withdrew most of their forces forty days later, following counterattacks by Hamza and the death of their commander, they left a strong garrison in the citadel, which Hamza was unable to dislodge.

In the midst of all this, Hamza rather unwisely fuelled the resentment felt by the Türkman and Tekkelu amirs. He imprisoned the governor general of Azerbaijan, Amir Khan, apparently for obstructing his attempts to find out who was responsible for the murder of his mother, Mahd-e Oliya. Amir Khan was the leading amir of the Türkman tribe, which had come to regard Azerbaijan as its fief. The other Türkman amirs were incensed not only by his imprisonment, but also by his replacement with an Ustajlu. The Türkman and their Tekkelu allies began to mobilise. Spurred on by the Ustajlu and Shamlu amirs around him, Hamza responded by executing Amir Khan. This led to renewed conflict. In the spring of 1585 the Türkman and Tekkelu amirs marched on Tabriz, where Hamza was besieging the Ottoman-held citadel. On reaching the royal camp, they burst in and demanded the removal from the court of the more influential Shamlu and Ustajlu amirs, including the new Ustajlu governor of Azerbaijan. They then seized the shah's youngest son, ten-year-old Prince Tahmasp, and took him to the capital, Qazvin, where they proclaimed him heir apparent in place of Prince Hamza.

Hamza defeated the rebels the following spring and imprisoned his young brother, Tahmasp, in the fortress of Alamut, in the Alburz Mountains north of Qazvin. But any hope he had of driving the Turks out of Tabriz now disappeared. After another assault on the citadel had failed, the approach of a fresh Ottoman army forced him to raise the siege. Despite opposition from the Qizilbash amirs, he responded favourably to peace proposals made by the new Ottoman commander, Farhad Pasha, even agreeing to send his own younger son, Prince Haidar, as a hostage to the Ottoman court.

But before Hamza could pursue this further, he was assassinated. One night early in December 1586, as he lay drunk in his tent, his personal barber crept in and cut his throat 'with all the skill of his barber's art'.[17] The barber fled to the tent of a prominent Shamlu amir, but was arrested and brought before the shah. He said others had put him up to it, but before he could reveal anything further he was silenced. According to one version, the Shamlu amir he had taken refuge with thrust a dagger into his mouth.[18] Another version is that 'a large packing needle was stuck through his tongue to prevent him making wild accusations against loyal servants of the crown'.[19] Either way, he was then quickly despatched. The leading Shamlu and Ustajlu amirs at court are believed to have been behind the murder, although their motives remain obscure.

At all events, these amirs now forced Sultan Muhammad Shah, against his will, to pass over his surviving eldest son, Prince Abbas, and to invest the latter's younger brother, eleven-year-old Prince Abu Taleb, as heir apparent. But the amirs who controlled the shah and the central government

28

soon fell out among themselves, creating further anarchy with rebellions on all sides.

In the meantime a new kingmaker had emerged in Khurasan. Murshid Quli Khan Ustajlu had managed to oust the new governor of Mashhad and to install himself instead. After rallying the Ustajlu and other amirs behind him, he had entered into conflict with his former ally, Ali Quli Khan Shamlu, the governor general of Khurasan and guardian of Prince Abbas. In the course of a battle between the two, Murshid Quli Khan had succeeded in seizing Prince Abbas and carrying him off to Mashhad.

Severely weakened by its internal problems and by the Ottoman invasion of its north-western territories, Iran now received a further hammer blow from the east. A new Uzbek leader, Abdullah Khan, had reunited the Uzbek clans and in December 1587 he swept into Khurasan, laying siege to Herat and threatening to overrun the whole province. He was spurred on by the Ottomans whose conquest of Shirvan and much of Azerbaijan had enabled them to put a fleet on the Caspian and enter into direct contact with their Uzbek allies for the first time. Shi'i Iran faced a real danger of being crushed between the two Sunni millstones.

The Uzbek invasion was a threat to Murshid Quli Khan in Mashhad, who realised this might be his last chance to exploit his possession of Prince Abbas. Other leading Qizilbash amirs gave assurances of their support for placing Abbas on the throne, and after learning that Sultan Muhammad Shah had left Qazvin to confront rebels in the south, Murshid Quli Khan decided to strike. He left his brother, Ibrahim Khan, to defend Mashhad against the Uzbeks and set out for Qazvin with the seventeen-year-old Abbas and a small force of some 600 horsemen.

As they rode west along the old Silk Road that threads its way between the foothills of the Alburz Mountains and the Great Salt Desert, Qizilbash amirs from the powerful Türkman, Afshar and Zul Qadr tribes, who controlled many of the key towns on the way, came to pledge their allegiance. By the time they approached Qazvin, their small force had swelled to some 2,000 armed horsemen. Called upon to surrender, the governor of Qazvin initially vacillated and many of the Qizilbash amirs in the capital urged resistance. But they gave up when crowds of ordinary citizens and soldiers, presumably anxious to avoid further fighting, came out onto the streets to voice their support for Abbas, who rode into the capital beside Murshid Quli Khan on a late September day in 1587.

The Qizilbash faction led by the Shamlu and Ustajlu amirs that had dominated the court was encamped with Sultan Muhammad Shah and

Prince Abu Taleb some 200 miles away, near the Shi'i holy city of Qom. Divided as ever, they had little choice but to accept the *fait accompli*. One or two began to leave for Qazvin to do obeisance to their new prince, then others followed and their army quickly disintegrated. Iskandar Beg Munshi writes:

> Soldiers of all ranks, not obeying anyone's orders, began to leave. Even the men in the royal workshops abandoned their gear and left. The men in the royal bandmaster's department decamped with the trumpets and kettledrums, and played a fanfare for Prince Abbas after they reached the city. On the day they struck camp and moved towards the city, only a handful of grooms, reinholders and stable boys were left to assist the shah and Prince Abu Taleb.[20]

The blind old shah is said to have been 'heavy-hearted at the harsh treatment meted out to him by events'[21] and anxious only to end his days in peace. On 1 October 1588, at a ceremony in the palace in Qazvin, he abdicated and placed the crown on the head of the seventeen-year-old son who had overthrown him and who now ascended the throne as Shah Abbas I. The former shah and all the other royal princes were then placed in detention.

Abbas showed no mercy towards the amirs who had backed his younger brother, Abu Taleb, and whom he held responsible for the murder of Prince Hamza. He had them disarmed and brought one by one into the audience hall of the palace, where they were killed. Afterwards, 'twenty-two of their heads stuck on the points of lances were exhibited from the palace windows to the populace below, a sight of terror that struck awe into the hearts of the boldest and most arrogant'.[22]

Abbas rewarded the amirs who had supported his cause by giving them offices at court and provincial governorships. Murshid Quli Khan, to whom Abbas owed his throne, was given the principal office – that of *vakil* or viceroy. But the amirs were soon to discover that Abbas had inherited all of his mother's will to rule, and none of his father's passivity. The days of the Qizilbash amirs lording it over the state were numbered. Abbas was determined to break their power once and for all, and was already devising the means to achieve this.

Chapter 3

Abbas Takes Control

There are no descriptions of Abbas's appearance when he came to the throne, but much that is found in later descriptions would have applied then too. The first thing to say is that, physically, he does not seem to have been a particularly regal figure. He was short of stature, with a low forehead, an aquiline nose and a pointed chin. His hands were short and plump, and were later compared to those of a workman. But he was strongly built and well-proportioned. One of his most striking features was his green eyes, which were penetrating and shining. He had a beard when he came to the throne, but two years later he shaved it off and grew a moustache, of which he was inordinately proud.

He already had one wife, a Circassian Christian woman who had just borne him his eldest son, Prince Safi. During the first year of his reign he strengthened his dynastic position within the Safavid house by marrying two women from the Safavid royal line, one of them being the widow of his murdered elder brother, Prince Hamza. The marriages were held together in Qazvin, and celebrated with three days of fireworks and illuminations.[1]

For the first eighteen months of his reign, however, Abbas had to live in the shadow of the Qizilbash kingmaker, Murshid Quli Khan Ustajlu. He disliked the Ustajlu khan, but he was conscious that, for the time being, he could not do without him. The kingdom remained very unsettled and the loyalty of many of the amirs was doubtful. Abbas needed Murshid Quli Khan to secure his position. So he bided his time.

It seems surprising that Murshid Quli Khan should apparently have had no idea of the real character of his young protégé, of Abbas's dislike of the dominant role of the Qizilbash and that he might eventually move against his former guardian and current *vakil*. Clearly Abbas was already a past master of deception.

Confident in his new-won power, Murshid Quli Khan took up residence with Abbas in the palace in Qazvin, before moving into a house next to the palace that had been the home of Abbas's forceful aunt, Pari Khan Khanum. At his residence, he issued daily orders to the state officials, promulgated decrees, and distributed civil and military offices and provincial governorships to friends and dependants – all in the name of the shah, but without consulting him. He took the richest province of Isfahan for himself. At the same time, he introduced one measure which must have made him fairly unpopular in the country: he raised taxes by 25 per cent.[2]

Two months after the coup, Murshid Quli Khan sent the former shah and the rest of the royal princes to join Abbas's brother, Prince Tahmasp, in the prison-fortress of Alamut in the mountains north of Qazvin, fearing that their presence in the capital might incite unrest. The princes included the former shah's paternal uncle, Sultan Ali, who had been blinded at the age of four by Shah Ismail II; Abbas's other younger brother, Abu Taleb; and the infant sons of the murdered Prince Hamza, Ismail and Haidar.

Murshid Quli Khan's monopoly of power and the arrogance with which he exercised it soon provoked opposition from other high-ranking Qizilbash amirs, even from those promoted to high office immediately after the coup. A number of them plotted to kill him, among them three of the most senior officers of the state: the *qurchi-bashi* or commander of the household cavalry; the *muhrdar* or keeper of the seal; and the *khalifat al-khulafa* (literally 'deputy of deputies'), who was in charge of the Safavid Sufi organisation. All three had been appointed after the coup, which indicates the degree to which Murshid Quli Khan had succeeded in antagonising his fellow amirs. But Murshid Quli Khan got wind of the plot and alerted Abbas. When the conspirators realised this they decided to put their complaints against the *vakil* to the shah and demand his removal. They knew that Abbas had no love for his *vakil* and assumed that he would do as they asked. In this, they were mistaken. Abbas was not yet ready to dispense with Murshid Quli Khan and was certainly not going to do so at the behest of a group of Qizilbash amirs who were at least partly responsible for the calamitous state of the country. He decided to stand by the *vakil* and instead to rid himself of the conspirators, whom he regarded as men who had risen to their positions through treachery to his father.[3]

The conspirators rode up to the palace with their retainers and burst in, still wearing their riding boots and carrying their weapons. Abbas kept his nerve and sent a messenger to demand the reason for this intrusion. Hesitating to launch an immediate attack on the *vakil*, they said had come to accompany him out of the city to welcome an important religious personage from Yazd – an occasion on which they had originally planned to kill him. Abbas sent back the reply that the *vakil* was too busy to go and dismissed them. Somewhat disconcerted, the conspirators withdrew to a nearby park, where they summoned more of their retainers and openly declared their opposition to the *vakil*. When Abbas sent to enquire further what their purpose was, they complained of the arrogant and oppressive behaviour of Murshid Quli Khan and said that working with him had become impossible. Abbas replied that if they had a complaint against Murshid Quli Khan or anyone else, they should make it politely and await the shah's command. He warned them that assembling troops and creating a disturbance was a sign of rebellion. Meanwhile, Abbas called on other Qizilbash to rally to him on the basis of *shahsevan* or 'love of the shah'. This was now replacing the outworn appeal to *sufigari* or 'conduct becoming a Sufi' as a more inclusive and effective bond between the shah and his subjects. As more and more Qizilbash came to the palace in response to this call, the conspirators sent a message to the shah stressing that they had no complaints against his person, but reiterating their objections to Murshid Quli Khan. Abbas said that he would summon Murshid Quli Khan in the morning.

The following morning the conspirators sent the governor of Shiraz, Mehdi Quli Khan Zul Qadr, to the palace as their spokesman. He demanded that the shah dismiss his *vakil*, allow the Qizilbash chiefs greater freedom and resume the practice of holding twice-weekly meetings of the Council of Amirs. The shah told him that his demands were unacceptable, because they amounted to 'that same independence and unjustified interference of the Qizilbash amirs in the affairs of state which weakened the central government and assisted the enemies of Iran in my father's time'. He went on: 'Now I dispose of the affairs of the country, and I have entrusted the administration of these affairs to Murshid Quli Khan, because of the trust that I place in him. Contrary to what happened in the past, you must dismiss ideas of independence and of creating discord, and if you are obedient to this state you will accept his [Murshid Quli Khan's] commands and recognise him as your chief.'[4]

Mehdi Quli Khan gave an impudent reply to the shah and began abusing Murshid Quli Khan, who was standing near the throne. Abbas rounded on him in a fury: 'You seditious little man! It was I who made you governor of Shiraz, with the rank of khan. What more do you want? What gives you the right to cause trouble among the Qizilbash? You, and people like you, are thorns in the side of the body politic.'5

Abbas then bestowed the governorship of Shiraz on another Zul Qadr chief, Yaqub Khan, and ordered him to execute Mehdi Quli Khan. He reassigned the posts of the other conspirators in similar manner, each new appointee being ordered to execute the conspirator who had been holding the post. When the conspirators learnt of this, they tried to flee, but most were caught and killed. Two of them managed to escape to Ottoman Baghdad, and two others, one of whom was the *qurchi-bashi*, were pardoned by the shah and imprisoned.

Meanwhile, Abbas's former guardian and the *vakil's* great rival, Ali Quli Khan Shamlu, was in desperate straits in Herat, where he had been under siege by the Uzbeks for months. Abbas remained as fond as ever of Ali Quli Khan, who had been like a father to him and had saved his life by not carrying out his uncle, Shah Ismail II's, order to kill him when he was still a child. He constantly pressed Murshid Quli Khan to assemble a relief force, but the *vakil* dragged his heels, unwilling to give succour to a man who was his enemy and a favourite with the shah. With no prospect of relief in sight and with famine and sickness taking its toll, Ali Quli Khan finally surrendered in February 1589, having endured a siege of more than a year. The Uzbek leader, Abdullah Khan, broke a promise of safe conduct and had Ali Quli Khan and the entire garrison slaughtered. Fired by Sunni zeal, he also had many of the city's Shi'i inhabitants killed. After plundering Herat and briefly besieging Mashhad, he withdrew into the desert to the north.

The fate of Ali Quli Khan deeply affected Abbas. He held Murshid Quli Khan responsible and brought forward his intention of ridding himself of his tutelage. He could no longer tolerate the *vakil's* habit of treating him like a child, by ignoring his wishes and views. Relations between the two were further strained when Abbas rejected a request by the *vakil* for the hand of a Safavid princess. Murshid Quli Khan, who had hoped to bolster his position in this way, was both angered and alarmed to find the shah opposing him. Feeling it might be necessary to replace Abbas, he sent orders for the deposed shah and his sons, the princes Abu Taleb and Tahmasp, to be brought from Alamut to Qazvin. But before these orders reached Alamut, Abbas had learnt of his intention and had had them moved instead to the fortress of Varamin near Tehran, where he appointed a trusted officer to watch over them.

Now that Ali Quli Khan Shamlu was no longer a threat to him, the *vakil* had no difficulty in rapidly assembling an army to shore up Safavid rule in

Khurasan. He and Abbas set off with the army in April 1589. Abbas had meanwhile found four officers who were willing to kill Murshid Quli Khan – one of them being a Georgian *ghulam*, or slave, by the name of Allahvirdi Khan, who was soon to rise to high office and become one of Abbas's closest associates. On the night of 23 July, when the army was encamped at Shahrud in the eastern foothills of the Alburz Mountains, the shah detained Murshid Quli Khan in conversation in the royal tent until he fell asleep. He then called in the four assassins, whose turn it was to guard the tent that night, and, after some hesitation, they fell on the sleeping *vakil*, but failed to kill him outright. Horribly wounded and streaming blood from his throat, he managed to get up and stumble out of the tent, where he was finished off at a signal from the shah by the keeper of the stables who brought a hammer down on his head.[6]

Criers were then sent through the camp to spread the news of the killing of Murshid Quli Khan, which was a turning point in Abbas's reign. Now, finally, at the age of eighteen, he was free to rule as he wished. He followed up the killing with a purge of Murshid Quli Khan's associates, a number of whom were rounded up and executed before the night was out. As a further warning to any recalcitrant amirs - and there were still plenty of them - he also executed the amir who had led the rebellion in 1585 in the name of Abbas's younger brother, Prince Tahmasp, and had his head paraded through the camp on a pike. At the same time, he gave suitable rewards to the four assassins. He made Allahvirdi Khan the governor of a town near Isfahan; it was the first step up the ladder.

As soon as Abbas arrived with the army in Mashhad, he removed Murshid Quli Khan's brother from his position as governor. But when he replaced him with an amir from another tribe he provoked furious protests from the Ustajlu, who considered Mashhad to be their hereditary fief. This time Abbas gave in to Qizilbash pressure and reappointed an Ustajlu, although that did not prevent the rebellion of a number of Qizilbash chiefs in Khurasan who had been close to Murshid Quli Khan. He had many grave challenges to deal with elsewhere as well. Local governors were in revolt in a number of provinces and powerful vassal rulers on the frontiers had thrown off their allegiance. On top of all this, Abbas received the news that the Ottomans were launching fresh offensives in the west. He had no choice but to abandon his intention of pushing on to Herat and to return instead to Qazvin. On the way he had his father, the former shah, freed from his prison in Varamin and brought before him. Abbas received him with respect and took him back to the capital with him. Later, however, his father was caught plotting with a group of Safavid Sufis, who regarded him as their true spiritual guide. Abbas dealt mercilessly with any challenge to his spiritual authority. He had the Sufis executed and confined his father thereafter to the harem. The former shah died in Qazvin of dysentery in 1595 or 1596.[7]

There had already been moves towards accepting Ottoman peace terms, but these had stalled as a result of the rapid changes of leadership. The Ottomans had now stepped up the pressure by launching a two-pronged attack, while Abbas was absent with the army in the east. One Ottoman army advanced from Erzerum in eastern Anatolia into the Safavid province of Qarabagh in the southern Caucasus, which was a fief of the Qajar Qizilbash tribe. The Ottomans occupied the province and drove the Qajar forces south across the River Aras. Another Ottoman army moved up from Baghdad into the Zagros Mountains, where they defeated and took prisoner the Shamlu governor of Hamadan, plundered the city and extended their occupation as far as the borders of Luristan in the south.

Abbas could not fight the Ottomans, the Uzbeks and his internal enemies all at the same time. So he decided to accept the Ottoman peace terms, however humiliating they were, but with every intention of resuming the fight once he was strong enough to do so. He sent an embassy to Istanbul led by the governor of Ardabil with rich gifts for Sultan Murad III, including 1,500 of the finest horses and an escort of 1,000 elite Qizilbash horsemen. Also accompanying the embassy was Abbas's young nephew, Prince Haidar. Abbas's murdered elder brother, Prince Hamza, had already agreed to send him to Istanbul as a hostage.

The Treaty of Istanbul, which put a temporary end to hostilities, was signed on 21 March 1590. Under its terms, the Ottomans kept all the Iranian territory they had occupied in the Caucasus, Kurdistan and Azerbaijan, including the former Safavid capital of Tabriz – although Abbas was left in possession of a small part of Azerbaijan centred on the Safavid shrine city of Ardabil. The shah agreed to end the persecution of Sunni Muslims, the ritual cursing of the first three caliphs[8] and the dissemination of Shi'i propaganda on Ottoman territory – all promises the Safavids had made before and had evidently failed to live up to. Prince Haidar was to remain at the Ottoman court as a hostage and a guarantee of Iranian good faith. He died there of the plague six years later.

Abbas was now free to concentrate on internal problems and the Uzbeks. As a long-term solution to the former, he had already begun to put through a programme of military and administrative reforms aimed at ending the domination of the Qizilbash, strengthening the central government and providing him with able servants he could depend on to carry out his policies. The reforms would take several years to complete and would transform the nature of the Safavid state.

Military reform was the key, because the Qizilbash could not be dislodged from their dominant position so long as they continued to provide the Safavid state with almost all its military forces. So Abbas set about a huge expansion of the small standing army he had inherited, which was paid for out of the royal treasury and owed allegiance to the shah alone. He more than doubled to over 12,000 the numbers of the *qurchis* or household cavalry. These, as we have seen, were Qizilbash tribesmen who had forsaken their tribal allegiance for allegiance to the shah alone. They were, in effect, in the contemporary terminology, *shahsevans* or 'lovers of the shah'. The tie that bound them to the shah was such that they were not allowed to marry without his permission. When a prominent *qurchi* died, the shah would often order him to be buried within the precincts of the Safavid shrine at Ardabil.[9] Abbas began appointing *qurchis* to important state and court offices previously held by Qizilbash amirs, and their commander, the *qurchi-bashi*, became one of the five most important state officials, a position he retained until the fall of the Safavid dynasty.[10]

The other main element of Abbas's military reforms was the creation of a corps of *ghulams* or slave soldiers.[11] This had existed in embryonic form under Shah Tahmasp, but Abbas now gave it official status as the corps of 'royal household slaves' (*ghulaman-e khassa-ye sharifa*) and greatly increased its numbers from a few hundred to between 10,000 and 15,000 – a build-up which obviously took some time. These slave troops were also known as *qullars* and their commander as the *qullar-aqasi*. Mainly composed of captured Christians from the Caucasus – Georgians, Armenians and Circassians – who were converted to Islam and trained at the court, they bore some resemblance to the Ottoman janissaries.[12] Indeed, Shah Abbas often referred to them as 'my mounted janissaries' – the Safavid *ghulams* being cavalry, whereas the Ottoman janissaries were infantry.

Abbas was determined that his new model army should be equipped with up-to-date weaponry. He is said to have considered bows and arrows useless as weapons of war[13] and was at pains to equip both the *qurchis* and the *ghulams* with muskets, in addition to their traditional weapons. More importantly, he created for the first time a substantial infantry corps of musketeers (*tofangchis*). Numbering 12,000, they were recruited mainly from the Iranian peasantry. He also formed an artillery corps of similar strength, though this remained the weakest element in the Safavid army.[14] Sir Thomas Herbert, who accompanied the English Embassy to Iran at the end of Shah Abbas's reign, said that the Iranians detested the 'trouble of cannon and such pieces as require carriage'.[15] They tended to turn to Europeans for help and advice in this field and they never developed much of a capacity for making their own cannons. Most of the *ghulams*, musketeers and artillerymen were not stationed in the capital, nor were they permanently under arms. They were distributed around the provinces and took some months to assemble for a campaign.

The creation of this much larger standing army did not mean that the Qizilbash tribal levies could be dispensed with altogether. Even after the reform, they were the largest element within the army, accounting for about half its total strength, and they remained its most effective fighting force. But Abbas was no longer wholly dependent on them.

In order to pay for his standing army and to create a more centralised state, Abbas began taking back so-called 'state provinces' (*mamalik*) which had hitherto been granted to Qizilbash amirs as administrative fiefs, and turning them into 'crown provinces' (*khassa*) under the direct control of the central government. The tax revenues of these 'crown provinces', which were administered by centrally appointed viziers, went into the government coffers, instead of being retained and spent in the province, as was the case with administrative fiefs. Among the first provinces to be taken back were Qazvin, Isfahan (after the murder of Murshid Quli Khan who had appropriated it) and Kashan. These were followed later by Yazd and Qum. The Caspian provinces of Gilan and Mazandaran were also administered as crown provinces after Abbas took control of them from their vassal rulers.

At the beginning of his reign, Abbas continued the practice of appointing royal princes to provincial governorships. In 1591 or 1592, he appointed his eldest son, Prince Safi, who was only four, as titular governor and commander-in-chief of the west-central province of Hamadan, which extended to the Ottoman frontier in Mesopotamia, with a Qizilbash amir as his guardian. Shortly afterwards, however, he recalled him and abandoned the practice altogether, so as to avoid the risk of the royal princes being used by powerful Qizilbash amirs to further their political ambitions, as he and his brothers had been. Many years later, following the example of the Ottomans, he had his sons and grandsons confined to the harem, where they were brought up and educated by their mothers and eunuch *ghulams*.

As this indicates, under Abbas the influence and importance of the *ghulams* extended far beyond the military sphere. Their slave status, which in Islam made them adopted sons of their owner,[16] created a unique bond of dependency and allegiance in their relationship to the shah. Abbas found in them the willing and able executors of his policies, men he could trust implicitly, and he made them a principal pillar of the more centralised and unified state he wished to establish. He increasingly appointed them to high offices at the court and in the administration previously monopolised by the Qizilbash, thereby diminishing the Qizilbash influence on the state. By the end of his reign, *ghulams* governed eight of the fourteen biggest provinces and held one-fifth of the high administrative posts.[17] Abbas even gave *ghulam* provincial governors control over local Qizilbash tribes and put them in command of Qizilbash forces. And in a gesture that symbolised the end of the special status of the Qizilbash, he allowed the *ghulams* to wear the scarlet bonnet with twelve gores, which had hitherto been the unique privilege of the Qizilbash.

Prominent *ghulams* came to be among Abbas's closest companions. Of these, none was closer to Abbas than the Georgian *ghulam* Allahvirdi Khan, whose first service to the shah was his participation in the murder of Murshid Quli Khan. Allahvirdi Khan remains a familiar name in Iran to this day because of the bridge he built over the Zayandeh River in Isfahan, which is one of the outstanding monuments to have survived from Safavid times.[18] Abbas appointed him commander of the military corps of *ghulams* (*qullar-aqasi*), before sending him to Shiraz in 1595 as the first *ghulam* provincial governor. Later he appointed him commander-in-chief (*sipahsalar*) of the army. Abbas always paid great attention to his views and once famously commented: 'All Iran obeys me, and I obey Allahvirdi Khan.'[19]

The new importance of the *ghulams* and their greatly expanded role was naturally much resented by the Qizilbash who viewed them with contempt.[20] As former Christians, the *ghulams* were also disliked by the more orthodox Shi'i clergy who considered them 'unclean' even after they had converted to Islam.[21]

Abbas's immediate challenge was to assert his authority within the country. At the end of December 1589, assured of a peace with the Ottomans even though the treaty was not yet concluded, he set off to deal with rebels in central and southern Iran. Over the following year, he crushed rebellions by the governors of Isfahan, Kerman and Fars and effectively ended the second civil war which had broken out after the death of Shah Tahmasp in 1576. He made Isfahan a crown province, while in Fars and Kerman he initially appointed new governors from the same Qizilbash tribe that had long been ruling the province – Zul Qadr in the case of Fars and Afshar in the case of Kerman. But these new governors were *shahsevans*, who put loyalty to the shah above loyalty to their tribe. A few years later, however, he deprived both tribes of these fiefdoms by appointing the royal *ghulam*, Allahvirdi Khan, to Fars and a Kurdish *shahsevan*, Ganj Ali Khan, to Kerman. Ganj Ali Khan, it will be remembered, had grown up with Abbas in Herat.

As he moved around the country to suppress these rebellions, Abbas had plenty of time for exploring parts of his kingdom he was seeing for the first time, as well as for his favourite pursuits of hunting and playing polo. In Fars, on his way to Shiraz, it seems likely that he visited the remains of the palaces of the ancient Iranian kings at Pasargadae and Persepolis. He certainly inspected the famous 'Dam of the Amir' (*Band-e Amir*) built in the latter part of the tenth century by the Shi'i Buyid amir, Adud ud-Daula, to provide irrigation for some 300 villages. This was the sort of infrastructure project that Abbas himself would later promote on a large scale. Later, when playing polo in Shiraz, he fell off his horse and injured himself. He took opium for fifty-seven days to alleviate the pain.[22]

He also made his first visit to Isfahan and seems to have been instantly attracted to the city that was to become his capital, replacing Qazvin. He stayed there for four months on his way south, and on the way back, in November 1590, he first ordered building work to be carried out in the city. This mainly involved the renovation and restoration of bazaars and caravanserais around the *Maidan* or Square of Harun-e Velayat, which was then the centre of the city. But he also ordered that a square to the south of this be levelled and covered with sand from the river, so that it could be used for horse racing and polo. This was the Maidan-e Naqsh-e Jahan ('The Square of the Map of the World'), which he was later to develop as the magnificent Maidan-e Shah ('The Royal Square') and the focal point of a new administrative, commercial and religious centre of the city.[23]

During his first stay in Isfahan, Abbas had his brothers, the princes Abu Taleb and Tahmasp, and his nephew Prince Ismail, brought from Varamin and imprisoned in a fortress in Isfahan. He feared that in Varamin they were too close to dissident Qizilbash amirs, who had fled to the Caspian province of Gilan and whose ruler, Khan Ahmad, was refusing to hand them over. However, when he returned to Isfahan something seems to have aroused his suspicions against the royal princes. According to one account, several Qizilbash amirs had made contact with them; according to another, the amir appointed to watch over them was suspected of preparing to use them in a rebellion. Whatever it was, Abbas's reaction was swift and violent.

40

He had the princes blinded and sent back to Alamut. As a result of his experiences during the civil war, Abbas's suspicions were easily aroused where royal princes or the Qizilbash were concerned. This was later to have tragic consequences for his own children. A Qizilbash amir who gently rebuked Abbas for his treatment of the princes paid for his temerity with his life.

Abbas was back in Qazvin by the middle of January 1591, having covered approximately 1,440 miles in 382 days. Some of the time he was accompanied only by a small escort and travelled at speed, but at other times he had to move at the slower pace of the army and the royal household.[24] Frequently on the move during his reign, Abbas came to be known for his habit of fast riding.

At the same time as he was busy dealing with rebels in the centre and south of the country, Abbas took a first step towards reviving the economy by introducing a new and sounder silver coinage. The highest denomination coin was known as an *abbasi*. It remained in use until the end of the eighteenth century and the French traveller Jean de Thévenot (1633–67), who visited Persia in 1664, described it as 'the best money in the world'.[25]

As Abbas gradually pacified the country, he also took measures to re-establish security on the roads, which was an essential condition for reviving long-distance trade. He had armed guards known as *rahdars* (literally 'road keepers') stationed at intervals along the principal roads to provide protection from thieves and robbers. It was an efficient system that came to be widely admired.

All the time he had been away, Abbas had been busy making new appointments – new provincial governors and viziers, a new steward of the royal household, a new master of the hunt, and so forth. He was constantly striving to have people in place whom he could trust. But it was not until the spring of 1591, during the Noruz, or New Year, celebrations in Qazvin, that he found the right person to fill the post of *vazir-e azam* or grand vizier. The grand vizier was the head of the bureaucracy and was responsible for overseeing the entire business of government. Engelbert Kaempfer, a highly educated German, who acquired much solid information on a visit to Persia towards the latter part of the seventeenth century, described the grand vizier as the shah's deputy and 'the axis of the state administration, around which all public life revolves'.[26]

The man Abbas chose for this post was Hatem Beg Ordubadi. He belonged to an old Tajik administrative family who traced their lineage back to the medieval philosopher Nasir ud-Din Tusi (1201–74), and had close ties to the Safavid court. The family owned large estates by the River Aras in north-western Azerbaijan and Hatem Beg's father had played host to Shah Tahmasp when he went on fishing expeditions on the Aras. Hatem Beg himself had climbed the administrative ladder, serving as a provincial vizier and then as head of the financial department of the central government. In this last position he had been charged with implementing a measure to restore order to the state finances by undertaking an exact survey of the revenues and expenditure of each province.

As the new *Etemad ud-Daula* ('Trusty Support of the State'), the honorary title by which the grand vizier was known, Hatem Beg proved to be an administrator of exceptional ability. He remained in office until his death nearly twenty years later and during this time he built up a very effective government bureaucracy which enabled the Safavid state to continue to thrive under much less able rulers than Shah Abbas. Iskandar Beg Munshi, who served under him, says he 'brought security into the lives of Iranians' and 'was a model for all in regard to the administration of justice, his knowledge of accounting procedures, and his organisation of divan affairs'.[27] He was equally admired by foreigners. The Carmelite friar Father Paul Simon, in a report to Rome in 1608, expressed amazement at the ease with which Hatem Beg discharged a heavy burden of work. The friar described how Hatem Beg 'used to despatch 200 petitions in a morning, and after having sat and given a hearing for six or seven hours would go out as serene as if he were coming from taking his horse for a walk'.[28] The English adventurer Sir Anthony Sherley, who met Hatem Beg several years earlier, describes him as 'a wise man, excellently seen in all Affairs, of great Experience'. But he adds that he was 'such a one as was only his [the shah's] creature, without Friends or Power'. Sherley says that Abbas now appointed throughout his kingdom 'those who must be most assured to him, their Fortunes depending only upon him, having no more strength, nor authority in themselves, than they received from him . . .'[29] Besides his civilian duties as grand vizier, Hatem Beg also took part as a military commander in the further pacification of the country. It was a sign of changing times that he apparently did so without incurring the anger of the Qizilbash, as his predecessor, Mirza Salman, had done.[30]

The year 1591-2 CE was the year 1000 of the Muslim lunar calendar.[31] This inevitably stirred up millenarian expectations among extremist religious groups like the Nuqtavis, who continued to have a strong presence in a number of cities, despite bouts of severe persecution. There were more executions of Nuqtavis in Kashan in 1586, in which two well-known musicians perished, and a Nuqtavi uprising in Fars in 1591 was savagely crushed on the orders of Abbas. The Nuqtavi poet Amri, who had been blinded by Shah Tahmasp for his heretical beliefs, was involved in the uprising and was literally torn to pieces afterwards at the behest of the Shi'i clergy.

However, Abbas was more ambivalent when it came to the large Nuqtavi community in Qazvin led by Darvish Khusraw, who was careful to appear to be an observant Shi'i Muslim. The numerous followers who gathered at his lodge – he had had to build a more spacious one to accommodate them – now included many Qizilbash, principally from the Shamlu and Ustajlu tribes. Their decision to desert their Safavid 'perfect guide', the shah, for Darvish Khusraw no doubt reflected their disillusionment with Abbas's anti-Qizilbash policy.[32]

Abbas himself eventually went along to see what was going on and began attending meetings at the lodge. He may have done so initially out of curiosity, since this was very much part of his nature, and some scholars believe that, for a while at least, he may have been genuinely attracted to the Nuqtavi teachings. Predictably, however, the Safavid chroniclers insist that he merely feigned an interest in order to find out what Darvish Khusraw was up to. At all events, Abbas soon came to be regarded by the Nuqtavis in Qazvin as a 'full trustee' (*amin-e kamil*), at which point he was made privy to the secret beliefs of the community. This was done by two of its most senior members, a quiver-maker by the name of Yusufi Tarkishduz who visited the palace regularly with quivers for the shah, and his companion Darvish Kuchak Qalandar Bahla-duz, a maker of falconers' gloves. The beliefs they revealed to him were mainly those associated with extremist movements, such as the denial of the resurrection and the day of judgement. What he had not expected to hear was a prediction that at the start of the coming Muslim year 1002 (27 September 1593) he would lose his throne to a Nuqtavi disciple.

Alarmed though he was, Abbas seems to have thought it prudent to take no immediate action. However, the seriousness of the Nuqtavi threat was underlined when he consulted Darvish Khusraw about a planned campaign against the rebellious chief of the Lur tribes in the Zagros Mountains of west-central Persia. The Nuqtavi leader warned him to return to Qazvin before the beginning of the Muslim New Year, which 'marks the beginning of our age' when 'one of our darvishes will take control of power'. Believing Abbas to be a committed Nuqtavi, he appears to have proposed that Abbas abdicate over the crucial period to allow the pre-ordained takeover to take place, and return to the throne afterwards.[33]

Abbas decided to march against the Lur chief nonetheless, but on the way he received another missive from Darvish Khusraw again urging him to return quickly, but also offering to provide troops to help the shah in his campaign. It seemed to Abbas that the Nuqtavi leader was now acting as if he was disposing of the affairs of the state and was intent on acquiring political power. His anxiety increased when his chief astrologer told him that 'the reading of the stars and the verses of the Quran' pointed to the execution of a ruler and that there was an unlucky conjunction of the planets in his horoscope.[34] He suggested that the shah give up the throne for three days during the most dangerous period. Abbas followed his advice and finally took action to extirpate the Nuqtavis.

He sent troops back to Qazvin with orders to round up and imprison Darvish Khusraw and his disciples as swiftly and discreetly as possible, before they were able to organise any serious resistance. This was done in a surprise dawn swoop and the only resistance was from disciples at the Nuqtavi lodge, a number of whom were killed or wounded. On Abbas's orders, some of the Nuqtavi leader's most trusted disciples were brought before him, among them the quiver-maker Yusufi Tarkishduz. When questioned by Abbas, Yusufi stood by the prediction that the shah would soon be supplanted by a Nuqtavi disciple. With his astrologer's suggested scenario in mind, Abbas replied that no one was fitter than Yusufi to fulfil that prediction and assume the crown.

For three days Yusufi was given all the trappings of kingship. The Safavid chronicler Iskandar Beg Munshi says that, on the day of his installation, he was clothed in gorgeous robes, with a crown on his head and other royal regalia, placed on a mule with a saddle and bridle studded with jewels, and escorted by all the court to his residence, where he was brought food and wine in abundance. Guarded at night by *qurchis*, 'the poor wretch realised what his fate was to be and decided to make the most of the three days'. 'Kingship, however ephemeral,' comments Iskandar Beg, 'is an enjoyable experience.'[35] At the end of the three days, Yusufi was taken out and shot. His companion, Darvish Kuchak Qalandar Bahladuz, the maker of falconers' gloves, committed suicide by swallowing poison, saying to his guard as he did so, 'We have gone, only to be back in the next cycle.'

On his return to Qazvin from Luristan, Abbas had Darvish Khusraw tried for heresy before the Shi'i clergy. As proof of Khusraw's disregard for the precepts of the Sharia, vats of wine were said to have been discovered in his lodge. Abbas then had him die a painful and humiliating death. He was tied by his throat to the saddle of a camel and dragged around the city, after which his body was exposed to public view for a week.

44

This act was followed by a country-wide massacre of suspected Nuqtavis, in which Abbas personally took part, killing the leader of the community in Kashan with his own hands by cutting him in two with his sword. Many Nuqtavis, however, managed to escape to India, where they found a safe refuge with the tolerant Moghul emperor, Akbar. It is an indication of the appeal of the movement to artists and intellectuals that many of these were poets.[36]

Abbas's ruthless purge of the Nuqtavis was prompted by his realisation that they were an extremist religious movement which was aiming at political power, just as the Safavid movement itself had done so successfully. It represented a clear rejection of the kind of heterodox religious beliefs that had brought the Safavids to power and a strong affirmation of the Safavid monarchy's close identification with 'orthodox' Twelver Shi'ism and the Shi'i clergy. From now on Abbas would make the Shi'i clergy, the *ulama*, a key pillar of the state, alongside the *ghulams*.

Chapter 4

The Recovery of Khurasan from the Uzbeks

Having established his authority in the interior of the country, Shah Abbas turned his attention to the vassal rulers on the frontiers who had thrown off their allegiance. Principal among these were Khan Ahmad, the ruler of the Caspian province of Gilan, and Shahvirdi Khan, the leader of the Iranian Lur tribes in the western Zagros Mountains, both of whom were neighbours of the Ottomans – a position they exploited in order to maintain their independence of the shah.

Gilan was a province of vital importance to Abbas, because it was the centre of silk production, which was Iran's main export commodity. One of Khan Ahmad's predecessors had sheltered Shah Ismail I from his enemies for several years before he began his conquest of Iran. But Khan Ahmad had had a difficult relationship with Shah Tahmasp, who imprisoned him for many years. Freed by Sultan Muhammad Shah, he had married one of Shah Tahmasp's daughters, but when war broke out between Iran and Ottoman Turkey he made overtures to the Ottomans.[1] Shah Abbas summoned him to appear at court after he refused to hand over some rebellious Qizilbash amirs and was reported to have offered to become a vassal of the Ottomans. Khan Ahmad ignored the summons, and in 1592 Abbas sent an army into Gilan. As a sign of the shah's displeasure with the Gilanis, he sent ahead as the vanguard of the regular army a 500-strong corps of men who had been used to suppress criminality in Qazvin and were notorious for their brutality. They had dagger-like moustaches and were dressed from head to toe in scarlet, which was 'the uniform of the executioners of the king's justice'.[2] In one town in Gilan they put all the

47

inhabitants they could lay their hands on to the sword, including women and children, and as the governor of the town had fled, they burnt his wife alive.

Khan Ahmad was defeated and fled to Istanbul, leaving his Safavid wife and their young daughter behind. Shah Abbas put them both in his harem and took the daughter as his wife. Gilan remained in a troubled state. There were further rebellions which were put down with great severity, and in 1595 Abbas annexed the province. But the Gilanis were a fiercely independent people and would continue to reassert themselves. That loyal Safavid bureaucrat, Iskandar Beg Munshi, no doubt reflected the prejudice of many at the court when he wrote:

> As everyone knows, the people of Gilan are dim-witted, ignorant and improvident. They are treacherous and disloyal by nature. .... For the sake of being king for a day, they are ready to destroy themselves. ... Providence dictates that one should avoid having dealings with such a people.[3]

After subjugating Gilan, Abbas turned his attention to the neighbouring Caspian province of Mazandaran, the home of his mother Mahd-e Oliya, which was ripe for conquest as it was divided between a number of warring dynasts. Local resistance was crushed in two campaigns in 1596 and 1597, paving the way for the annexation of the province. Abbas became very attached to Mazandaran, where he later built a number of magical palaces by the Caspian Sea.

He also mounted two campaigns against the Lur leader, Shahvirdi Khan, who sought refuge with the Ottomans, but was finally captured and put to death in 1597 or 1598. All the other Lur chiefs who were suspected of disloyalty to the shah were also executed. Abbas then divided the province of Luristan by putting a small part that was close to Ottoman Baghdad under a Qizilbash amir, while entrusting the rest to a maternal relation of Shahvirdi Khan's. This branch of the family continued to govern the province as obedient vassals until the fall of the Safavid dynasty more than a hundred and twenty years later.[4]

Abbas entrusted most of these campaigns to a Qizilbash amir, Farhad Khan Qaramanlu, who was his commander-in-chief with the honorary title of *rukn as-saltana* ('pillar of the sultanate'). Farhad Khan was descended from one of Shah Ismail I's commanders and was part of that Qizilbash establishment that Abbas had otherwise come to mistrust. But he became a close ally of the shah at a time when Abbas's power was still insecure and was rewarded with fiefs that stretched right across northern Iran. By the time he completed his pacification of Mazandaran, Farhad Khan was presiding over a brilliant court of his own and was seen as such a powerful figure that he was commonly known as 'the khan of the age'.[5]

The Uzbeks took advantage of Abbas's preoccupation with internal problems to intensify their attacks on Khurasan. In 1590 they renewed their attack on the Shi'i holy city of Mashhad, and this time succeeded in capturing it after a four-month siege. The Uzbek troops led by Abdullah Khan's son, Abd ul-Mumin, engaged in an orgy of killing, raping, burning and looting. Some of the population thought to save themselves by taking refuge in the shrine of the Imam Riza, only to be massacred there. The shrine was pillaged, its priceless library destroyed and its graves desecrated, including the grave of Shah Tahmasp. Thousands of people were carried off into slavery. After leaving a garrison in Mashhad and other towns, Abd ul-Mumin again withdrew into the desert. For the next seven years the Uzbeks remained in control of most of Khurasan.

Shah Abbas had his gold and silver plate melted down to meet the cost of a protracted war. He quoted his father approvingly as saying that 'good pay had brought about as many or more victories as ever good fortune had alone accomplished'.[6] He also introduced severe penalties for any Qizilbash who shirked military service. He mounted repeated counterattacks in alliance with the rebel Uzbek khan of Khwarazm to the north of Khurasan, but met with only temporary successes. On occasion he challenged the Uzbek leader, Abdullah Khan, to settle their differences in single combat – a challenge that was not taken up – and he ordered his general, Farhad Khan, not to engage the Uzbek forces if they were led by either Abdullah Khan or his son Abd ul-Mumin, 'because it was contrary to protocol for amirs to give battle to kings'.[7] But otherwise there was little room for chivalry in a war made more savage by the bitter Shi'i-Sunni antagonism, where atrocities were committed on both sides.

Abdullah Khan, meanwhile, urged both the Ottoman and Moghul empires to join him in a holy war against the 'heretical' Shi'i state. But the Ottomans were unwilling to tear up the newly signed peace treaty with Iran, while the Moghuls regarded the growing power of the Uzbek khanate as a potential threat to themselves. The Moghul emperor, Akbar, was also far from sharing Abdullah Khan's Sunni fanaticism. He told him that although the Safavids were not Sunnis, they were descendants of the Prophet, and had long been linked with the Moghuls by ties of friendship. But this friendship did not extend to helping Abbas to drive the Uzbeks out of Khurasan, as the shah requested in an embassy he sent to India in 1591. Nor did it prevent Akbar from exploiting the situation to take back Qandahar while the shah was distracted elsewhere. He did this entirely peacefully, by offering attractive financial rewards to the Safavid governor of Qandahar, Muzaffar Husain Mirza, who was facing the ever-present danger of an Uzbek attack with no prospect of receiving help from Shah Abbas.

By 1597 the Uzbeks were carrying out raids further west, deep into the heartlands of Iran. But the following year there was a dramatic reversal of fortunes. Abdullah Khan died in February 1598, shattered by the rebellion of his son, Abd ul-Mumin, who was assassinated shortly afterwards. With the Uzbeks thrown into disarray, Farhad Khan was able to occupy Mashhad and was joined near Herat by Shah Abbas and the commander of the *ghulam* troops, Allahvirdi Khan. Together they routed the Uzbek army in a pitched battle on the morning of 9 August, after which the shah made a triumphal entry into Herat. Soon Iranian rule was restored throughout most of Khurasan, though the Uzbeks retained control of the important commercial centre of Balkh in the east.

On the morrow of his great victory Abbas struck a further blow at the Qizilbash by ordering the assassination of his army commander, Farhad Khan. He had this carried out by the Georgian *ghulam* Allahvirdi Khan, who eight years earlier had been detailed to take part in the assassination of the over-mighty *vakil* Murshid Quli Khan. A number of allegations were made against Farhad Khan, including that he had shown cowardice during the battle and was conspiring with the Ottomans. Neither carries much credibility. As we have seen, Abbas had a suspicious nature that was easily aroused, especially where a Qizilbash amir was concerned. It is probable that, like the *vakil*, the general had become arrogant with power, and the shah saw him as a threat. Allahvirdi Khan, who was already commander of the *ghulams* and governor general of Fars, was rewarded with the additional office of commander-in-chief. Significantly, Abbas brought back an old Persian word – *sipahsalar* – for the office of commander-in-chief, in place of the Arabic term *amir al-umara* or 'amir of amirs', which had been used hitherto, when this office was normally held by a Qizilbash amir.

Abbas gave thanks for his victory to the Shi'i Imams and his people. He stayed for about three months in Mashhad and during this time he went every morning and evening to the shrine of Imam Riza, where he swept the carpets in an act of humility. He made rich gifts to the shrine – jewelled chandeliers, gold and silver candlesticks and fine Kerman carpets – and brought the numbers of clerics employed there up to strength.[8] He also reorganised the daily distribution of food to the poor, which was a regular charitable activity of great shrines. To show his gratitude to his people, Abbas rescinded the 25 per cent tax increase introduced by Murshid Quli Khan, and as a special gesture to the people of Khurasan he completely abolished the sheep tax in the province.[9]

He also remitted all taxes for a year in Isfahan, which he had now decided to make his new imperial capital. The city had appealed to him ever since his first visit in 1590, during his campaign to crush rebels in the centre and south of the country. It had a pleasant climate, a good supply of water from the Zayandeh River that flows down from the Zagros Mountains to the west, and plenty of fertile land around it to feed a large urban population. He had spent the previous winter in Isfahan, and before setting out for Khurasan he had approved plans for its further development. Since 1590 considerable work had already been carried out. Much more would be done over the rest of Abbas's reign, with the aim of creating a capital that would be the equal of Delhi or Istanbul and the architectural embodiment of his vision of a strong, centralised state. After Tabriz and Qazvin, Isfahan was the third and would be the last Safavid capital. It represented a move deeper into the Iranian heartlands and yet further away from north-western Iran with its strong Turkoman and Qizilbash presence. It also represented a new orientation towards the south and the Persian Gulf, where Abbas had ambitions to extend his authority.

But it was to Qazvin that Shah Abbas now returned in triumph, to find a somewhat unusual foreign mission waiting for him.

Chapter 5

English Adventurers
at the Service of Shah Abbas

The mission that awaited Abbas in Qazvin was led by two English adventurers, Sir Anthony Sherley,[1] who was then thirty-four, and his younger brother Robert, who was not more than eighteen. They were accompanied by a suite of twenty-four followers, six of whom were gentlemen and the rest servants. They had arrived in Qazvin three weeks earlier after travelling through Ottoman territory from Aleppo to Baghdad and then joining a caravan of Iranian pilgrims returning home.

The original purpose of their mission remains something of a mystery. Sir Anthony says they went there with two aims in mind: to persuade Shah Abbas to seek an alliance with the Christian powers of Europe against the Ottomans, and to promote commercial relations. The alliance aim is hard to understand, as it ran completely counter to the foreign policy of Queen Elizabeth I's government, which was to seek friendship with the Ottomans, on the principle that 'my enemy's enemy is my friend'. From the point of view of London, the Ottomans were playing a very useful role in tying down the Spanish fleet in the Mediterranean. The second aim is also puzzling. Direct trade between England and Iran would mean reopening the route through Russia, which the tsar had shown no inclination to agree to and which had anyway proved to be hazardous at the best of times. Trade through the Persian Gulf was ruled out as it was still controlled by Portugal, which since 1581 had been united with Spain. Any direct trade with Iran would also undermine the newly founded Levant Company, which bought goods originating in Iran and further east from Turkish merchants in Aleppo.

The Sherley mission had no sanction whatever from the English government. If it represented anyone other than Sir Anthony Sherley himself, it was his patron, the Earl of Essex, who was Queen Elizabeth's favourite but was soon to lose his head in an ill-conceived coup attempt. Essex sent the Sherley brothers and their companions to Italy to help the illegitimate son of the Duke of Ferrara in a quarrel over his inheritance with the pope. When they got to Venice they found the dispute had been settled. Sir Anthony claimed he then received instructions from Essex to lead a mission to Iran. Essex does seem to have supported the mission, but the idea is likely to have originated with Sir Anthony himself. While in Venice he got into conversation with an Iranian merchant as well as with an Italian, Angelo Corrai, who had just returned from the Safavid court. Corrai, who was to join the mission as interpreter, told Sir Anthony that Shah Abbas 'was a gallant soldier, very bountiful and liberal to strangers', and assured him that 'if he would go thither, it would be greatly for his advancement'.[2] It is quite possible that Sir Anthony went to Iran in the first instance with little more in mind than seeing what opportunities might be offered by this 'bountiful and liberal' prince, and thought out what he could usefully propose to the shah once he was there. He was every bit the Elizabethan adventurer – resourceful, persuasive, proud and boastful, always with an eye to the main chance and not above embroidering the truth. His mission is important because it initiated the most intensive diplomatic contacts there had ever been between Iran and Europe.

Shah Abbas was naturally informed of the presence of the Sherley brothers before he reached Qazvin. He ordered that they and their suite be given horses so they could ride out with the official welcoming party to meet him. They dressed magnificently for the occasion, as only Elizabethan gentlemen knew how to. Sir Anthony and Robert Sherley both wore cloth of gold with rich turbans on their heads. Sir Anthony had boots embroidered with pearls and rubies and a sword studded with pearls and diamonds hanging from a sash around his neck. The interpreter, Angelo Corrai, and five gentlemen wore cloth of silver, while the servants were dressed some in crimson velvet, some in blue and yellow damask and others in carnation taffeta. One of the gentlemen acted as marshal and rode ahead of Sir Anthony with a white staff. The governor of Qazvin and an Iranian official described as the Lord Steward rode beside the Sherley brothers.

They met up with the royal army a short distance from the city, where they saw 'such a prospect as is not usually seen'. The vanguard was composed of 1,200 horsemen carrying the heads of slaughtered Uzbeks on their lances, 'and some having the ears of men put on strings and hanged about their necks'. Then came the trumpeters, 'making a wonderful noise ... these trumpets being two yards and a half in length, with the great end big, and so much compass as a hat'. They were followed by the drummers, beating brass kettledrums carried upon camels. Next came six standard-bearers, then twelve pages with lances, and a good distance after them came the king, 'riding alone with a lance in his hand, his bow and arrows, sword and target hanging by his side, being a man of low stature, and swarthy of complexion'. He wore 'an old brocade doublet and tight breeches of the same material. On his head was a turban, adorned with many precious stones and rich plumage.' His general, Allahvirdi Khan, rode behind him, with 'all his bows in rank like a half-moon', and after them came his officers and the rest of the army, 'to the number of twenty thousand soldiers, all horsemen'.[3]

The Sherley brothers and their retinue approached to within five or six paces of the shah, where they dismounted and kissed his boot, which he held out to them. Sir Anthony made a short speech saying he had come from a far country 'to be a present spectator' of those 'royal ventures' of which he had heard so much. Abbas's reply was, in Sir Anthony's words, 'infinite affable'.[4] He told him he was heartily welcome and invited the Sherley brothers and their companions to accompany him into the city. On the way they saw 'a great troop of courtesans ... come riding richly apparelled to salute the King and to welcome him from his wars'. They wore breeches and rode astride like men, 'and came with such a cry as the wild Irish make'.[5] Huge crowds lined the way, and 'the people would kneel and kiss the earth' as the shah passed by.

They alighted at a palace in the main square where Sir Anthony made another speech, this time emphasising their ill treatment at the hands of Ottoman officials when they were on their way to Iran. This elicited an expression of sympathy from the shah, who conversed with Sir Anthony about his travels, his native country of England, and its manner of government. A banquet was served, after which Abbas invited Sir Anthony to watch from a window while he played polo – a game then unknown in England. The shah joined eleven other horsemen in the square who were divided into two teams, each player 'having in their hands long rods of wood, about the bigness of a man's finger, and on the end of the rods a piece of wood nailed on like unto a hammer'. When they turned to face one another, 'there came one into the middle, and did throw a wooden ball between both the companies, and having made goals at either end of the plain, they began their sport, striking the ball with their rods from one to the other ... and ever when the King had gotten the ball before him, the drums and trumpets would play one alarum, and many times the King would come to Sir Anthony to the window, and ask him how he did like the sport'.[6]

One of the discomforts all Europeans had to endure in Iran, where chairs were not normally used, was sitting cross-legged or kneeling on a carpet for extended periods of time. On this occasion it seems that Abbas provided his English guests with stools. One of the gentlemen in the retinue of the Sherley brothers, George Manwaring, says this was only after an Ottoman ambassador who was present told Abbas that 'it was the fashion of England to sit on stools, for he had been oft-times in the English merchants' houses in Constantinople'. Abbas rewarded the ambassador's helpful intervention with an anti-Turkish outburst. Drinking a health to Manwaring, he said, 'I do esteem more of the sole of a Christian's shoe, than I do of the best Turk in Turkey.'

Later, Abbas escorted Sir Anthony and his party back to their lodgings, where they had supper and were about to retire to bed when he sent for them again. They found the shah waiting for them in the covered bazaar which had been festooned and painted in celebration of the victory over the Uzbeks and was now lit up with 'an infinite number of candles and lamps'. All the goods were beautifully displayed and the shopkeepers themselves were 'apparelled very gallantly'. Drums and trumpets announced another banquet, this time with musicians and twenty richly dressed women singing and dancing. This took place in the middle of the bazaar on 'a round kind of stage covered with costly carpets'. Afterwards, the king took Sir Anthony by the arm, his nobles each took one of the English company by the hand, and together they walked through the city, 'the twenty women going before, singing and dancing . . . and at every turning there was variety of music, and lamps hanging on either side of their streets of seven heights, one above another, which made a glorious show'.[7]

The victory celebrations went on for eight days and nights, but the court remained in Qazvin for another six weeks. The shah seems to have taken a genuine liking to Sir Anthony, no doubt in part because the Englishman helped to feed his insatiable curiosity. Sir Anthony later recalled approvingly that Abbas did not waste time with talk 'of our apparell, building, beauty of our women, or such vanities', but instead wanted to hear 'of our proceeding in our warres, of our usuall Armes, of the commodity and discommodity of Fortresses, of the use of Artillery, and of the orders of our government'.[8] Warfare was a subject on which Sir Anthony was something of an expert, having fought in France and the Low Countries and led a naval expedition to the Caribbean. He had also brought some books with him on military science which the two pored over together. Abbas is said to have sent for Sir Anthony at least once a day and sometimes to have summoned both the Sherley brothers to his bed-chamber at midnight to continue their discussions – all this, of course, through the tireless interpreter, Angelo Corrai.

There was the usual exchange of presents between the shah and a visiting envoy, with Sir Anthony giving the shah a number of jewels and precious objects and receiving in return much of what he needed for his further travels in the way of horses, mules, camels, tents and carpets. Sir Anthony says that while he was with the shah in Qazvin he refrained from mentioning the main purpose of his mission – the anti-Ottoman alliance. He says he wanted first to find out what was in the shah's mind and to gain his affection, as well as that of 'his Great men; especially of those whom I did imagine would be best and strongest assisters of my purpose'. He may also have been deterred by the presence of the Ottoman ambassador.

In January 1599 Abbas and the court left for Isfahan, accompanied by the Sherley brothers and their entourage. During the journey Abbas told the Sherleys of the hostility of the Ottomans towards him and of his belief that his former general, Farhad Khan, had been an Ottoman agent. He also said that 10,000 Kurds had fled from Ottoman territory and had asked for permission to settle in Iran. Sir Anthony observed that it was almost impossible for two such great potentates as the Safavid shah and the Ottoman sultan to remain friends. He still did not raise the idea of an anti-Ottoman coalition with Abbas, but he says that he put the plan to the shah's general, Allahvirdi Khan. The general expressed his support, but warned Sir Anthony to expect opposition from the grand vizier, the court chamberlain and the commander of the household cavalry, the *qurchi-bashi*.

Two weeks after arriving in Isfahan, Sir Anthony Sherley finally broached the matter while walking with the shah in the palace gardens. The chief Iranian officials were present and an animated debate ensued. As Allahvirdi Khan had predicted, Sir Anthony's arguments in favour of a concerted attack on the Ottomans were vigorously opposed by the grand vizier, Hatem Beg Ordubadi. He accused the Sherley brothers of being self-seeking adventurers, and argued that the blessings of peace far outweighed the risks of war. He said that Iran was unprepared, that it was humiliating to seek the friendship of Christian princes, and that 'if the Porte was decadent it would be wise to let it decay still more'.[9] Instead he favoured an expedition against the Portuguese in the Persian Gulf. The court chamberlain spoke in similar vein. They were answered by Allahvirdi Khan who backed the alliance proposal and said an expedition against the Portuguese would be much more risky. Abbas brought the discussion to an end with a survey of the state of the Ottoman Empire, but gave no indication whether he favoured war or peace. Over the next few months the shah showed no inclination to reopen the debate and it began to look as if the peace party had gained the upper hand. Sir Anthony became ill with anxiety and took to his bed, but the shah showed his consideration for him by visiting him regularly.

There can be no doubt that Abbas intended to go to war with the sultan sooner or later to recover the lost territories. It also looks as if he was already thinking in terms of a Christian alliance when the Sherley brothers arrived, judging by the report that he was planning to send an embassy to Spain.[10] Abbas was very conscious of the military strength of the Ottoman Empire and that he would stand a much better chance of achieving his aim if the Ottomans had to fight on two fronts. If he still hesitated it was because, as he admitted to Sir Anthony, efforts to build such an alliance had a long and disappointing history. He also needed to assure himself that the Sherley brothers were not simply self-seeking adventurers, as his grand vizier alleged. Here apparently Sir Anthony used a little inventiveness to enhance his standing. He told Abbas he was a cousin of King James VI of Scotland (the future James I of England) and 'all the kings of Christendom had recognised him as such, and had now empowered him as their ambassador to treat with the King of Persia'.[11]

Abbas was not the sort of ruler to ignore the views of senior councillors, like the grand vizier. But the latter were finally persuaded by the shah and Allahvirdi Khan to agree to Sir Anthony Sherley's proposal. Sir Anthony himself says the Ottomans played into his hands by sending another ambassador to Isfahan with a series of unacceptable demands. After admonishing the shah to keep the peace, the Ottoman ambassador demanded that he restore Khurasan to the Uzbeks, return the Kurds who had taken refuge in Iran, and send his eldest son to the Ottoman court as a hostage to replace his nephew, Prince Haidar, who had died there. Abbas was so angry he had the ambassador's beard shaved off and told him to give it to the sultan with his compliments and tell him to eat it.

At first, Abbas wanted to send Robert Sherley on a mission to Queen Elizabeth and to make use of Sir Anthony in Iran in a military capacity. But Sir Anthony persuaded him that he himself should be sent instead 'to all the princes of Christendom'.[12] He also asked the shah to appoint an

Iranian of rank to accompany him. Abbas chose a Qizilbash noble, Husain Ali Beg Bayat, and seems to have made him the official leader of the mission. But either this was never made clear to Sir Anthony or he simply refused to accept it. The mission was to be dogged by bitter disputes between the two of them over precedence

The shah gave them letters for the Habsburg emperor; the kings of Spain, Poland and Scotland; the pope; the Venetian Senate; the Queen of England; Henry of Navarre (the future Henry IV, the first of the Bourbon kings of France); the Medici Grand Duke of Florence; and the Earl of Essex. Besides these letters, which were general expressions of friendship, Sir Anthony was instructed to make a verbal offer of an alliance against the Ottomans.

Robert Sherley was to remain behind in Iran as a hostage against his brother's return. Five members of their suite were to stay with him, among them a gunner whose expertise Abbas clearly hoped to make use of. The rest of the Sherleys' followers accompanied the envoys to Europe. Finally, Abbas issued a decree giving Christian merchants freedom to trade and to practise their religion throughout his empire, with full protection for their lives and property.[13]

There followed a month of feasting that Sir Anthony was to remember fondly when he fell on harder times later in life. It took place 'in a great garden of more than two miles compass, under tents pitched by certain small courses of running water, like divers rivers, where every man that would come, was placed according to his degree, [and] provided for abundantly with meat, fruit, and wine, . . . a royalty and splendor which I have not seen, nor shall I see again but by the same King'.[14]

Shortly before the envoys were due to leave, two Portuguese friars arrived from Hormuz. They introduced themselves as emissaries of the pope and the King of Spain. One of them, an Augustinian called Nicoloa de Melo, used Sir Anthony's good offices to obtain an audience with the shah, at which he then did his best to disparage Sir Anthony and to get himself appointed in his place. Sir Anthony bought him off by including him in the embassy and obtaining letters from the shah for him to present to the pope and the King of Spain. But he was to prove a headache for Sir Anthony on the journey.

Abbas was able to indulge his passion for religious debate with Nicoloa de Melo. He questioned him on the pope's power to remit sins, which Abbas insisted only God could do, adding, 'as for Christ, I do hold him to be a great prophet, yea, the greatest that ever was; and I do think verily, that if any man could forgive sins, it was he'. He presented the friar with a golden crucifix encrusted with precious stones that was said to have belonged to Prester John, the legendary Christian emperor in the East. He also told him how he hated the Jews for crucifying Christ and would allow none to live in his country, which was quite untrue, although he did later persecute them. George Manwaring, who was present, says: 'The friar was stricken mute; and we all did wonder to hear the King reason so exceeding well, in regard he was a heathen; but he told Sir Anthony he was almost a Christian in heart since his coming unto him.'[15]

Much of Abbas's praise of Christ was entirely in line with Islamic teaching, where he is the penultimate prophet in a long line of prophets culminating in Muhammad, who is 'the seal of the prophets'. But Europeans at that time would not have been aware of the high regard Muslims have for Christ, so they read more into what Abbas said about him than they should have. On the other hand, Abbas does seem on occasion to have expressed an enthusiasm for Christ and Christianity that was contrary to Islamic teaching, as here, for instance, where he is quoted as calling Christ 'the greatest prophet', which a Muslim could only say of Muhammad, and as referring to the crucifixion of Christ, which is explictly denied in the Quran. It seems likely that Abbas pretended to be more sympathetic to Christianity than he really was in the belief that this would encourage the Christian princes of Europe to become his allies against the Ottomans. His words certainly made a great impact on his Christian interlocutors. De Melo wrote excitedly to Pope Clement VIII, telling him of the favourable climate for a Christian mission to Iran. His letter was carried posthaste to Rome by the Sherleys' interpreter, Angelo Corrai. Two months later, two Portuguese, one a Jesuit, Francesco da Costa, and the other a soldier, Diego de Miranda, travelled separately through Iran, where they heard about the Sherley embassy and the shah's positive attitude towards Christians. Diego de Miranda also met an Iranian merchant in Venice called Asad Beg, who claimed to be on a secret mission for the shah. Asad Beg even went so far as to tell de Miranda that Abbas intended to become a Christian; all he needed was some Catholic missionaries to convert a sufficient number of Iranians first, so that his own conversion would not provoke a rebellion. When Pope Clement heard this he could hardly contain himself. He immediately wrote to Abbas saying he had heard of his 'ready inclination towards the Christian religion', of his wish to see churches built and to have priests sent out to preach the Gospel. 'This, O King', he said, 'is great news and the start of greater things', and he promised to send missionaries. He also wrote to one of the shah's Christian wives - the Circassian mother of Prince Safi - urging her to help bring the shah 'to the wondrous light of Christian truth and faith'.[16] Pope Clement gave the letters to Francesco da Costa and Diego de Miranda, and sent the pair back to Iran in February 1601 as his ambassadors. He told da Costa he should offer to instruct the shah in the catechism.

Sir Anthony Sherley and Husain Ali Beg Bayat left Isfahan on 9 July 1599 with their respective retinues and the two Portuguese friars. Sir Anthony was accompanied by nineteen members of his original suite, while Husain Ali Beg took with him a number of Iranian secretaries and servants, including his nephew, Ali Quli Beg Bayat, and another Bayat noble, Uruch Beg, who acted as first secretary. Apart from their own considerable baggage, there were thirty-two chests of gifts for the European rulers which the shah had entrusted to Sir Anthony. In view of the nature of their mission there was no way they could travel through Ottoman territory, so they went via Russia. It took them a good six weeks to cross the Caspian Sea, battling against the storms for which it was notorious in a very basic Iranian ship with no deck and only one sail. When they reached Astrakhan at the mouth of the Volga they met up with another Iranian envoy, who had been sent by Abbas to congratulate the new tsar, Boris Godunov, on his accession. The envoy, Pir Quli Beg, had a suite of forty persons, including several Iranian merchants and the shah's falconer. He was also carrying a large consignment of fine Iranian textiles which the shah had ordered him to barter for woollen cloth, coats of mail, furs, falcons and other birds for hawking. The two embassies set off up the Volga in five boats as far as Nizhni Novgorod, where they were met by a courtier sent by the tsar who conducted them overland to Moscow.

Sir Anthony and Husain Ali Beg spent the winter in Moscow, where they quarrelled over who should have precedence. The tsar's court decided in favour of Husain Ali Beg and even imprisoned Sir Anthony after the Portuguese friar, Nicoloa de Melo, made accusations against him. When Sir Anthony was brought before a commission appointed by the tsar to investigate the charges, he became so enraged that he punched de Melo and knocked him down. This impressed the Russians, who promptly freed Sir Anthony and arrested de Melo. The friar later died a prisoner in a monastery in Archangel.

In the spring of 1600 the shah's two envoys left Moscow and took a ship from Archangel across the Barents Sea and down the coast of Norway to the Elbe. Sir Anthony told Husain Ali Beg he had sent the thirty-two chests of presents on ahead by boat. But they were never seen again and his Iranian companion later accused him of selling them and pocketing the proceeds.

The route they took meant that they did not visit the Polish court, as originally intended, perhaps because of pressure from the tsar. Instead they called at various German courts before arriving in Prague in the autumn of 1600. There they were given a lavish reception by the emperor, Rudolph II, who was at war with the Ottomans in Hungary and had a more direct interest in their mission than any of the other Christian princes. However, in the letter he had drawn up for the shah, the emperor resisted pressure from Sherley to pledge not to make peace with the Ottomans without first consulting the shah. He merely promised to pursue the war against them with great vigour.

There was puzzlement in Prague and elsewhere in Europe that Sherley, an Englishman, should be working for the shah to drum up an alliance against the Ottomans, since everyone knew that Queen Elizabeth was pursuing a pro-Ottoman policy. Many suspected that England was secretly trying to gain control of the Iranian and Asian trade, either by diverting it through Russia or by working with Shah Abbas to oust Spain-Portugal from the Persian Gulf. No one imagined that Sir Anthony Sherley was acting on his own initiative – except, that is, Queen Elizabeth, who was furious at his actions. Anthony wrote to her chief minister, Sir Robert Cecil, saying he had only sought to 'bring general profit to my country' and requesting permission to return. This was refused and the English ambassador in Istanbul was instructed to reassure the sultan of the queen's continuing friendship. There was a real fear, particularly on the part of the Levant Company, that commercial relations with the Ottomans might suffer.

About this time Sir Anthony Sherley became a Roman Catholic, which was not calculated to improve his chances of being allowed back into England. After Prague he and Husain Ali Beg went to Munich to visit the Duke of Bavaria, then on across the Brenner Pass into Italy where they were well received by the Gonzagas in Mantua and the Medicis in Florence. But the Venetian Senate refused to see them. For some years now Venice had been seeking to foster friendly relations with the Ottomans in order to safeguard its commercial interests in the Levant. In addition, an Ottoman ambassador was in the city at the time.

Relations between Sir Anthony Sherley and Husain Ali Beg now broke down altogether. They had a violent altercation in Siena over the missing presents, with Husain Ali Beg calling Sir Anthony a thief. Their entry into Rome on 5 April 1601 was greeted with a salute from the guns on the Castel Sant' Angelo, but all the time they were engaged in a furious argument over precedence, eventually becoming so heated they began lashing out at each other. When they were shown their quarters in the magnificent Palazzo della Rovere, they began fighting over who should have the better apartment and had to be separated. Their quarrel soon became the talk of Rome. The Spanish ambassador reported that it divided the entire court 'from the men of rank to the cobblers and the very servants of the Pope . . . some favouring the Englishman and others the Moor'.[17] The two envoys bombarded the papal authorities with messages pressing their rival claims. The French ambassador, Cardinal d'Ossat, commented caustically:

> Perhaps someone may be found who shall tell them that since they being but two and sent by the same prince on the same mission cannot agree between themselves, they will find it difficult to bring about a union of so many Christian princes and others in order to ruin the empire of the Turk.[18]

In the end Pope Clement VIII settled for the only possible diplomatic solution and decided to receive them separately. Although they spent much of their audiences denigrating each other, they confirmed the reports the pope had already been receiving about the shah's desire for an alliance against the Ottomans, his sympathy for Christians and his wish for missionaries. Sir Anthony even said he believed the whole of Iran might be converted. The pope was delighted and gave them a letter for the shah, in which he thanked him for his favours to Christians, promised to send missionaries soon and to work for the co-operation of the Christian princes against the Ottomans.

At the end of May, Sir Anthony Sherley and Husain Ali Beg finally parted company. Sir Anthony left Rome saying he intended to return to Iran, but for some reason changed his mind and went to Venice, where he became involved in other matters. Although he later gave advice on Iran to the Emperor Rudolph and the Spanish government, he never went back there. After more unsuccessful ventures, he ended his days in Madrid as a pensioner of the King of Spain, forever dreaming of some fantastic exploit that would make his fortune.

Husain Ali Beg, meanwhile, had a new problem. While he was in Rome, three members of his entourage – an under-secretary, the cook and the barber – were converted to Catholicism and left the mission. He continued with the remainder to the Spanish court in Valladolid, where he was graciously received by King Philip III (r.1598–1621). Here, besides the Ottoman question, Husain Ali Beg raised an issue which was beginning to cause friction. This was the alleged ill treatment of Iranian merchants by the Portuguese authorities on Hormuz. Portugal's overseas possessions had become as much a Spanish as a Portuguese responsibility now that the two countries were united under the Spanish Crown, and King Philip promised to address the Iranian complaints. He also assured the Iranian envoy that he intended to continue the fight against the Ottomans with all the means at his disposal.

Husain Ali Beg now suffered further embarrassment. The three principal members of his suite, including his nephew, Ali Quli Beg, fell under the influence of the Jesuits and also became Catholics. Ali Quli Beg and another convert, Uruch Beg, were baptised as Don Philip and Don Juan in the Chapel Royal, with the King and Queen of Spain acting as sponsors. They wore white satin suits for the occasion. The third convert, Bunyad Beg, was baptised in a similar ceremony as Don Diego. Husain Ali Beg was livid, but, unable to do anything about it, he sailed for Iran from Lisbon early in 1602. The three converts were given lodgings and a generous allowance by King Philip. Don Juan published his memoirs in Spanish in 1604, but the following year he was involved in a street brawl in Valladolid and stabbed to death. This was the rather embarrassing end for Shah Abbas of his first embassy to Europe.

Chapter 6

Maintaining the Offensive: Khurasan, the Persian Gulf and a Challenge to the Ottomans

After driving the Uzbeks out of most of Khurasan, Abbas was impatient to build up, train and equip his new model army for the greater challenge of taking on the Ottoman army, which was regarded as the most efficient fighting force of the time. This seems to have been principally the work of the shah himself assisted by his general, Allahvirdi Khan, although the Sherley brothers almost certainly gave some help and advice. Robert Sherley even fought with great valour in the Iranian army – the first, but by no means the last, Englishman to do so. The Sherleys did not introduce artillery into Iran, as was once thought,[1] but Shah Abbas clearly looked to the English gunner who remained behind with Robert Sherley to help develop this arm. Unfortunately, while he was accompanying the shah's army to Khurasan he was killed by an Italian, who was possibly also employed as a gunner.

The Ottoman sultan, Mehmet III, was perfectly aware that Abbas intended to try to recover his lost territories, as his envoy's warning to the shah to keep the peace made clear. But the sultan could do little more than warn and threaten, since his forces were fully engaged in fighting the Austrians in Hungary and in combating a series of large-scale rebellions in Anatolia. Abbas drew the sultan's attention to his own new-found strength by sending an ambassador to Istanbul in the summer of 1599 with gold and silver keys to the cities he had taken from the Uzbeks.

For the time being it was the Uzbeks who continued to claim the shah's attention. After his recapture of Herat in 1598, Abbas had moved thousands of Kurds from their homelands in the west to northern Khurasan to help defend the province from further Uzbek attacks. It was the first of a number of major deportations of peoples carried out by Abbas. He did them for a variety of reasons: to strengthen the defences of a frontier, as in this case; to remove a potential threat; to punish or weaken a tribe; or to secure an economic benefit.

The Uzbek khanate, strong in its Sunnism, remained a potentially formidable enemy and still possessed a foothold in eastern Khurasan in the great trading city of Balkh. Abbas's strategy was to exploit divisions among the Uzbeks in order to promote princes loyal to himself, with the aim of turning the khanate into an Iranian satellite. The attempt failed, mainly because of the skilful and determined resistance of a new Uzbek leader, Baqi Muhammad.

After the departure of his embassy to Europe, Abbas returned to Khurasan, where he captured the northern city of Marv and brought it under Iranian rule for the first time since the reign of Shah Ismail I. In the summer of 1600 he succeeded in installing another Uzbek puppet in Balkh, who he hoped would then be able to establish himself in the Uzbek capital, Bukhara. But his puppet made himself thoroughly unpopular, and when he died of smallpox a few months later the Uzbek ruler in Bukhara, Baqi Muhammad, moved swiftly and took control of the city. Abbas now decided to throw his weight behind two Uzbek princes who had escaped from Balkh and taken refuge in Iran.

He tried to persuade Baqi Muhammad to hand Balkh over to them. When that failed, he decided to use his reformed army to install one of the princes in Balkh by force. It was to be the most disastrous campaign of his reign.

But before he embarked on this, Abbas carried out one of the most striking acts of his reign. Leaving Isfahan some time in the autumn of 1601, he made a pilgrimage on foot all the way to the shrine of Imam Riza in Mashhad, covering about 625 miles in sixty-six days, some of it across the extremely inhospitable Dasht-e Kavir, the Great Salt Desert.[2] Two or three courtiers walked with him, but the rest accompanied him on horseback. Two Nuqtavi dervishes also joined him early on, but as soon as they revealed their heretical beliefs they were shot. Ever with an eye to improving the country's economic infrastructure, Abbas ordered a stone causeway and accommodation for travellers to be built over the section of desert which he crossed. The English embassy that visited him at the end of his reign rode along this and was impressed by the 'extraordinary labour and expense' the work must have required.[3]

66

Contemporary Persian sources say Abbas made the walk in fulfilment of a vow, though without specifying what occasioned the vow. The more likely motive that has been suggested is that he wished to invoke the aid of Imam Riza in his forthcoming campaign against Balkh.[4] During the winter he now spent in Mashhad, Abbas made frequent visits to the shrine of the Imam, where 'on the most holy days . . . [he] kept vigil from early evening until sunrise, performing various menial tasks at the shrine such as snuffing the candles'. He also laid out plans for the embellishment of the shrine, which was becoming of increasing symbolic importance for the religious underpinning of his rule.

In the spring of 1602 Abbas moved to Herat and set out from there for Balkh in April. His army now included much larger units of *ghulams* and *qurchis* alongside the traditional Qizilbash tribal levies. Abbas's chronicler, Iskandar Beg Munshi, puts the total number of troops at 50,000 and says they took with them 300 cannons and mortars. These would have been siege cannons, the main form of artillery then used by the Iranians, although it is unlikely that Abbas took so many of them as they were very heavy to move. The only foot-soldiers were the musketeers and artillerymen who numbered 10,000, according to Iskandar Beg Munshi. The rest of the army were mounted, so there were a huge number of horses, as well as camels and other pack animals carrying equipment and supplies. As usual, the army was accompanied by a horde of camp followers.

This vast assemblage of men and animals threw up a blinding and choking cloud of dust as it moved. A mixed vanguard of cavalry and infantry was out in front, the shah and his generals were in the centre, and twelve trumpets were constantly sounding from the rear to prevent any of the units from falling behind. The army marched by day to avoid the danger of a surprise night attack as it advanced into enemy territory. But the extreme heat meant that it could only cover a short distance each day and took its toll on the soldiers. Many fell sick and there was an outbreak of dysentery caused by the brackish water encountered on the way.

After three weeks they reached Balkh to find that the Uzbek leader, Baqi Muhammad, had taken up a strong position in front of the city. Although his army was half the size, it was protected in front by a ditch and in the rear by the fort and walls of the city. It also occupied the cultivated area around Balkh, so that it had plentiful supplies of food and fodder.

Abbas was a naturally cautious commander and saw that it would be rash to attack. For a month the two armies confronted each other, before Abbas decided he had no choice but to withdraw. He was running out of food, one-third of his army was sick and another third was unfit to fight. As the army retreated, the heat, hunger, dysentery and Uzbek attacks claimed many more lives.

Fortunately for Abbas, Baqi Muhammad was keen to end hostilities so that he could concentrate on recovering his eastern province of Badakhshan, which had declared allegiance to the Moghul emperor, Akbar. He therefore ordered his amirs on the frontier to contact their Iranian counterparts with a view to preventing incidents and ensuring the free passage of caravans. When a chastened Abbas heard this, he responded in kind by ordering his own frontier amirs to strive for peace and not to molest merchants or other travellers. But as an insurance for the future, the Uzbek leader turned to Bukhara's old allies, the Ottomans, for military assistance. The sultan, Mehmet III, was only too happy to oblige and ordered the Ottoman governor of Shirvan to provide the Uzbeks with whatever weapons they required. Not long afterwards, the Uzbeks received twenty cannons and 200 arquebuses, specifically for use against the Iranians.[5]

In the course of his retreat from Balkh, Abbas took captive many of the Sunni inhabitants of the town of Andekhud and gave them to his soldiers to take to their homes in western Iran, where at best they would have been servants. Iskandar Beg Munshi is rather defensive about this action, which he justifies on the grounds that the Ottomans and the Uzbeks had treated the civilian inhabitants of Iranian towns even worse, by selling them into slavery, and that in this way 'several thousand women and children were brought up in Shi'ite and God-fearing homes, and adopted the Shi'ite faith'.

Shah Abbas had meanwhile been active with rather more success in the region of the Persian Gulf, where up till now the Safavids had exercised little control – a situation he was determined to put right. In 1601 he annexed the vassal kingdom of Lar, on the Gulf coast, across from the Portuguese island of Hormuz. The last of the hereditary rulers of Lar, Ibrahim Khan, submitted to an invading force under the governor general of Fars, Allahvirdi Khan, and was then made to join the ill-fated expedition to Balkh in the course of which he died, at the age of thirty-five – 'an able youth of simple habits, a lover of poetry . . . an expert musician', but also an opium addict, according to Iskandar Beg Munshi. The conquest of Lar put the Safavid government in control of the main overland trade route from the gulf entrepôt of Hormuz to the Iranian interior.

The same year Allahvirdi Khan seized the island of Bahrain with its valuable pearl fisheries. The island belonged to the King of Hormuz and therefore effectively to Portugal, since the king was no more than a Portuguese puppet. Although Allahvirdi Khan may have acted on his own initiative, he did so knowing he had the shah's approval. On the face of it, it was a surprising move at a time when Abbas was trying to persuade Spain-Portugal to join him in a military alliance against the Ottomans. But Abbas resented Portugal ruling over territories he regarded as rightfully his and enjoying the substantial customs revenue from the trade that passed through Hormuz and the neighbouring mainland port of Gamru, or Gombroon as the Europeans called it, which Portugal also controlled. His resentment was exacerbated by continuing tales of Portuguese ill treatment of Iranian merchants on Hormuz. From now on he would be putting increasing pressure on the Portuguese position in the Gulf.

The immediate reaction of the Portuguese authorities on Hormuz was to prepare a naval expedition to retake Bahrain. The Iranians countered by laying siege to Gombroon and blockading the caravan routes. At this point three Portuguese Augustinian friars led by Antonio De Gouvea arrived in Hormuz from the Portuguese headquarters in Goa, in India. They brought with them a letter for Shah Abbas from King Philip III of Spain, which was the first official response to the shah's European embassy. Before travelling on to meet the shah, who was then engaged before Balkh, De Gouvea managed to defuse the crisis over Bahrain, at least in the short term. He persuaded the Iranians to lift the siege of Gombroon in return for a Portuguese undertaking to halt their military preparations. But the caravan routes remained closed.

De Gouvea sent an Armenian messenger to Khurasan with a letter informing the shah of the arrival of the embassy. The shah was initially reluctant to receive the Portuguese friars because he thought they were coming to demand the return of Bahrain,[6] but he relented when he heard they were bringing a letter from the King of Spain. On 4 September 1602 they reached Mashhad, where the shah was holding his court after the retreat from Balkh. Among the courtiers sent to escort them into the city was Robert Sherley, who was disappointed to find they had no news of his brother.

The account of what follows is given by De Gouvea who was almost certainly wrong in supposing that he influenced the timing of Abbas's attack on the Ottomans, although he certainly encouraged Abbas in his hope that when he did attack the Ottomans, the Christian powers in Europe would do so too. Like most of the European Christians who met Abbas, De Gouvea read more than he should have into the shah's frequent expression of pro-Christian sentiments, which were calculated to win him sympathy and support in Europe.

De Gouvea and his companions, accompanied by their Armenian interpreter, were summoned to an audience the next day. They found the shah seated on the carpet in a great square gallery which reminded De Gouvea of the cloisters of a convent. He sat in the midst of his grandees, courtiers and officials, who were ranged in two rows on all four sides of the gallery. In fact, Abbas had to be pointed out to the friars, because he always dressed plainly and there was nothing to distinguish him from the rest of the company. Instead of prostrating themselves and kissing the shah's feet, as was the Iranian custom, the friars approached him as they would the King of Spain, going down on one knee, taking his hand and kissing it. Some of the courtiers looked disapproving, but the shah received them warmly and thereafter made a point of giving them his hand.

They handed the shah the letter from Philip III, which Abbas said he valued more than a great treasure. But he paid no attention to the gifts they had brought, which were paraded through the gallery and carefully shown to everybody. They had been sent by the Portuguese viceroy in Goa, but the Iranian officials insisted they be described as gifts from the King of Spain, 'so as to show their enemies the esteem in which the King of Spain held the shah, his friendship and his alliance'.[7] Abbas showed much more interest in a richly bound book of the life of Christ which the Augustinians presented to him. After studying it closely and inquiring about the mysteries contained in it, he delighted De Gouvea by asking to have an explanation of these written in Persian in the margins. His curiosity on religious matters now thoroughly aroused, Abbas questioned the Augustinians on their manner of living and on the difference for Christians between the clergy and the laity. This led to a protracted discussion, after which cloths were laid on the carpets and dinner served – the shah eating in a separate room with his eldest son, Prince Safi, and the son of the King of Georgia, Prince Constantine. When the Augustinians retired to their lodgings, they were advised to be up early so as to leave with the court for Isfahan.

The shah set off the following morning with between 5,000 and 6,000 soldiers, having disbanded the rest of the army. De Gouvea says he travelled slowly, because he was suffering from gout. On the way, the Augustinians had another audience with Abbas in his tent, at which De Gouvea pressed him to make war on the Ottomans. He reminded him of the rich provinces the Turks had seized from the Iranians, pointed out that the Ottoman Empire was being weakened by internal revolts, and insisted the Christian princes were waiting, sword in hand, for him to move against the common enemy. When one of the Augustinian fathers worried that it might be dangerous to talk about this so loudly, the shah said it did not matter because his hatred of the Turk was well known and there was nothing he desired more passionately than the utter ruin of the Ottoman Empire. For the benefit of the Augustinians, he said he hoped before long to see all the mosques of the Turks turned into Christian churches. Despite this, De Gouvea expressed concern that he was postponing taking action. The shah answered that it was no longer the campaigning season and that he was awaiting the return of his embassy to Europe, which he hoped would be soon. But he promised the Augustinians that he would launch the war before they left Iran.

During the journey Abbas encouraged the Augustinians to believe that his conversion to Christianity remained a real possibility. When one of the fathers praised his qualities and said the only thing he lacked was the Christian faith, he laughed and said God alone knew what was in the heart. On another occasion he hinted that his conversion was happening 'little by little'. One evening he summoned all the Georgian and other Christians in his suite to his tent and told the Augustinians that it was these Christians he trusted most. Then, after making everyone sit down, 'he began to talk very particularly of some mysteries of our faith', De Gouvea recalled later, 'and it was wonderful to hear how well informed he was'. Abbas spoke about the death and resurrection of Christ and the survival of the soul. The evening ended with him asking the fathers to show him how to make the sign of the Cross and requiring all his courtiers to do the same. 'It was a thing of great satisfaction', writes De Gouvea, 'to see all the grandees and the closest confidants of the King wanting to make the sign of the Cross and begging the Christians present to show them how.'

The shah approached the city of Kashan with the Augustinian fathers riding on either side of him. A large and excited crowd of men and women, including the usual bevy of courtesans on horseback, came out to meet him. Some threw themselves on the ground to kiss the place where his horse would pass, while others offered calves for sacrifice or released pigeons to signify the liberty he had given them by enabling them to live in security. Some of the women beat their breasts and called on God to shorten their lives so as to increase the life of the shah. The press of people around the shah became so great that his officers had to beat them back. Abbas, with tears in his eyes, took hold of the sleeve of De Gouvea's black habit and said his heart was even blacker with sadness when he considered how unworthy he was of all this joy and happiness. 'How much better it would be for me', he said, 'to be a private person who only needs a piece of bread to subsist, than to be king of so many people and so many towns that I possess unworthily.'

Meanwhile, one of the envoys sent by the pope, Diego de Miranda, had already met up with the shah during the march; the other envoy, Francisco da Costa, was waiting for him in Kashan. They proved to be a very bad advertisement for the papacy. Throughout their journey they behaved shabbily and dishonestly, and quarrelled incessantly till they finally separated. Reports of their behaviour reached the pope, who tried in vain to have them recalled. Diego de Miranda arrived at the royal camp with a luxurious equipage and a large retinue of pages and grooms – all paid for from the proceeds of goods he had seized from a Venetian merchant in the name of the pope. When he produced the pope's letter from the back pocket of his breeches, the shah rebuked him for showing a lack of respect and referred to him thereafter as 'the fool'.[8] Da Costa made a better impression to begin with, but soon shocked Abbas by his dishonest and violent behaviour. The two papal envoys accompanied the shah to Isfahan, where they remained for several months before each was sent back to Europe in the company of an Iranian ambassador.

Isfahan was reached on 10 November. De Gouvea was much impressed by the improvements Abbas had already made to his new capital, in particular the broad avenue of the Chahar Bagh – 'a street of admirable artifice and beauty', the Allahvirdi Khan Bridge with its many arches, and the spacious Maidan-e Shah or Royal Square. But the Shah now became cooler towards the Augustinians, partly because he had received reports that the Portuguese were sending reinforcements to Hormuz with the aim of recovering Bahrain, and partly because of Shi'i hostility to the Augustinians. He had agreed to allow the Augustinians to establish a permanent residence in Isfahan, but they had also requested permission to build a church. The Shi'i clergy were bitterly opposed to this and had gone in a body to the shah to protest.

The storm clouds eventually blew over. A small Portuguese squadron from Goa did arrive at Hormuz and the governor general of Fars, Allahvirdi Khan, responded by ravaging the territory on the mainland that belonged to Hormuz. The Augustinians complained to the shah, who ordered Allahvirdi Khan to desist. Eventually it was decided that De Gouvea would return to Goa accompanied by an Iranian ambassador to Spain, somewhat confusingly named Allahvirdi Beg. On the way, De Gouvea was to have talks in Hormuz aimed at preventing a Portuguese attack on Bahrain. If he was successful, Allahvirdi Khan would hand back all the territory he had seized from the

King of Hormuz. De Gouvea's two Augustinian companions were to remain behind in Isfahan where the shah, overriding the objections of his clergy, now gave them permission to build a church.

Towards the end of his stay in Isfahan, De Gouvea spent an evening with Abbas in his most relaxed mood. The Augustinians joined the shah in a delightful pavilion where there were pools of water fed by hidden channels, and musicians and singers were providing entertainment. At one point in the evening Abbas asked De Gouvea for a song in Portuguese. The Augustinian fathers obliged instead with a rendering of the psalm 'Laudate Pueri Dominum'. The shah said he had never heard anything so beautiful. He then took up an instrument himself and sang some verses of his own composition. When he had finished he turned to a Venetian who had been at his court for twelve years and asked him to confirm to the fathers that he had never done that for any other ambassadors.

All the time De Gouvea continued to urge Abbas to begin his campaign against the Ottomans. The shah repeated his promise to do so before De Gouvea left Iran. He told him he was delaying his departure from Isfahan till he received news of the capture of the town of Nahavand, in the Zagros Mountains about 40 miles south of Hamadan, which the Ottomans had taken from the Iranians in the last war. The Safavid governor of Hamadan had involved himself in a domestic Kurdish dispute and was besieging Nahavand with the help of a local Kurdish leader. Abbas had approved the action, but had told the governor to keep this quiet as he did not want to be seen to be violating the peace agreement with the Ottomans.

In fact, De Gouvea left Isfahan before any such news arrived. As he set off, the shah lifted the embargo on commercial traffic to Hormuz, with the result that De Gouvea was accompanied on his journey by a large caravan of merchants. The embargo had been in place for more than a year and had done great harm to the economy of Hormuz, which depended entirely on trade.

Merchant caravans were now able to move in safety along the roads of Iran, as De Gouvea testifies. Shah Abbas, he writes, 'is the mortal enemy of thieves and robbers, whom he has punished very severely, by means of which he has so well cleansed his kingdom that I believe there is no other place in the world where travellers go with more safety'.

On his way back, De Gouvea did his best to smooth relations between the Portuguese authorities on Hormuz and the powerful governor general of Fars, Allahvirdi Khan. While De Gouvea was in Shiraz, Allahvirdi Khan crushed a revolt in the newly conquered province of Lar, which he initially suspected had been stirred up by the Portuguese. But when he had satisfied himself that this was not the case, he gave De Gouvea a place of honour at a triumph he held for his son, Imam Quli Khan, to whom he wished to give the credit for the victory. He was anxious that the shah should have a good opinion of his son and eventually make him his successor, which Abbas did. De Gouvea says the victory celebrations went on for several days and reminded him of the grandeur of the ancient Persian kings. Both Allahvirdi Khan and his son Imam Quli Khan were famous for their extravagance. Allahvirdi Khan is once said to have served a banquet on '3,000 dishes all of gold with lids of the same'. As for Imam Quli Khan, Shah Abbas is said to have asked him jokingly to 'spend one dirham less per day, that there may exist some slight difference between the disbursements of a khan and of a king'.[9]

Before De Gouvea left Shiraz, a courier arrived from Isfahan with the news of the fall of Nahavand. The courier had been sent by Abbas to inform Allahvirdi Khan and to tell him to pass on the news to De Gouvea so that he might know the shah had kept his word. Clearly his hope was that the Europeans would now keep theirs.

Shortly afterwards Abbas set off with his army to drive the Turks out of Tabriz. The Ottoman-Safavid conflict had been renewed in earnest and was to continue with brief intervals for the next thirty-five years.

Chapter 7

Abbas Expels the Ottomans

We have a description of Abbas as he would have appeared when he went to war with the Ottomans in September 1603. It is by an Englishman, John Cartwright, who saw the shah in Isfahan about two years earlier. Cartwright observed:

> This Prince is very absolute both in perfection of his body and his mind (but that he is in religion a professed Mohammadan), excellently composed in the one, and honourably disposed in the other. Of an indifferent stature, neither too high, nor too low, his countenance very stern, his eyes fierce and piercing, his colour swarthy, his moustaches on his upper lip long, with his beard cut close to his chin, expressing his martial disposition and exorable nature, that at first a man would think to have nothing in him, but mischief and cruelty. And yet he is of nature courteous and affable, easy to be seen and spoken withall . . .[1]

The timing of the war could hardly have been more favourable to Abbas. His authority was no longer challenged within Iran and the Uzbek threat had been banished for the time being, despite the setback at Balkh. The Ottoman Empire, on the other hand, was severely weakened by war and internal revolts. For the past ten years the Ottoman army had been engaged in a constant round of sieges and battles with the Austrians in Hungary. Discontent with the war, combined with deteriorating economic conditions, had caused large-scale rebellions in Anatolia, which continued almost without interruption from 1596 to 1608. No sooner was one revolt suppressed than another broke out. It was an ideal moment for Abbas to strike.

Abbas had always intended to break the peace treaty as soon as he was ready. Iskandar Beg Munshi says this was justified by the lawless behaviour of the Ottoman pashas on the frontier.[2] The Ottoman governor of Van had executed a royal merchant and confiscated money he was carrying that belonged to the shah. The Ottoman authorities in Shirvan had also mistreated agents sent by the shah to purchase mules and hunting animals. Protests by the shah had brought no response.

The shah similarly dismissed Ottoman protests over the seizure of Nahavand and found an opportunity shortly afterwards to begin the war himself. It was provided by one of the Kurdish chiefs who preserved a semi-independence by switching their allegiance between the Ottomans and the Safavids. This Kurdish chief, Ghazi Beg, rebelled against his immediate overlord, the Ottoman governor of Tabriz, and entered into a secret alliance with Abbas. The governor of Tabriz, Ali Pasha, set off with many of his troops to teach his rebellious vassal a lesson, leaving the city virtually undefended. Ghazi Beg immediately sent a messenger to inform Abbas of this.

The shah assembled the troops he had available, but concealed his intentions by spreading the rumour that he was marching south to oppose a Portuguese attack on Bahrain. Then, on 14 September 1603, he marched rapidly north to Qazvin. After a brief halt he pushed on towards Tabriz, ordering the governor of Ardabil and the constable (*darugha*) of Qazvin to follow after him with their forces.

Abbas took the Ottoman garrison in Tabriz completely by surprise. Many of them were doing their shopping in the market when he entered the city. This was a simple enough matter now that there was no Ottoman army to oppose him, since Tabriz, like many cities in Iran, had no defensive wall around it.[3] In a situation like this, the garrison would try to hold out from within the citadel until a relief force arrived. This is what the Ottoman garrison now did. They rushed back into the citadel, which was in the centre of the city, and hurriedly closed the gates behind them.

In the absence of the Ottoman governor, Ali Pasha, his son was in command, but did not realise at first who the attackers were. He sent a message to his father saying they were being besieged by a band of marauders. When he realised it was the shah, he had to send two messages to this effect before Ali Pasha would believe him. The Ottoman governor hurried back, but was defeated outside the city by Abbas, who by now had received reinforcements from Qazvin and Ardabil. The citadel then surrendered after a short siege, in which the Iranians used cannons operated by Portuguese gunners from Hormuz.[4] The shah is said to have treated the garrison kindly, offering to take any who wished into his service at double the pay they had received from the Ottomans. He is also said to have made Ali Pasha one of his companions at private banquets, because he admired his courage and found him 'a sociable and extremely witty man'.[5]

Others were not so lucky. The Ottomans had proved to be rapacious rulers and the Shi'i population of Tabriz took a savage vengeance for eighteen years of occupation. Angry crowds chanting the Qizilbash war cry of 'Allah! Allah!' attacked and killed any Ottoman soldiers they could find. Soldiers who had married local girls are said to have been dragged from their houses and slain by their in-laws.

While Shah Abbas was in Tabriz, he received an envoy from the Habsburg emperor, Rudolph II. The envoy, Georg Tectander von der Jabel, was one of only two survivors of an embassy sent by the emperor in response to the visit to Prague of Sir Anthony Sherley and Husain Ali Beg. All the others, including the ambassador, had died of fever in the humid heat and insect-infested swamps of Gilan. Tectander himself was in a very weak state when he arrived and had an unnerving experience when he met the shah. An Ottoman prisoner was brought in and Abbas called for two swords, which he then proceeded to examine. He chose one and sliced off the prisoner's head. Tectander feared the shah had heard that the Emperor Rudolph was making peace with the Ottomans and would use the second sword on him. Instead Abbas turned to Tectander with a smile and said that was how the Christians should treat the Turks.[6]

In the middle of November, Abbas led his army north and crossed the Aras River into Armenia. One town after another opened its gates, as the Ottoman garrisons abandoned their fortresses and fell back on the strongly defended Armenian capital of Erivan. Ottoman rule was if anything even more unpopular with the Armenians than with the Shi'i Muslims of Azerbaijan. Tectander, who accompanied the shah, says Abbas was welcomed at every town or village by groups of men, women and children dancing and singing. Towns were illuminated in his honour.[7] Pro-Safavid sentiments were particularly strong in Julfa on the north bank of the Aras. Many of the town's wealthy Armenian merchants did business in Iran and some even knew the shah personally. When the inhabitants heard of his approach, they rose in revolt and slaughtered the Ottoman garrison of about a hundred soldiers. They brought the heads of the soldiers and the keys of the town to the shah, who promised to treat them well.[8] Abbas advanced unopposed as far as Erivan, where his forces occupied the town and laid siege to a chain of three forts held by the Ottomans. At this point Tectander, accompanied by an Iranian envoy to the emperor, returned across the Caucasus to the Caspian on the long journey back to Prague. He had enjoyed his time with Abbas, whom he describes as 'a friendly and entertaining gentleman' ('ein freundlicher und lustiger Herr'). He also tells an amusing story of how, at Erivan, he was once sitting on carpets on the ground next to Abbas when several Ottomans came to beg for mercy, but threw themselves at Tectander's feet because he was better dressed and had a foot sticking out further than the shah, as he found it uncomfortable to sit cross-legged. The incident caused the shah much merriment, but whether he was merciful to the Ottomans is not recorded.

It was already late in the year, but Abbas decided to continue the siege through the winter of 1603–4, confident that the Ottomans would run out of supplies. During the winter he was joined by Allahvirdi Khan, who brought with him some 18,000 horsemen and was accompanied by an ambassador from the Moghul emperor, Akbar. The ambassador carried a letter from Akbar warmly congratulating Abbas on his victories over the Uzbeks and the Ottomans, as well as over his internal enemies.[9] He brought rich gifts, but Abbas paid no attention to them except for a sword which he took as a good omen, coming as it did from a descendant of the great Tamerlane. The Moghul embassy remained at the shah's camp until after the fall of Erivan four months later, when it was given permission to leave. Abbas was perfectly friendly, but did not treat the embassy with any special ceremony. At the beginning of his reign he had been anxious to court Akbar's favour. But he was in a stronger position now and also resented the Moghul emperor's possession of Qandahar. Over the winter, the king of eastern Georgia, Alexander II, also arrived at the shah's camp with a small force. He had been an Ottoman vassal, but after receiving a warning from Abbas not to withhold support, he had massacred the Ottoman garrison in his capital, Tbilisi.[10]

For his assault on Erivan, Abbas brought up heavy siege guns and rounded up some 12,000 Armenian peasants from the surrounding countryside to build breast-works opposite the walls of the three forts. The harsh winter weather took a heavy toll on the besiegers; every morning a number of Iranian soldiers were found frozen to death. But it was the Armenians building the breast-works who suffered most, being exposed both to the cold and to the fire from the forts. When the breast-works were completed, Abbas placed cannons and musketeers on them to keep up a steady fire into the forts. Starvation and sickness began to take their toll on the Ottoman garrison, which finally capitulated towards the end of May 1604, after the Iranians captured one of the forts in a night attack.[11]

Meanwhile, the reports of the Iranian offensive and the siege of Erivan had stirred the Ottoman authorities in Istanbul into action. In the spring of 1604 Sinan Pasha was appointed to lead an army against Abbas. He was a Genoese who had entered Ottoman service after being taken prisoner and had risen to the highest positions in the state, becoming grand vizier and commanding Ottoman forces on land and sea. But he was more successful as an admiral than as a general, and his harsh punishment of the Ottoman feudal cavalry for fleeing during a battle in Hungary had caused many of them to desert and join the first great rebellion in Anatolia in 1596.

Sinan Pasha set off from Istanbul in June 1604 with an army that included a large force of janissaries. By this time Abbas had advanced beyond Erivan to Kars, on the frontier of Georgia. When he heard that Sinan Pasha was on the march, he ravaged the countryside between Kars and Erzerum to impede Sinan Pasha's advance. He also extended a warm welcome to a Spanish ambassador, Louis Pereira de Lacerda, who visited his encampment in October. Abbas was now more anxious than ever to see the Christian powers step up their pressure on the Ottomans in the west. Between 1603 and 1604 he sent several ambassadors to Europe with this end in view. But Lacerda's mission had nothing to do with the Ottoman war. He had been sent without Madrid's knowledge by the Portuguese viceroy of Goa to improve relations with the shah and thereby, it was hoped, ward off a possible threat to Hormuz.[12]

Sinan Pasha's progress through Anatolia was extremely slow. He halted for some time in Erzerum, where he made terms with a rebel leader and received reinforcements. It was by now late in the year, but instead of settling down to spend the winter in the region and resume his campaign in the spring, he pushed on towards Kars. This surprise move led Abbas to make a hurried withdrawal south across the Aras River, intensifying his scorched-earth tactics in the process.

Orders went out for the immediate evacuation of the entire population, most of them Armenian Christians, over a wide area to the north of the Aras River and embracing the three towns of Erivan, Nakhichivan and Julfa. The inhabitants were given forty-eight hours to leave, failing which they would be removed by force. Their homes and farms were destroyed, along with any food or supplies that could be of use to the Ottoman army. Some 60,000 families were herded across the Aras and then sent eastwards along the river to various locations where they settled in as best they could during

79

the harsh winter months. Many died from exhaustion, starvation and the bitter cold. Only the Julfa Armenians, who were especially useful to Abbas, were treated with any consideration and provided with camels, horses and mules for the journey.[13] Armenian merchants from Julfa had become the principal intermediaries in the export of raw silk, Iran's most valuable commodity, to Europe, where it was greatly in demand. They took it overland to Aleppo, where they sold it to European merchants in return for the silver coin which Iran, and Abbas, so badly needed. Abbas had also used Julfans as royal merchants, sending them to Venice to sell silk on his private account.[14]

The deportation of the Armenians shocked Robert Sherley, who was with the Iranian army. In May 1605 he wrote of Abbas in a letter to his brother Anthony:

> In all his actions, he publisheth to the world the hatred he bears to the name of Christians, for every day he maketh slaves of the poor Armenians, which are daily brought like sheep into every market, burning and pulling down all churches, to the great infamy of all the Christians that live here.[15]

For Abbas, however, it was strategic necessity and certainly not hatred of Christians that prompted his action. It would have made little sense deliberately to maltreat the Armenian Christians at a time when he was looking to Christian Europe to support his war against the Ottomans. On the other hand, there is no doubt that some of his soldiers and officials were less tolerant of Christians and carried out his orders with a brutal zeal.

To begin with, Abbas seems to have assumed that the Armenians would return to their homes, or what was left of them, once the Ottoman danger was past.[16] But when he realised that the prevailing insecurity made this difficult, he issued a decree stating that they were under no obligation to return, and began making arrangements to settle some of them in Iran. Abbas saw that the skills of the Armenians as merchants, artisans and farmers would increase the wealth of the kingdom and help to provide him with badly needed revenue. That year, 1605, he settled several thousand Armenians in and around Isfahan. He continued to bring in others during his reign. Some were settled inside the city, some in surrounding villages, but the most famous settlement of all was the new suburb which was created on the south bank of the river for the Armenians from Julfa, who in future would carry on their vital trade in Iranian silk from there. The suburb was named New Julfa, but in time it came to be known simply as Julfa. Abbas helped the Armenians with interest-free loans and grants of land and livestock, and they quickly became a flourishing community. Other settlements soon followed elsewhere, though not all were so successful. European observers were so impressed by what they saw in Isfahan that they almost felt Shah Abbas had done the Armenians a favour by deporting them. This was also the view of Abbas's chronicler, Iskandar Beg Munshi. It was not one shared by the Armenians themselves, who retained a bitter memory of the mass deportation and the terrible suffering it involved.

Sinan Pasha reached Kars, which the Iranians had evacuated, towards the beginning of November 1604. He wanted to continue on into Shirvan, but his officers objected, so instead he headed south across the Aras and established his winter quarters in Van.[17] This was a short distance to the west of the shah's camp near Tabriz. When the spring came, Abbas learnt from his spies that Sinan Pasha was waiting for reinforcements. He immediately sent Allahvirdi Khan to attack Van before these arrived. Allahvirdi Khan defeated a Kurdish force camped outside the fortress, routed a sortie by Ottoman troops inside and ambushed some Ottoman units attempting to link up with Sinan Pasha. The Ottoman commander now withdrew across Lake Van into northern Mesopotamia, while Allahvirdi Khan returned to the shah with the usual trophy of the heads of slaughtered Ottomans. These were paraded before Abbas during a highly symbolic visit to the battlefield of Chaldiran – the scene of Shah Ismail I's defeat by the Ottomans in 1514.

After being strongly reinforced, Sinan Pasha returned to the attack, advancing into Azerbaijan and finally confronting Shah Abbas at Sufiyan near Tabriz early in November 1605. Abbas's spies reported that the Ottoman army was about 100,000-strong, compared to just over 60,000 on the Iranian side. In the face of such odds, Abbas hesitated to risk losing all that he had won and considered withdrawing to Tabriz. On the eve of the battle he climbed with his most trusted commanders to the top of a hill to assess for himself the enemy numbers. His commanders concurred with what his spies had reported. But Abbas ordered them to tell their soldiers the numbers were far less. He then went to consult his aunt, Zainab Begum, a daughter of Shah Tahmasp, whose advice he frequently sought. She poured scorn on his anxieties and urged him to fight – advice he accepted.[18]

Despite the disparity in numbers, the battle of Sufiyan which took place the following day, 6 November 1605, was one of Shah Abbas's greatest victories over the Ottomans. As the huge central column of Ottoman cavalry advanced towards the Iranian lines, he ordered some detachments of light cavalry to sweep round the Ottoman left flank and deliver a feint attack in their rear. Sinan Pasha was deceived into thinking this was the direction of the main Iranian attack and detached a large body of his advancing horse to meet it. This caused confusion, with many on both sides believing they were fleeing. Abbas now hurled the full weight of his Qizilbash cavalry into the battle. In a series of furious charges they fell upon the dispirited Ottomans and after some hard fighting scattered them in all directions.

Many of the Ottoman commanders – governors of great cities and provinces of the empire – were either killed or taken prisoner. One of the prisoners who was led before the shah, 'an Ottoman of huge physical stature',[19] drew a dagger he had concealed and threw himself on Abbas. The shah wrestled with the man until he made him drop the dagger. The prisoner was hacked to pieces by the shah's attendants.

Sinan Pasha fell back on Van with the remnants of his army. There he found the Pasha of Aleppo who had refused to commit his troops, and had him executed, prompting his son in Aleppo to throw off Ottoman rule. Sinan Pasha continued his retreat to Diyarbakr, where grief at his defeat hastened his death on 2 December 1605. Some reports say he took his own life.

Faced with this disaster, the Ottomans used a rather unusual channel to try to persuade the shah to make peace.[20] The sultan's mother, the saltana, decided to approach the shah through his aunt, Zainab Begum. She chose as an intermediary another woman, Gulsara, who was the wife of a Georgian king held prisoner in Istanbul – promising her that if she was successful, her husband would be freed. The saltana wrote a letter to Zainab Begum, asking her to use her influence with the shah to stop a war that was so damaging to Muslims, who ought not to fight one another. When she received the letter from Gulsara, Zainab Begum promised to do her best and showed it to the shah. But the answer the shah sent back was uncompromising: he would only lay down his arms if, as he put it, all the lands trodden by Shah Ismail's horse were restored to him. This was more than the Ottoman government was prepared to concede.

Abbas gave his army little rest after Sufiyan. Three months later, with the winter barely over, he invested Ganja in northern Azerbaijan, capturing the fortress after a six-month siege. He then advanced into Georgia, where he took control of the main city, Tbilisi. In the winter of 1606 he invaded Shirvan, overriding opposition from his officers who complained that the army had been too long in the field, that many horses had died or been weakened by a lack of fodder and that the men's equipment was in poor shape. Many more animals were lost as they struggled to negotiate the ice floes on the River Kur, on the frontier of Shirvan, after the Ottomans destroyed the bridge. Then the Iranian camp outside the capital, Shamakhi, which they laid siege to, was turned into a muddy quagmire by more than two months of almost nonstop rain. But the key cities of Darband and Baku on the Caspian soon fell to pro-Safavid uprisings and in the spring of 1607 the walls of Shamakhi were breached by the Iranian siege guns and the city was taken by assault. With the conquest of Shirvan, Abbas had recovered all the territory he had been forced to cede to the Ottomans in 1590.

In gratitude for his victories over the Ottomans, Abbas made a pilgrimage in September 1607 to the shrine of the Eighth Imam, Ali ar-Riza, at Mashhad, with whom he was increasingly associating his rule. He also gave thanks both to the Eighth Imam and to his Safavid ancestors in the form of two major endowments – one for the shrine of the Imam at Mashhad, the other for the Safavid shrine at Ardabil.

The endowment for the shrine at Mashhad was dedicated to 'the Fourteen Immaculate Ones', who were the Prophet Muhammad, his daughter Fatima and the Twelve Shi'i Imams. It consisted of the revenue from all of Abbas's private estates and from the shops, bathhouses and caravanserais which he had recently had built in Isfahan. The shah stipulated that the substantial sums involved were to be spent 'for administrative expenses and subsistence allowances for the employees at each location [i.e. where there was a shrine, mosque or religious college] and for subsistence allowances for those living in the neighbourhood of these locations, for pilgrims, scholars, pious men and students of theology'.[21] He also donated his collection of books in Arabic, which were mainly religious works. These included copies of the Quran, commentaries on the Quran, works on Shi'i jurisprudence and collections of traditions of the Prophet Muhammad and the Imams, which were an important source of religious law.

To the Safavid ancestral shrine at Ardabil, on the other hand, he gave all his books in Persian. These were books of a secular nature – mainly works of history and collections of Persian poetry.[22] He also gave to Ardabil his outstanding collection of Chinese porcelain,[23] his jewels, jewelled weapons and bowls of gold and silver, his studs of horses, his herds of camels and flocks of sheep and goats. At the same time, Abbas ordered extensive renovation work to be carried out at the Ardabil shrine.

These endowments represented an assertion of the twin sources of Abbas's legitimacy as ruler – the one, Ardabil, being dynastic, and the other, Mashhad, religious.

It is significant too that the chancery scribe and Abbas's official historian, Iskandar Beg Munshi, who accompanied Abbas throughout these campaigns, compared his achievement to that of Timur (Tamerlane), with whom Abbas also liked to associate himself, thereby sharing in the same source of legitimacy as the Moghul emperors.

'Not since the time of Timur, 250 years ago,' writes Iskandar Beg, 'had any ruler kept his armies in the field for five continuous years and achieved such an uninterrupted run of victories.'

After such a long absence, Abbas finally returned to his capital of Isfahan, where several days were given over to celebrations.

Chapter 8

The Search for European Allies

After all the pressure put on him by De Gouvea to make war on the Ottomans, now that he had done so Abbas was understandably disappointed to have received no help from Spain. In 1605 he had sent an ambassador to Madrid to remind King Philip of his promise to fight the Ottomans. Now came much worse news from Europe. While he was at Shamakhi he heard that the Habsburg emperor, Rudolph, had made peace with the Ottomans behind his back. The shah had been getting reports of possible peace moves, but had not believed them. He had trusted in the emperor's promise, conveyed through Husain Ali Beg, to prosecute the war with vigour, and was no doubt further reassured by Tectander's embassy. De Gouvea says Abbas respected the emperor so much for waging war against the Ottomans that he kept a portrait of him at the entrance to his bedroom, which he bowed his head to whenever he went in. Abbas felt personally let down. He would have felt even more deceived had he known that on the very same day that the emperor authorised peace negotiations with the Ottomans – 31 October 1605 – he repeated his promise to continue the war at a farewell audience in Prague to three Iranian ambassadors. But the ambassadors were held up in Russia and did not return to Iran until four years later. The Peace of Zsitvatorok of November 1606 put an end to hostilities between the Habsburg and Ottoman empires for more than half a century. That allowed the Ottomans to concentrate on dealing with the internal unrest in Anatolia and on meeting the new challenge from Iran. It was no wonder that Abbas described it as 'this infamous peace'.[1]

The Portuguese Augustinians tactlessly chose this moment to approach the shah with a series of requests concerning his Armenian subjects. Led by an envoy from Goa, they asked him to insist the Armenians recognise the pope as their head, free all enslaved Armenians and give the Armenian community in New Julfa ground on which to build churches, a monastery and a school. While he was still hopeful of Christian support against the Ottomans, Abbas had appeared to favour the idea of the pope taking charge of all the Christians in his empire. Now he simply stared in disbelief at the Augustinians. 'At a time when the Christian princes are not keeping their word, do you want to have churches in my kingdom?' he demanded, 'Do you want the Armenians to submit to you? Do you want to ring the church bells? You are lucky I don't have your bells smashed, and have you driven from my territory.'[2]

The shah's anger was also felt by a new papal mission to Iran. The mission composed of friars from the order of Barefoot Carmelites had been sent from Rome over three years earlier by Pope Clement VIII. Its purpose was to establish a permanent presence in Isfahan and to encourage the shah in his war with the Ottomans. A Spanish soldier was sent with the mission to find out what kind of military advisers the shah needed, but he died on the way. The Carmelites were held up by civil war in Russia and did not reach Isfahan until December 1607. By that time both Clement VIII and his successor Leo XI had died and Paul V had become pope. The friars – there were three of them – were accompanied from Qazvin by Robert Sherley, who warned them that the shah was 'greatly disgusted at the news of the Emperor having made peace with the Turks',[3] as well as at not having heard from the pope for four years or having had any news of his own ambassadors to the emperor. In Isfahan, the Carmelites had to wait a month before Abbas agreed to see them.

They were finally summoned to an audience on 3 January 1608, in a courtyard of the royal stables, where the shah was choosing the horses for his forthcoming campaign. The informal setting was typical of Abbas and was not intended as a snub. They arrived to find him 'seated on a mound, on a carpet of little value, clothed in black cloth', as it was the fasting month of Ramazan. His son and various nobles were standing nearby, and two Ottoman pashas were sitting behind him. There was a large crowd outside the stables, many of them soldiers.

The Carmelites handed three letters to Abbas. One was from the now-deceased pope, Clement VIII, another was from the new pope, Paul V, and the third was from the Emperor Rudolph. Abbas immediately brought up the peace the emperor had made with the Ottomans, 'contrary to promises several times made, while he [Abbas] had persevered in the war for ten years continuously'.[4] The leader of the Carmelite mission, Father Paul Simon, attempted, rather unconvincingly, to reassure the shah. The friars then presented their gifts, which included a fine illustrated Bible. Abbas opened it by chance at a picture of St Michael brandishing his sword over a prostrate Lucifer. He asked who the vanquished figure was, and on being told it was the Devil, he laughed and said he thought it was the Turk - glancing over his shoulder, as he said this, at the Ottoman pashas, 'for he lost no opportunity to mock them'.

The Carmelites had a second audience two days later, which was just as informal. This time the shah was watching bull and ram fights in the Royal Square. He paid them little attention until Father Paul Simon told him that the pope was trying to get the Christian princes to make war on the Ottomans, particularly by sea, and urged him 'to continue to fight valiantly against the common enemy'. The idea of a Christian naval offensive excited Abbas and revived his hopes of combined action against the Ottomans. He replied that he was a staunch friend of the Holy See and was planning to attack Baghdad that winter, after which he would march on Istanbul.

At a third audience shortly afterwards, Abbas responded to the pope's appeal to him to treat all Christians kindly, and especially his Armenian subjects. He insisted he had always done so and had never coerced them into becoming Muslims. But he complained bitterly about the Portuguese on Hormuz who, he said, seized young slaves, purchased in India, from Iranian merchants and forced them to become Christians. As for the Armenians, he asked whether the pope had ordered the Augustinian Fathers to change the faith the Armenians had kept for a thousand years and turn them into Portuguese. Father Paul Simon said there had been no such orders and that the pope would be displeased at any annoyance caused to the shah.

Abbas then drew up a letter for Father Paul Simon to take to the pope. In it, he put forward his own plan for a Christian offensive in the Mediterranean. He proposed that Christian forces land on the Syrian coast and attack Aleppo, while he advanced on Diyarbakir in Anatolia.[5] He also asked the pope for his help in protecting Iranians on Hormuz. Father Paul Simon set off with the letter for Rome, travelling through Ottoman territory disguised as a poor Armenian. The other two Carmelites remained in Isfahan, where Abbas ordered them to be given a better house with room for a chapel. There were now two permanent Catholic missions in Iran - the Augustinians and the Carmelites. Their prospects of converting Muslims, for whom death was the price of apostasy, were minimal, and such missionary effort as they engaged in tended to be concentrated on the Armenians.

Their role was primarily a diplomatic one, with the Augustinians representing Spain and Portugal, and the Carmelites the papacy. Relations between the two were often strained.

Hard on the heels of Father Paul Simon, the shah despatched Robert Sherley on an embassy similar to the one undertaken by his brother with so little success nine years earlier. Up till now he had refused all Robert Sherley's requests to be allowed to return to Europe. But in the light of what the Carmelites had told him, Abbas felt it was worth stepping up diplomatic pressure on the Europeans. He had been further encouraged – and Robert's standing had been improved – by the news that Sir Anthony Sherley had been given command of a Spanish fleet to attack the Ottomans in the Mediterranean. Robert seized on this to press his case with the shah, arguing that now was the time to negotiate a league against the sultan, and he was the man to do it. Both the pope and the emperor had also asked the shah to allow Robert to leave.

Robert Sherley had served the shah well. He is said to have fought valiantly in the Ottoman wars and to have been wounded three times at the battle of Sufiyan. The shah, for his part, never punished him for Anthony's failure to return. He paid him an annual allowance, though Robert apparently had to enrol himself as a *ghulam* or slave of the shah to avoid having 10 per cent deducted. But when the Carmelite fathers met him in Qazvin, they found he had rather fallen out of favour. He complained that the shah and some of the nobles were forever putting pressure on him to become a Muslim. Perhaps because he refused, his allowance was no longer being paid regularly or in full. He begged the Carmelites to ask the shah to let him go, which they duly did.

Shortly before he left on his embassy, Robert Sherley married the daughter of a Christian Circassian chieftain, called Teresa, who had been brought up at the Safavid court where her aunt was one of the shah's favourite wives. The couple were married by the Carmelites, who received them into the Roman Catholic church, together with several of Robert's English companions. Teresa is described as handsome and a fine horsewoman. Robert was then of medium height, fair and beardless, and wore a ring with a tiny diamond in one ear. They set off from Isfahan on 12 February 1608 with an imposing retinue, travelling by the northern route to Europe through Russia.

In Madrid, in the meantime, Sir Anthony Sherley had come up with a scheme to improve relations between Spain and Iran, which he saw was necessary to protect Hormuz. Iran had already put renewed pressure on the

Portuguese island by demanding the payment of protection money for the trading caravans passing through Lar on their way to and from Hormuz, on the grounds that this had been paid in the past to the kings of Lar. In 1608 the Safavid governor of Lar, Camber Beg, occupied the neighbouring island of Qishm, which supplied Hormuz with much of its water. If Iran were now to make peace with the Ottomans there was a danger it might seek to drive the Portuguese out of Hormuz by allying itself with Portugal's new rivals in the east, the English and the Dutch. There was, as before, a strong peace party at the Safavid court, and Abbas had listened to them to the extent of sending an ambassador to Istanbul after he received the news of Zsitvatorok. The authorities there kept him in isolation in a futile attempt to prevent him learning how weak the Ottoman Empire had become. But the shah's demand that all the territories ceded in 1590 be restored to him was still too much for the Ottomans to accept.

Sir Anthony Sherley proposed that Iran's main export commodity, silk, should in future be exported to Europe by sea through Hormuz and Goa, rather than by the traditional overland routes through Ottoman territory to the Mediterranean.[6] When he presented the scheme to the Spanish government in January 1607, he argued that it would secure the shah's friendship because it would deprive the Ottomans of a valuable source of customs revenue. The initial reaction in Madrid was cautious, but Sir Anthony then enlisted the enthusiastic support of the Spanish viceroy in Naples, the Count of Benevento. The two sent letters to Iran, to the shah and Robert Sherley, advocating the scheme. These were delivered by a Hormuz merchant in the summer of 1608. By that time Robert Sherley had long departed, and Antonio De Gouvea was back in Iran with a new Augustinian embassy from Goa.

De Gouvea had been sent to take charge of the permanent Augustinian mission in Isfahan and to deliver a letter to the shah from King Philip III of Spain. When he and his companions arrived in Isfahan towards the end of June 1608, they found the shah determined to remind them of his earlier displeasure with the Augustinians. After ignoring their presence for several days, Abbas left to join his army near Hamadan, where he awaited an opportunity to descend on Baghdad. He was already in contact with prominent citizens there who wanted to throw off Ottoman rule.

Having made his point, Abbas summoned the Augustinians to an audience at his encampment. The Ottoman state was gaining the upper hand over the rebels in Anatolia, and as soon as it had crushed them it would be able to throw its full weight against Iran. In these circumstances, Abbas could not afford to abandon his effort to win European allies. He continued to look to Spain, in particular, to take the lead in an attack on Aleppo.

Abbas received the Augustinians in his tent at eight o'clock in the morning, invited them to lunch, and kept them till four o'clock in the afternoon. As soon as they arrived, he made it clear he wanted to put the past behind him. He said he was not going to talk about the peace the emperor had made with the Turks because he would rather argue with the Turks than with the Augustinians. However, the letter De Gouvea gave him from King Philip was hardly encouraging. The king congratulated the shah on his victories, but offered no military support. At the same time, he complained that the shah had not handed back Bahrain. Undeterred, Abbas asked De Gouvea to go to Europe to persuade King Philip and the pope to make war on the Ottomans. De Gouvea demurred, saying the King of Spain wished him to remain in Isfahan.

Abbas now received the letters from Anthony Sherley and the Spanish viceroy in Naples, the Count of Benevento, proposing that the Iranian silk exports to Europe be diverted to the sea route from Hormuz. He appeared delighted with the idea and was soon talking of not letting 'a single thread'[7] go via Aleppo, where the silk exports to Europe were normally traded. Besides the financial loss it would mean for the sultan in customs and transit charges, it would also compensate for the temporary closure of the export route to the north due to internal conflicts in Russia. But Abbas is unlikely to have envisaged any long-term concentration of silk exports on Hormuz, as this would have made him too dependent on Spain-Portugal and deprived his own Armenian silk merchants of their livelihood.[8]

After a period of illness, De Gouvea had another audience with the shah at which he questioned the need for sending so many envoys to Spain. Abbas replied that he was putting pressure on the Christian princes to fight the Turks as they ought to, because he was now standing alone and did not know whether his forces would be sufficient, especially as he had the Uzbeks to deal with in the east. There had been two Uzbek raids on Khurasan the previous autumn. De Gouvea said that if it was up to him he would have all the princes of Europe fighting the Ottomans, and he announced that he was now willing to go to Spain on behalf of the shah. Abbas immediately summoned a secretary and dictated letters for the pope and the King of Spain.

He urged King Philip to make war on the Ottomans and said he was very happy to deprive them of their profits from the silk trade. But he asked the king to send someone to see that the Iranian merchants were fairly treated in Hormuz. He assumed Philip was fully behind the proposal to divert the silk exports to Hormuz, although in fact the Spanish government had not yet committed itself. He also asked Philip to send a consul to Iran to judge foreign Christians according to their own laws.[9] In a reversal of the position he had taken earlier with the Augustinians, he asked for a Roman Catholic bishop to reside in the Armenian religious centre of Echmiadzin, near Erivan, and to oversee all Christians in Iran, including the Armenians.

Abbas appointed an Iranian merchant, Dengiz Beg Rumlu, to accompany De Gouvea and gave them a consignment of silk to take to Spain. This was to cause serious misunderstanding and to cost Dengiz Beg his head. According to De Gouvea, when Abbas found there was only a modest amount of silk in his warehouses – 100 bales – he told them to present it to the King of Spain as a gift and a sample of what Iran had to offer. Other accounts say it was De Gouvea who persuaded Dengiz Beg to make a gift of the silk, assuring him that King Philip would reciprocate with a present worth twice the value.

In his discussions with the shah, De Gouvea also complained about the aggressive actions of the governor of Lar, Camber Beg, in particular the occupation of Qishm and the construction of a fortress on the mainland opposite Hormuz. Abbas promised to deal with the matter, but in the event nothing happened.

That Christmas, 1608, Abbas made another of his extraordinary displays of pro-Christian sentiment. No sooner had the Augustinians told him that in Portugal they ate a pig for Christmas, than he had one sent to them.[10] He explained that he was given a pig every year by the Christian vassal ruler of Georgia and kept them in a nearby village. He also ordered wine for the Augustinians in the presence of senior Shi'i clerics, and regardless of the fact that it was the Muslim fasting month of Ramazan. Abbas asked De Gouvea to recount all this to the pope, and to 'tell him how close I am to being a Christian, and how much I deserve his favours'.

On Christmas day, the shah visited the Augustinian convent with his eldest son, Prince Safi, and several other great lords. He looked at everything in the church with great interest and bowed reverentially before some pictures on the altar of the Virgin Mary and Christ. When the fathers, assisted by some Portuguese and Armenian children, sang complines to the accompaniment of various instruments, including a harp, Abbas went and sat on the steps of the altar to have a closer view of the harpist. He stayed for about three hours. At one point he reminded De Gouvea that churches were not allowed in Iran in the past as they were now, to which the friar replied that former Iranian kings were not like the present one. 'I have great hope,' De Gouvea wrote later, 'that if at the hour of his death there are Christians near him, he will not die a Mahommedan.' Abbas probably genuinely enjoyed the experience, but he was certainly mindful of making a favourable impression in Madrid and Rome.

De Gouvea and Dengiz Beg left with their 100 bales of raw silk towards the end of 1609. De Gouvea says there was then serious talk at the court of making peace with the Ottomans. To counter this, he made sure that his embassy to Europe and the plan to divert the silk trade to Hormuz became common knowledge in the Safavid army. The idea was that this would be picked up by the Ottoman spies and relayed to Istanbul, where it would undermine any peace moves by Abbas. Ottoman spies would almost certainly have found out anyway, and the news was more likely to increase pressure on the Ottoman government to make peace with the shah.

By now Father Paul Simon had delivered the shah's letter to Pope Paul V and had gone on to Madrid, where he urged the Spanish government to fight the Ottomans in order to prevent the shah making peace with them and threatening Hormuz. Robert Sherley too had been making an altogether more flamboyant progress through Europe. His reputation as a kind of Lawrence of Arabia of his time had gone before him, with wildly exaggerated accounts circulating of his exploits in the Ottoman wars.[11] He played the part by dressing in a splendid Iranian costume. After spending some time at the Polish court in Cracow, where he left Teresa in a convent to join him later, he went on to Prague and was made a Count Palatine by the Emperor Rudolph. He was given a warm welcome in Florence by the Medici Grand Duke of Tuscany and finally arrived in Rome on 27 September 1609.

At his audience with Pope Paul V, Robert Sherley wore a turban surmounted by a golden crucifix. He was accompanied by his suite of ten Europeans and eight Iranians – all, like himself, in rich oriental costume. The pope, for his part, was flanked by twelve cardinals. Sherley presented the letters from the shah, which applauded the pope's commitment to form a Christian League against the Ottomans and asked him to put pressure on Christian princes and merchants to cut their ties with the Ottoman government. Abbas also asked the pope to persuade Spain to seize Cyprus and use it as a base for an attack on Aleppo. He again invited the pope to send an archbishop to Echmiadzin to take charge of all his Christian subjects. Sherley then iced the cake by asserting that once Abbas had destroyed the Ottomans and captured Constantinople, he would become a Christian. The letter the pope drew up in reply was friendly, but offered nothing concrete. He honoured Robert Sherley by making him a Count of the Sacred Palace of the Lateran.

From Rome, Sherley travelled to Madrid, where the Spanish authorities said they 'had no great opinion of his wisdom for coming with a turban on his head'.[12] He spent the next eighteen months in a fruitless attempt to draw the Spanish government into an active alliance against the Ottomans. He canvassed the idea of an attack on Cyprus and the despatch of a Spanish fleet to the Red Sea to interrupt the supply of spices that brought Christian merchants to Alexandria. Both were turned down. Philip III's chief minister, the Duke of Lerma, was resolutely opposed to further foreign adventures at a time of economic difficulties at home.

Robert Sherley's problems in Spain were compounded by quarrels with his brother Anthony and by the arrival in February 1611 of a new Iranian embassy that superseded his own – that of Dengiz Beg and Antonio De Gouvea with their 100 bales of silk. They refused to co-operate with Robert Sherley, who also tried to negotiate an agreement on the diversion of the silk trade. It is not clear what instructions Sherley had received about this from Isfahan, but it now became central to his diplomatic efforts.

When he still failed to make any headway in Spain, he decided to turn to his 'natural sovereign', the King of England, James I. He told the English ambassador in Madrid, Francis Cottington, that the shah was ready to offer the English East India Company two ports on the Persian Gulf, consular jurisdiction and freedom from customs, if it would take on the silk trade, because 'by it will be diverted that great course of traffick to Constantinople and Aleppo, to the great loss of his enemy the Turk'. He said he had been unable to get the Spaniards to accept similar trade proposals, because he was making it a condition that Spain fight the Turk, which would not be the case with England. Cottington reported the offer favourably to King James's chief minister, Robert Cecil, Earl of Salisbury. But Robert Sherley's intention of going to England was strongly opposed by his brother Anthony, who warned the Spanish government it could be damaging to its interests. Although Madrid was unwilling to reach any agreement itself with Robert Sherley, it did not like the idea of him encouraging the English to muscle in on the trade in the Persian Gulf. So it dragged out the discussions with him as long as possible.

After being joined by his wife, Teresa, Robert Sherley finally left Spain in June 1611. But he did not go straight to England. Instead he first went secretly to Rotterdam to pursue a plan he had concocted with a Dutch merchant he had met in Spain to import Iranian silk into Holland. The scheme was considered by the States General and the Dutch East India Company, but both mistrusted Sherley and his partner and turned it down. Sherley then went to England, where he arrived on 1 August. He got off to a difficult start, as King James was not best pleased to see one of his subjects turn up as the envoy of a foreign power. He had to wait two months for an audience, which he was only granted on condition he take off his turban and dress as an Englishman. But he asked forgiveness with such eloquence at Hampton Court that the king began to regard him with some favour. Sherley also gained a firm supporter in the king's eldest son, Henry, Prince of Wales. However, the English mercantile community was less welcoming. His proposals for importing Iranian silk met fierce opposition from the Levant Company, which saw its trade with the Ottoman Empire threatened. The proposals also aroused no enthusiasm at this juncture with the directors of the more recently established East India Company. The death of the Prince of Wales and of the king's chief minister, Lord Salisbury, who had thought the project worth exploring, ended any hope of getting it accepted and in June 1613 the Sherleys began the return journey to Iran on an East India Company ship.

De Gouvea and Dengiz Beg had some success in Madrid, although King Philip was so underwhelmed by his gift of raw silk that he asked whether Shah Abbas took him for a silk-weaver. De Gouvea secured an agreement in principle for the despatch of two ships a year from Goa to Hormuz to carry Iranian merchants with their silk to Lisbon, where they would sell it. The merchants were to be well-treated and to pay no imposts in Hormuz, but would pay a freight charge for the voyage and customs duties in Lisbon. However, the agreement proved to be of no value as it was never adopted by the Spanish government. De Gouvea and Dengiz Beg also urged a Spanish blockade of the Red Sea, but in this they were no more successful than Robert Sherley. They sailed for Iran from Lisbon in March 1612.

In the meantime, the pope had responded to the shah's repeated request for a senior Latin prelate to take charge of his Christian subjects by appointing De Gouvea Bishop of Cyrene and Apostolic Visitor over all the Christians in Iran. Pope Paul V urged De Gouvea to work to preserve 'the goodwill of the most puissant King of the Persians, when We have received so many and so clear indications of his kindness to the Christian faithful'.[13] He also asked De Gouvea to explain carefully to the shah that the pope greatly regretted his inability to fulfil all Abbas's requests as he would like to have done – a reference to his failure to persuade the Christian princes to join together in fighting the Ottomans.

The shah was already well aware of this and once again felt badly let down by the European powers. In March 1609 he had received a pessimistic assessment of the prospects for a European alliance against the Ottomans from his envoy, Zainal Beg, who had been visiting the courts of Europe for the past six years. In a letter to the shah, Zainal Beg said that the professions of friendship by the Christian princes were false, 'and that all they wanted was for the Turks and Persians to destroy each other, and the Muslim religion included'.[14]

In June of the same year, three Carmelite friars brought him the reply to the letter he had sent to Pope Paul urging an attack on Aleppo. The shah received the friars out in the open at a villa near Isfahan, on a very hot day. The pope's letter contained nothing new. Barely a quarter of it had been translated, 'when the Shah began to toss his head, saying that those were mere words. Then, breaking out very angrily, he began to complain bitterly of the Pope and of the other Christian Princes, who for more than ten years past had given him [nothing but] words and mocked him with promises that they would declare war on the Sultan of Turkey'. When the interpreter resumed his translation, Abbas interrupted again, this time becoming even more worked up, and saying that all those were empty words and lies and that they were deceiving him and the Christians did not want to fight the Turks', while he was then going off to the army, 'just clothed like any poor soldier, and with a pair of rope shoes, to which he pointed as he spoke, resolute to expose himself to any fatigues and dangers, and to remain out in the wind and rain with a morsel of bread like the rest of his soldiers and in a tent'. The friars did their best to defend the pope and the discussion went on for more than an hour, 'with the Shah standing the whole time under a very fierce sun, so that his face was bathed in perspiration, which from time to time he wiped off with his hand'.[15]

After this tempestuous audience, Abbas sent a threatening message to the Carmelites. He told them 'to write promptly to Rome all that he had said, and put it plainly to the Pope that unless action were taken, and the Christian Princes made war on the Sultan of Turkey, he [the pope] should not afterwards complain if the King of Persia used harsh measures with Christians from Europe'. He had already provided a taste of this by sending soldiers to turn the Carmelites out of the house he had given them in Isfahan and telling them to move in with the Augustinians. The Augustinians refused to have them, and for a while the Carmelites had to lodge in a caravanserai. Abbas then relented and found the Carmelites a spacious new house. It stood in the middle of a large garden, and had its own freshwater spring and stables with room for fifty horses.

A few weeks later, Abbas was all charm again when he met two of the Carmelites in a garden near Isfahan as he was preparing to leave on campaign. He was sitting on the bank of a large fishpond with a number of grandees and two Ottoman pashas. After ascertaining that the friars were more than happy to eat fish, he had some caught and a fire lit, and set about cooking the fish himself. Carpets were then spread out and supper served. When the wine was brought, the shah announced 'in a loud voice that he was drinking to the health of the Sovereign Pontiff', and he insisted on sending for the two Carmelite fathers who had brought the pope's letter from Rome to join the company. He wanted to impress on the Ottoman pashas that he had powerful allies in Europe, who might yet join the battle against them.

As night fell, the attendants lit a great number of candles around the fishpond

and above an arch and portico near where the Shah was sitting and the reflections in the water made the scene beautiful beyond measure; some musicians of the Shah too from time to time were singing and playing on certain barbaric instruments used in this country, and to the sound of this, seeming as if transported in ecstasy, the Shah with his hand and his head was making movements like those of a man bereft of his natural senses . . .[16]

The gathering broke up around midnight, when the shah rode back to Isfahan.

Abbas sent another letter to the pope later that year through one of the Carmelites. To stir the Pope into action, he promised to deliver Jerusalem into his hands should he conquer it – an utterly incredible pledge that was never likely to be put to the test. The pope replied with more words. Just over a year later, early in 1611, the shah sent another Carmelite on a mission to Moscow, Poland and Rome. In Moscow he was to negotiate over increasing trade across the Caspian, thereby again reducing dependence on the trade routes through Ottoman Anatolia; in Poland and Rome he was to press for military action against the Turks. But he never got further than Astrakhan, the Russian port on the Caspian, where he was detained for three years, after which he returned to Isfahan.

Abbas saw no alternative to continuing the search for allies in Europe so long as there was no prospect of peace with the Ottomans. Ottoman and Safavid ambassadors had travelled to and fro between Istanbul and Isfahan, but the obstacle to peace was the Ottoman refusal to accept Abbas's territorial gains. The Ottomans appealed for peace on the grounds of Muslim solidarity, arguing that a continuation of hostilities 'would only weaken the Muslim forces engaged in the struggle with the Frankish princes, who were in a constant state of war against the Muslim world, and would produce malicious joy among Christians and other infidels'.[17] This argument undoubtedly carried weight with some at the Safavid court, particularly among the Shi'i clergy, who disliked the shah's policy of allying with Christian states against a Muslim one, albeit a Sunni one. This was the peace party which Sir Anthony Sherley had had to confront. Support for the war was strongest among the *ghulams*, like Allahvirdi Khan, and some of the Qizilbash amirs, who inherited a long tradition of fighting the Ottomans.

Abbas could not ignore altogether the views of the peace party. Adopting a conciliatory tone, he replied that if the sultan would relinquish any further claim to the territories which he had taken back and which he regarded as his by inheritance, then he was 'ready at any time to discuss peace for the benefit of all Muslims'. 'What could be better', he asked rhetorically and somewhat ingenuously, 'than that Muslim rulers should live together in peace and harmony, and thus frustrate the designs of the enemies of the faith?'[18] He followed this up by instructing his ambassador to the Ottoman government to press for peace on the basis of the treaty of 1555 between his grandfather, Shah Tahmasp, and the Ottoman sultan, Sulaiman the Magnificent, which recognised the territories Abbas had been fighting for as rightfully belonging to the Safavids.[19] This was noticeably more modest than his previous claim to all the lands trodden by Shah Ismail I's horse, which would have included Baghdad and the rest of Mesopotamia.

In 1608 the Ottoman grand vizier, Murad Pasha, defeated the last of the great rebel leaders in Anatolia, who fled to Iran with thousands of his followers. Two years later, at the age of ninety, he led an army against Tabriz. Abbas ordered the rural population and all stores of grain to be moved out of his path, and evacuated the civilian population from Tabriz. But after skirmishing with Safavid forces near the city, Murad Pasha withdrew to winter quarters in Diyarbakir. There he died, putting an end to the campaign. The shah in the meantime had offered to pay an annual tribute of 200 bales of silk as compensation for the territories he had won, and this opened the way in November 1612 to a peace agreement on the basis of the status quo. In practice it was little more than a truce, as the Ottomans remained determined to reverse the Safavid conquests, and it was not long before war broke out again.

Chapter 9

Pressure on the Gulf, Mass Deportations and the Murder of a Son

Abbas could now devote himself, for a while at least, to peacetime pursuits. Building was always one of his great passions and with the cessation of hostilities he set in motion another great burst of construction in Isfahan. For many years now Isfahan had been a vast building site and much work had already been done in extending the city to the south. New features included a vast Royal Square designed to be the focus of government, religious and commercial activity, as well as of sporting and other entertainments, a broad tree-lined avenue with a water channel and fountains known as the Chahar Bagh, or Four Gardens, which was about one-and-a-half miles long, and a majestic bridge which carried the avenue over the Zayandeh River, as well as new residences, elegant pavilions and well-watered parks and gardens. Now, in 1611–12, Abbas ordered work to start on a large congregational mosque at the southern end of the square and on a new residential quarter on the north bank of the river for people he brought in from Tabriz, among them many experienced merchants who would add to the prosperity of Isfahan.

After this, however, Isfahan ceased to be the main focus of his building enthusiasm or even his principal residence. He turned his attention instead to the northern province of Mazandaran, where in the following years, 1612–13, he began the construction of two new palace complexes at the south-east end of the Caspian Sea. They were called Farahabad ('The Abode of Joy') and Ashraf, and for the remaining seventeen years of his reign they became his principal residences, where he regularly spent the winter months. During the whole of this time, he made only five relatively short visits to Isfahan.

Around each of these palace complexes he created a town, where his courtiers and officials built residences of their own and which quickly attracted craftsmen, shopkeepers, merchants and others who benefited materially from the presence of the court. He also further populated both the towns and the surrounding countryside with peoples he deported there from the Caucasus, mainly Georgian and Armenian Christians.

Abbas seems to have made the move to Mazandaran for a variety of reasons. He probably felt he had more or less realised his vision for Isfahan, even if much of the work remained to be completed, and he needed a new outlet for his restless desire to build. Mazandaran seems to have had an emotional pull on him because it was his mother's homeland. It also offered excellent hunting, which was his main recreation. The Caspian coast with the Alburz Mountains rising up behind was an obviously attractive site, while its plentiful rainfall and lush vegetation offered new scope for laying out the gardens that so appealed to him. Besides the extensive gardens he created at Farahabad and Ashraf, he laid out four more with pavilions or small palaces in other nearby locations.

Before his move to the Caspian, however, Abbas laid on a splendid reception in Isfahan for the Uzbek khan, Vali Muhammad, who fled to Iran in March 1611 after his nephews, Imam Quli Khan and Nadir Muhammad Khan, took up arms against him. It was Abbas's policy to weaken the Uzbek khanate by encouraging dynastic rivalries and this was too good an opportunity to miss.

Abbas immediately sent Vali Muhammad everything he needed for a royal progress to Isfahan and ordered his governors to entertain him generously on the way. When the fugitive khan reached the Iranian capital in the middle of June, all the shops, coffee-houses and caravanserais around the Royal Square were specially decorated in his honour. In a gesture of respect, Shah Abbas rode out 10 miles to meet him, accompanied by his amirs and principal officers of state. He warmly embraced Vali Muhammad and escorted him into the city along a route lined with musketeers, while the ground beneath their horses' feet was covered with rich cloth. As they rode together, stopping occasionally to be served wine, Abbas asked the khan solicitously about his experiences. A huge press of people turned out to watch the spectacle.

The next day Abbas visited Vali Muhammad in his residence and continued their conversation. 'If the Shah perceived from time to time some signs of melancholy on the part of the khan as he reflected on the way fate had treated him,' writes Iskandar Beg Munshi, 'he would banish such cares by the warmth and expansiveness of his manner.' Abbas arranged a private banquet for Vali Muhammad with singers and musicians, at which he condoled with him in a way calculated 'to soothe grieving hearts'. He also 'praised the men who had accompanied him for their loyalty and promised them handsome rewards'. In the days that followed, Abbas laid on other diversions, including polo matches, archery competitions and fireworks displays in the Royal Square. The Uzbek khan watched in amazement as fireworks lashed to one of the royal elephants were ignited, cannons were fired, and 'the huge beast performed strange antics and made terrifying charges'. When the fireworks were over, Abbas led him on a tour of the bazaar to see the shops and caravanserais which were all lit up. Vali Muhammad seems to have particularly enjoyed the pre-Islamic Iranian Festival of the Sprinkling of the Waters (*Abpashan*), which Abbas is said to have revived.[1] Shah Abbas took Vali Muhammad to see the fun in the great avenue he had laid out, the Chahar Bagh, which was packed with people thoroughly enjoying themselves as they ran around pouring water over one another.

Vali Muhammad remained only a month in Isfahan, before returning to recover his throne. Abbas was keen to have a friendly ruler in Bukhara and offered every assistance. But the Uzbek khan said he had received pledges of support from his subjects and that he would risk losing this if he were seen to be relying on the military power of Iran. He accepted only a small contingent of 200 Iranian troops and returned with these to the khanate, where he rallied enough support to retake Bukhara towards the end of August 1611. But he then treated those who had opposed him so harshly that he forfeited much of his support. As Iskandar Beg Munshi put it, he failed to show 'the tolerance and flexibility that are desirable, nay essential, characteristics in a ruler'. His Sunni clerics declared him a heretic because of his close association with Shi'i Iran and threw their weight behind his nephew, Imam Quli. Later that summer, Vali Muhammad was defeated and captured outside Samarqand by Imam Quli, who promptly had him executed. About fifty of his Iranian troops managed to get back to Khurasan safely by disguising themselves as merchants. Many of the others were killed by Sunni fanatics.

In 1613 Abbas lost one of his most devoted servants with the death of Allahvirdi Khan, the Georgian *ghulam* and governor of Fars, who had been his principal general as well as his close companion, confidant and adviser. Allahvirdi Khan died while on a visit to Isfahan and Abbas showed his deep affection and respect for him by accompanying his bier to the place where the corpses of the dead were ritually washed and personally overseeing all the preparations for the burial. He also visited his house in Isfahan to offer his condolences to Allahvirdi Khan's family. Allahvirdi Khan's son, Imam Quli Khan, was already governor of the southern province of Lar, but Abbas now appointed him governor of Fars as well.

Allahvirdi Khan's body was taken to Mashhad and buried in an elegant tomb that had been built for him within the precincts of the shrine, which was a singular honour. The story is told that a few days before his death the official who had been supervising the construction of the tomb came to Isfahan and Allahvirdi Khan asked him how the work was getting on. The man replied that the vault and portico had been finished and were beautifully decorated, and were just waiting for Allahvirdi Khan to set foot in them.[2]

Allahvirdi Khan's tomb can still be seen today, a two-storey octagonal structure abutting the north-eastern wall of the shrine. Another of Abbas's officials who appears to have been similarly honoured with a personal mausoleum within the shrine is his famous grand vizier, Hatem Beg Ordubadi, who had died three years earlier, in 1610.[3] As he did with Allahvirdi Khan, Abbas appointed the grand vizier's son, Mirza Abu Taleb Beg Ordubadi, as his successor. Iskandar Beg Munshi says this was in recognition of Hatem Beg's outstanding services as vizier. He adds that despite his youth, Mirza Abu Taleb 'was his father's equal in practical matters and his superior in learning'. Nonetheless, both deaths must have been felt as a severe loss by Abbas.

Now that he was no longer at war with the Ottomans, Abbas became less interested in a European alliance or in diverting the silk exports away from Ottoman territory. This was reflected in his treatment of his two envoys to Spain, Dengiz Beg and De Gouvea, who arrived back in Iran as the peace was being concluded.

His ambassador, Dengiz Beg, was the first to present himself at the court in the spring of 1613. As he went down on his knees to kiss the shah's foot, Abbas kicked him and gave the signal for his execution. He was given no opportunity to answer the charges against him, which derived from reports the shah had received from Europe – no doubt from someone appointed to his suite with the express task of spying on him. Among other things, Dengiz Beg was accused of wearing mourning for the death of the

Spanish queen although his own master was in good health, and of treating members of his mission so badly that several converted to Christianity and remained behind in Europe. This last was considered a capital offence. But other envoys had been instructed to conform to European customs and Sir Anthony Sherley's fellow ambassador, Husain Ali Beg, was not executed after members of his mission converted and settled in Spain. The shah's anger with Dengiz Beg was probably increased by King Philip's failure to respond positively to his overtures and by the reawakening of his resentment of Portuguese control over Hormuz. He was now furious that the silk had been given to the Spanish king as a gift instead of being sold, and that Dengiz Beg had received nothing of equal value in return. There was also a rumour that Dengiz Beg had sold half the consignment and pocketed the proceeds.[4] This is hard to credit because, had he done so, he certainly would not have dared to return to Iran.

De Gouvea arrived at the Safavid court in June with presents of spices, jewels and various curiosities. Abbas immediately wanted to know what represented payment for the silk and what was a gift from King Philip. When De Gouvea replied that the spices were payment for the silk, Abbas had them valued, and on being told that they were worth much less than the silk, he demanded that De Gouvea pay the difference. He also made him agree to send a letter to Spain explaining that the silk had been a commercial consignment and not a gift.

Abbas's patience with Spain was wearing thin, after its persistent failure to give him the support against the Ottomans that he had constantly asked for and been promised. In July 1613 he sent another Augustinian, Belchior dos Anjos, with a blunt message for King Philip. 'There can be two reasons for kings to be friends,' he said, 'either on account of belief, if they both profess the same faith, or for reasons of state.' The first, he went on, did not apply in their case 'because there was such great difference in belief, and if the other reason was not present either, there was no basis for friendship.'[5] That did not bode well for the Spanish-Portuguese presence in the Persian Gulf.

But it was the Armenian community in Isfahan that was the first to suffer as a result of the shah's disillusionment with the Christian powers of Europe and his temporary truce with the Ottomans. The Armenians themselves realised at once that the arrival of De Gouvea claiming authority over them as their Apostolic Visitor was likely to cause trouble in the prevailing climate, and they hurried to assure Abbas that it was none of their doing. De Gouvea only made matters worse by referring to the

Armenians in the presence of the shah as 'my subjects'.[6] Abbas allowed pressure to be put on the Armenians to convert to Islam. He also forbade them to have contact with Europeans and demanded they repay the money he had advanced when he resettled them in Isfahan, or hand over their sons and daughters. The Carmelites and Augustinians put up some money, but this was returned by Abbas who said he was astonished that De Gouvea should once again meddle in the sovereign's dealings with his own vassals.[7] De Gouvea made a hasty departure for Hormuz, while the rest of the Augustinians withdrew temporarily to Baghdad and all but one of the Carmelites also thought it prudent to leave Isfahan for the time being.

But Abbas stopped the persecution the following year, 1614, as he could not afford to alienate his Armenian merchants, who played such a valuable role in the export of Iranian silk. He now directed his anger against Spain and Portugal by again attacking the Portuguese port of Gombroon on the Persian Gulf, which was used by all the merchant caravans bringing goods to and from Hormuz. The Portuguese commander on Hormuz had angered the shah by ill treating some Arab merchants he had seized. As before, the Iranians began by preventing the movement of caravans. Then, at the end of September, they laid siege to Gombroon, which was defended by only some eighty Portuguese soldiers and a larger number of locally recruited troops. The port fell a few days before Christmas. The Iranian campaign was led by Imam Quli Khan, the new governor general of Fars as well as of Lar, in which Gombroon was situated.

An attack on the island of Hormuz itself was not possible without warships, which the Iranians lacked. But Hormuz was also saved from further harassment by worsening relations between Iran and the Ottomans. Shah Abbas needed to have his hands free to deal with a resumption of the Ottoman war and was again interested in diverting the silk exports to Europe away from Ottoman territory. He opened negotiations with the Portuguese on Hormuz through the Carmelites, though he made it clear he had no intention of handing back any of the places he had seized.

The Ottoman grand vizier, Nasuh Pasha, who had been the architect of the peace agreement of 1612, was executed in October 1614. His successor, Mehmed Pasha, was determined to make a renewed attempt to drive the Iranians out of the territories they had recovered. He justified breaking the peace on the grounds that the shah had failed to deliver the promised 200 bales of silk and had raided Ottoman territory in Georgia.

This incursion took place in 1613–14, after two Georgian princes who owed allegiance to the shah rebelled and took refuge with a neighbouring

Georgian vassal of the Ottomans. Abbas marched into eastern Georgia, turning churches into mosques and ravaging those districts suspected of aiding the rebel princes, including part of the territory of the Ottoman vassal. His troops also seized 40,000 sheep and cattle and took 30,000 prisoners who were brought back to Iran and forcibly converted to Islam.

In anticipation of a renewed conflict with Turkey, Shah Abbas deported 15,000 families from the Caucasus to Mazandaran in order to populate and develop the Caspian coastal region, where he was building his new palaces and towns of Ashraf and Farahabad. These deportees were non-native inhabitants of Georgia – Muslims, Jews and Armenians – and sections of the population of Shirvan and Qarabagh, who were suspected of having collaborated during the Ottoman occupation. Abbas also accused elements in the Safavid Sufi order in north-west Iran of collaboration and had them executed. He considered their disloyalty all the more serious as it was a violation of the absolute obedience they owed him as their Sufi master.

Abbas's tendency to suspicion and mistrust seems to have become intense at this time. Combined with the usual court intrigues, it proved fatal to the shah's eldest son, Prince Safi. The prince was extremely popular not only with many of the courtiers and nobles but also with the population at large. Like any influential figure at court, however, he had his enemies. Some of these insinuated that he was conspiring to seize the throne and produced servants and retainers to back up their allegations in front of the shah, while he was campaigning in Georgia. Iskandar Beg Munshi who, being close to the shah and the court, was in a good position to judge, makes it fairly clear that he considered these allegations to be baseless since he attributes them to 'court sycophants and place-seekers' who set out, he says, 'to poison the Shah's mind against his son'. Abbas, however, believed the allegations and had the prince assassinated.[8] This provoked riots and the shah himself is said to have felt remorse afterwards, though that did not prevent him from later turning savagely against his two remaining sons and having them blinded. He had already abandoned his predecessors' practice of appointing the royal princes to provincial governorships. He now went further and confined them to the harem, where their only companions were eunuchs and women. It was not proper, said Abbas, to expose them too much to the view of the people, who generally worship the rising sun.[9]

Ottoman preparations for war encouraged fresh resistance on the part of many Georgians, who rejected the quislings and Muslim converts the shah sought to impose on them. They rallied round one of their rebel princes, Taimuras, the ruler of the eastern principality of Kakhetia, and in

1616 inflicted a severe defeat on a 15,000-strong Iranian force. Abbas was so enraged that he 'ordered his men to spare no male Georgians, to take prisoner the women and children, and to plunder their possessions, in accordance with the Koranic injunction, "Slay all those who attribute partners to God"'[10] – a reference to the Christian doctrine of the Trinity. More than 60,000 Georgians were killed and over 100,000 deported to Iran. Iskandar Beg Munshi thought it unlikely that Kakhetia 'had ever suffered so much destruction since the advent of Islam'.[11]

The terrible brutality with which this mass deportation was carried out is described by the Italian traveller, Pietro Della Valle, who arrived in Iran shortly afterwards:

> Murders, people dying of starvation, robberies, rapes, children stifled in despair by their own parents, or thrown by them into rivers, others massacred by the Persians for want of good complexions, others again torn from their mothers' breasts, and thrown into the streets and highways, to become the prey of wild beasts, or be trodden to death by the horses and camels belonging to the army, which for a whole day together trampled upon carcases: such is the picture of this shocking expedient; and afterwards, how agonising the separation of parents from their children, husbands from their wives, brothers from their sisters, divided from each other, and forwarded to different provinces! So numerous were these wretched ruined people on this occasion that they were publicly sold at a cheaper rate even than beasts.[12]

Many of the Georgians were resettled as peasant farmers in Mazandaran and other parts of Iran that Abbas was keen to develop. The rest of the male deportees became slaves or *ghulams* of the shah, or of whoever bought them, while the best-looking women were a valued addition to the harems of Iran. The most celebrated victim of Abbas's punitive policy was the Georgian queen-mother, Princess Ketevan. Still a beautiful woman, she had been sent by her son, Taimuras, to intercede with the shah. Abbas demanded that she become a Muslim and enter his harem, and when she refused had her imprisoned in Shiraz. She died there in 1624, still refusing to abjure her faith despite being tortured, and was recognised as a martyr of the Georgian church.

A large Ottoman army under Mehmed Pasha laid siege to Erivan at the end of August 1616. Shah Abbas harried the Ottoman supply lines and in November, with winter approaching, Mehmed Pasha lifted the siege and withdrew, many of his soldiers dying of cold on the way. This failure led to Mehmed Pasha's downfall. His successor as grand vizier, Khalil Pasha, led a fresh assault on Iran in 1618, supported this time by Tartar and Georgian contingents. But first of all he sent an ambassador to the shah in Qazvin, offering to withdraw if Abbas surrendered his conquests.

Once again Abbas had to contend with an influential peace party among his senior officials, which he overcame this time by making a direct appeal to popular sentiment. In a carefully staged propaganda exercise, he received the Ottoman ambassador in the main square of Qazvin, with both men on horseback and a large crowd of citizens looking on. When the ambassador presented a letter which Abbas knew contained conditions of peace he would be unwilling to accept, he brushed it aside, declaring in a loud voice that, 'He did not wish to hear any more, nor to see any further letters, but that all might be finally concluded in a few words, if the Turks were satisfied with keeping what belonged to them, and ceased to dispute the possession of what belonged to the Persians.'[13] But he warned that if he was forced to war by the arrogance of the Turks, the blood of the myriad innocent people which would be shed would be upon their heads. In that case, he would place himself at the head of his troops and the Turks might put their trust in their wealth and their many soldiers, but he had God, Muhammad and Ali on his side. When the ambassador, speaking so quietly he could barely be heard, replied that the Turks could not make peace on such terms, Abbas declared that there was then no alternative to war and went on to compare the martial qualities of his soldiers to 'your Turks, who wear large turbans and keep their hands in their sleeves for fear of the cold'. After a mocking reference to the previous unsuccessful campaign of Mehmed Pasha, 'when your troops galloped off crying like women', Abbas turned and rode away to enthusiastic cries of 'Allah! Allah!' from the crowd.

The shah mobilised his forces and marched into Azerbaijan to meet the Ottoman attack. He went with part of the army to the Safavid shrine city of Ardabil, where he rebuffed another Ottoman envoy. He refused to entertain a peace offer, even after the envoy shelved the territorial demands and asked Abbas simply to pay the silk tribute and to send his son to Istanbul as a hostage. 'This is my son,' he said, drawing his sword, 'if you can wrest him from me.'[14] He ordered his main forces under his new commander-in-chief, Qarachaqay Beg, an Armenian *ghulam*, to devastate the countryside and to attack enemy foraging parties, but to avoid a major confrontation until the winter set in and the Ottomans began to suffer from hunger and cold. He allowed the enemy to occupy Tabriz, after the population had been evacuated, and was on the point of giving up Ardabil as well, when he received news that Qarachaqay Beg had won a complete victory over the vanguard of the Ottoman army. It mattered little, in view of the outcome, that he had disobeyed Abbas's orders and been drawn into a full-scale battle. Khalil Pasha was ready to abandon the campaign and towards the end of September 1618 another peace agreement was concluded, which left Abbas in possession of all his conquests and reduced his annual tribute to 100 bales of silk.

This had been achieved despite attempts by the Uzbeks to give military support to the Ottomans. Led now by Vali Muhammad's nephews, Imam Quli and Nadir Muhammad, the Uzbeks carried out a series of wide-ranging attacks on Iran in 1617. These extended beyond the usual target of Khurasan to the shores of the Caspian and as far west as the central Iranian city of Yazd. At the end of that year, however, the Safavid governor of Marv defeated an Uzbek force entering Khurasan and took prisoner several high-ranking Uzbeks. He sent them to the shah, who was spending the winter at his palace at Farahabad on the Caspian, while Khalil Pasha was making preparations for his invasion of Iran. Abbas treated the prisoners kindly but held them as hostages to deter the Uzbeks from supporting the Ottoman grand vizier with an attack of their own. In June 1618, after the Ottoman army had withdrawn and peace negotiations were safely under way, he sent them back to Bukhara with an offer of friendship. Imam Quli responded by sending an ambassador to Isfahan, who was well received. After protracted negotiations through ambassadors, a peace settlement was finally reached in 1623 which held for the rest of Abbas's reign. Under its terms, Abbas agreed to end the support he had been giving to Vali Muhammad's son, Rustam Muhammad, to carry out attacks on Uzbek territory from a base inside Iran.

After he had made peace with the Ottomans, Abbas returned to Qazvin to receive quite the most splendid embassy of his reign. It was sent by the Moghul emperor, Jahangir (r.1605–27), and led by a Moghul nobleman, Khan Alam, whose family had served Timurid rulers since the days of Timur himself. The Spanish ambassador, Figueroa, who visited Abbas's court at the same time, says Khan Alam was about sixty years old, wore pearl earrings, carried a dagger adorned with precious stones and was described as fabulously rich by the Indian merchants in Isfahan. Khan Alam was accompanied by about 800 attendants and an exotic collection of Indian fauna escorted by several hundred keepers. Iskandar Beg Munshi, who saw the embassy arrive in Qazvin, says there were 'ten huge elephants, equipped with gold howdahs and embellished with all kinds of trappings, and a variety of animals, including tigers, leopards, antelope, Indian lambs, cheetahs, rhinoceroses, talking birds and water-buffalo which pulled various types of litters'. Also accompanying the embassy was the Moghul court painter, Bishan Das, who did a number of portraits while he was in Iran which he brought back for Jahangir, including one of Shah Abbas which delighted the Moghul emperor.

The embassy was clearly intended to impress the Iranians and to convey to Abbas the esteem in which he was held by the Moghul emperor, no doubt partly in the hope that strengthened bonds of friendship would dissuade the shah from pursuing his long-stated aim of recovering Qandahar, with its valuable customs revenue from the caravans plying their trade between India and Iran. If so, that hope was to prove a vain one. Nonetheless, Abbas was anxious to retain the friendship of the Moghuls, as this made it less likely that they would form an alliance against him with the Uzbeks. Having grown up in the former Timurid capital of Herat, he also instinctively admired the Moghuls because of their descent from Tamerlane. Abbas regarded this as an important source of legitimacy and increasingly sought to associate his own dynasty with the great Mongol conqueror.[15] He took the sword which was among the gifts brought by the Moghul embassy that visited him while he was besieging Erivan in the winter of 1603-4 as a good omen, because, he said, it came from a descendant of Tamerlane. One of the gifts which Jahangir sent with Khan Alam – no doubt aware of Abbas's interest in the Timurids – was a rare collection of 240 portraits of Timur and his descendants.[16]

Abbas gave Khan Alam a warm welcome both in Qazvin and later in Isfahan, where more ceremony was laid on with ranks of soldiers two deep lining his route from a considerable distance outside the city. Huge crowds on foot and on horseback went out to watch the arrival of such a magnificent and colourful embassy. Afterwards there were banquets and a variety of entertainments, including nocturnal bullfights in the Royal Square, which was lit up with thousands of lamps and candles.

Figueroa, who attended these festivities, says that Khan Alam was a good-humoured man and very good company. Abbas got on well with him. According to Figueroa, the shah 'often teased him and played with him, not only with words, but also seizing hold of his beard and clapping him on the shoulders'. The only thing Abbas disliked was Khan Alam's habit of smoking, which he did with a two-foot-long gold pipe, expelling clouds of smoke 'so that even those sitting far away were inconvenienced'. Although Abbas was very civil to his guests, says Figueroa, he had difficulty concealing his irritation.[17]

In his discussions with Khan Alam, Abbas again raised the question of Qandahar, claiming that it was part of Khurasan which was his hereditary territory. The interests of both parties, he said, required that the emperor give back to him a territory which was far from the frontiers of India and a stumbling-block to their friendship.[18] This message was again conveyed, politely but firmly, to Jahangir by the Iranian ambassador, Zainal Beg, Abbas's former roving ambassador in Europe, who was chosen to accompany Khan Alam back to India in 1619. Iskandar Beg Munshi says that Abbas

> selected Zainal Beg as possessing the necessary qualities for an ambassador: intrinsic suitability, shrewdness, magnanimity, natural good manners and excellence of conduct. In addition, he was a man in whom the Shah had complete trust. For his part, Zainal Beg resolved, on the basis of the faithful and devoted conduct expected of a Sufi, not to spare either life or property in the service of his supreme spiritual director (morshed-e kamel) and benefactor.[19]

Zainal Beg's embassy was fitted out with great magnificence so that Abbas should not appear to have been outshone by the splendour of Khan Alam's embassy.

Ambassadors from the Shi'i Deccan states of Golconda, Ahmadnagar and Bijapur had also been visiting Abbas's court to seek his help in opposing Moghul attempts to take them over. Like his predecessors, Abbas maintained regular contacts with these states and was sympathetic to their cause. He had already interceded on their behalf after Jahangir launched military offensives against them led by his son, Prince Shah Jahan, but had been unable to prevent the Moghuls taking some territory when peace was made in 1617. It is doubtful whether Abbas's intercession, which the Moghuls regarded as interference, was of any real help. But he continued to maintain the close tie with the Deccan states, giving their ambassadors leave to depart and appointing Iranian ambassadors to accompany them to their respective courts.

Abbas was visited too at this time by a Russian embassy sent by the first of the Romanov tsars, Mikhail.[20] Since Abbas came to the throne a number of envoys had been exchanged between the two countries. These missions had been small-scale and mainly of a commercial nature, with Iranian merchants selling silk on the shah's private account and purchasing in return such items as furs, hunting falcons and weapons. There had also been an intermittent interest on both sides in possible co-operation against the Ottomans. On the other hand, Abbas had been concerned at Russian moves to extend their influence in the Caucasus. In general, however, the Iranians tended to have a low opinion of the Russians, considering them to be boorish and lacking any refinement. Iranian interest in Russia had also declined during the period of anarchy that had preceded the accession of Tsar Mikhail. This latest embassy, led by Ivan Ivanovich Chicherin, brought hunting falcons as a gift for Abbas, who gave them to Khan Alam. Abbas treated the embassy in a very offhand manner. He remained much more interested in developing relations with Europe, which would soon bring about one of the great triumphs of his reign.

Chapter 10

An Anglo-Iranian Victory: the Capture of Hormuz

The renewed Ottoman attacks between 1616 and the restoration of a fragile peace in 1618 had persuaded Abbas to resume his European diplomacy. Robert Sherley had returned to Isfahan in March 1615, despite every effort by the Spanish and the Portuguese to prevent him from doing so. They feared he brought with him some agreement on the part of the English to provide the shah with ships for an attack on Hormuz. The English were now regarded as an imminent threat to Portuguese hegemony in the Persian Gulf and the Indian Ocean. Two East India Company ships had defeated a Portuguese fleet off the mouth of the Indus in 1612 and the following year the company had obtained permission from the Moghul emperor, Jahangir, to establish a factory or trading base at the nearby port of Surat, a few hundred miles up the coast from the Portuguese headquarters at Goa. After Robert Sherley arrived in India, the Portuguese attempted to kill him by blowing up his house, but he and his wife escaped unhurt. He was well-received by Jahangir and was able to make his way overland to Isfahan.

Shah Abbas was on the point of sending an Iranian as his latest ambassador to Europe, but as soon as he knew Sherley was back he asked him to go instead, 'not caring to dispatch a Muslim on account of the bad reports he had had of all those who had gone to Europe, how they committed a thousand outrages and got drunk to the great disgust of the European sovereigns and to his own discredit and dishonour'.[1] Sherley took some persuading after all he had been through. Eventually he agreed to go, but insisted one of the Carmelite friars, Brother Redempt, go with him.

Despite his previous disappointment, Abbas still saw Spain-Portugal as the only power that could offer military assistance against the Ottomans, through naval action in the Mediterranean, and also help to deprive them of the customs and transit dues from Iran's silk exports. Robert Sherley's instructions seem to have been to make one last effort to reach an agreement with Madrid. But if the negotiations failed, Sherley was to turn to England, not only with a renewed offer on the silk, but this time to obtain warships as well – the purpose of which could only be to wrest Hormuz from the Portuguese.

Just as Robert Sherley was about to leave on his diplomatic mission, a new trading partner for Iran appeared on the scene in the shape of the English East India Company. Two representatives of the company, Richard Steele and John Crowther, arrived in Isfahan from the company's Indian headquarters at Surat to explore the Iranian market and obtain permission to trade. They wanted to use the port of Jask, which was outside the Persian Gulf and about 90 miles east of Hormuz. Like the Muscovy Company more than fifty years earlier, the East India Company was looking in the first place for a market for English woollen cloth. Its factors in Surat found they had overestimated the demand for the cloth in India, which had left them with large stocks on their hands. But they rightly judged that they should do better on the high Iranian plateau with its cold winters. Steele and Crowther carried letters from the factors in Surat asking Robert Sherley to use his influence at the Safavid court to help them. He was reluctant to do so at first lest the Spanish and Portuguese got to hear of it, but then decided he owed it to them 'as an Englishman'.[2] Taking care to conceal his actions from the Carmelites, he secretly introduced Steele and Crowther to the grand vizier and helped them to obtain a favourable *farman* or edict from Shah Abbas. In it the shah ordered his officials

> to receive kindly and entertain the English Frankes or Nation, at what time any of their ships or shipping shall arrive at Jasques, or any other of the Portes in our Kingdom; to conduct them and their Merchandise to what place or places they themselves desire; and that you shall see them safely defended about our Coasts, from any Frank or Franks whatsoever.[3]

The last point was clearly aimed at the Portuguese.

Robert Sherley finally left Isfahan at the beginning of October 1615. To facilitate a rapprochement with Spain-Portugal, he took with him all seventy Portuguese soldiers taken captive at Gombroon. This persuaded the

Portuguese authorities on Hormuz to put aside their former animosity towards him. He took ship to Goa, but had to wait there nearly a year to catch the annual convoy to Lisbon. In Goa, he crossed paths with an elderly Spanish ambassador, Don Garcia de Silva y Figueroa, who was on his way to Iran, returning the embassy of De Gouvea and Dengiz Beg to Madrid. Figueroa voiced his suspicion that Sherley was secretly working for the English, with the result that Sherley was kept under virtual house arrest until his departure, for fear he might otherwise gather information on Goa's defences. Ironically, the newly appointed English ambassador to the Moghul court in India, Sir Thomas Roe, was at the same time berating the East India Company factors in Surat for having dealings with Sherley who, he insisted, was working entirely in the Spanish interest.

Robert Sherley reached Lisbon in the summer of 1617 and remained in Portugal and Spain until 1622, trying to secure an agreement under which Spain-Portugal would take the Iranian silk exports and would also put further economic pressure on the Ottoman government by blockading the Red Sea. The Spanish government mistrusted him and his brother Anthony again appeared on the scene to fan that mistrust. Madrid was certainly interested in an agreement because that would spoil the English East India Company's attempt to move into Iran, the news of which had reached Spain and had caused some alarm. But it insisted on the return of Gombroon, Qishm and Bahrain as preconditions, which was unacceptable to Abbas. Despite this, a draft agreement was drawn up and two copies sent to Iran. One copy was sent overland. The other was taken by the Carmelite friar, Brother Redempt, who had accompanied Robert Sherley, and who sailed for Hormuz from Lisbon in April 1619 with a fleet of five galleons under the command of the Portuguese admiral Ruy Freire de Andrada. Ruy Freire had orders to prevent any other European power trading with Iran and to build a fort on the island of Qishm. This last order would amount, if implemented, to an act of war, as the Iranians had seized the island from Hormuz five years earlier.

For much of this time the Spanish government was also trying to negotiate with the shah through its ambassador to Iran, Don Garcia de Silva y Figueroa. He was appointed as far back as 1612 as an immediate response to De Gouvea and Dengiz Beg's embassy to Spain. But his mission was subject to endless delays and he did not reach Iran until October 1617. His initial brief was to encourage the shah to continue the war with the Ottomans by promising a greater Spanish effort in the Mediterranean. He was also to negotiate on diverting the silk trade through Hormuz. But by the time he arrived, Gombroon had fallen and the English East India Company was threatening to take the Iranian trade away from Portugal.

Following up the visit of Steel and Crowther, the East India Company factors at Surat had sent a first consignment of goods and a further mission to Iran on board the company ship, the *James*, which reached Jask on 2 December 1616, after successfully evading Portuguese attempts to intercept it. The leader of the mission, Edward Connock, caught up with Shah Abbas while he was campaigning on the Ottoman frontier. He found him very friendly and obtained a new *farman* extending specific privileges to the company. He also reported that the shah was willing to sell the company up to 3,000 bales of silk at reasonable prices and on credit. Connock was euphoric and held out the prospect of the company taking the entire Iranian silk export, which he calculated to be worth a million pounds sterling a year.

In view of these alarming developments, Figueroa was given new priorities. These were to demand that the shah return all the territories he had seized from Hormuz and exclude the English from trading in Iran. Figueroa took a gloomy view of the prospects for his mission from the start. He felt the Iranians were no longer impressed by Spanish power after the loss of Gombroon and that the shah was hiding his hostility under an appearance of good will. He believed the most he could hope to achieve was to prevent or delay the loss of Hormuz itself. He had little faith in the ability of the Portuguese to defend the island. On his arrival there he criticised the poor state of the fortifications and the inept behaviour of the Portuguese authorities in wantonly antagonising Muslims by tearing down a mosque.

One thing in Figueroa's favour was that he was not in holy orders. After his experience with De Gouvea, Abbas had requested not to be sent any more Augustinian friars as ambassadors because, as he put it, 'a Religious out of his cell was like a fish out of water'.[4] But Figueroa was not someone likely to strike up a warm, personal relationship with the shah. Aged sixty-seven, he was an old man and looked it, having lost all or most of his teeth. What is more, he did not drink and did not much enjoy parties. During his progress through Iran to meet the shah, the Iranian authorities thoughtfully offered to bring him some women. He thanked them, but said he was so old that the company of women was no longer able to divert him. Figueroa says the Iranians found this hard to believe, 'although they saw he had grey hair and his beard was completely white'.[5]

Shah Abbas was at his palace of Ashraf on the Caspian when he received news of the arrival of Figueroa in Isfahan. He asked the Italian traveller, Pietro Della Valle, who was present at a banquet there, about the new

Spanish ambassador. Was he a great man? Was he a man of truth and integrity? Della Valle, himself a high-born Roman, assured the shah 'that his house and kinship were of the most noble in Spain', but admitted he had never dealt with him personally. Abbas then asked why the King of Spain did not wage war against the Ottomans, to which Della Valle replied that the king harried them by sea. That was of little use, said Abbas. It was necessary to take Cyprus and recover the Holy Land. If he had been the King of Spain, he would have wanted either to die or to recover Jerusalem. Warming to his theme, he said

> that the King of Spain should be a soldier and ride out in person. It was not necessary to rely on viziers or ministers, because such as these only wanted to prosper themselves and live comfortably. It was needful to do as he did, who went forth in person, wishing either to lose his life or subdue all his enemies.[6]

Figueroa had his first meeting with Shah Abbas in Qazvin on Sunday 17 June 1618, a few days after the shah issued mobilisation orders and held his theatrical public audience with the Ottoman ambassador, at which he refused to make peace by surrendering his conquests. Figueroa was escorted to the palace by the governor of Qazvin, officers of the royal household and a large company of soldiers. More than 600 men carried the great array of presents he had brought for Abbas. These included a seventy-piece travelling dinner service, fifty damascened arquebuses with gold inlaid stocks, portraits of the Spanish Infanta and the Queen of France, and 'the strongest and most ferocious mastiff ever seen'.[7] There was also a big chest full of carpenter's, locksmith's and surgeon's tools, as Abbas was known to be fond of exercising such skills. In addition to all these gifts, Figueroa had brought 300 camel-loads of pepper, which he had left behind in Isfahan.

They made their way with difficulty through the crowds that had gathered to see the ambassador and his suite. A great public reception had been laid on in the palace gardens for more than a hundred guests 'of various nations, languages and dress'. Figueroa had to wait outside the palace in some discomfort for about half an hour so that he should arrive at the same time as the Ottoman ambassador. He was then led into the palace grounds, down avenues lined with cypresses and plane trees, and told to wait in front of a pavilion surrounded by water and reached across a little bridge. The shah, who was in the pavilion, was told of his arrival and came out to meet him. Figueroa did reverence Spanish-style, taking off his hat, bending his knee, kissing his right hand, touching the sleeve of the shah's gown, kissing his hand again as well as the letter from his master, the King of Spain, which he handed to the shah. Abbas welcomed him warmly and led him into the pavilion, which was open on all sides, and where he was seated on the carpet between two young nobles. The Ottoman ambassador followed, looking very grave, and was similarly seated. He wore a long, brown satin robe and a white turban. The shah carried one of the arquebuses Figueroa had given him, which he was delighted with as it was just the right size. He asked how it was used by the Spanish and Figueroa explained that it was an infantry weapon and that the cavalry had a shorter version. After inspecting it carefully, the shah handed it to one of his pages.

Abbas was plainly dressed, as usual. He wore an ordinary gown of green cloth with the Qizilbash 'crown of Haidar' on his head – the red felt bonnet of twelve folds wound round with a turban and with a stick emerging from the top.[8] His turban, which was wound around the bonnet, was of green and scarlet silk. By his side he had a plain scimitar with a black leather sheath. Figueroa says he was a little above average height, slim, vigorous and robust, with an aquiline nose, a sour look and very alert eyes. His naturally fair complexion was tanned and worn by long exposure to the sun and the elements. His most unattractive feature, according to Figueroa, was his short, fat, blackened hands, like those of a peasant.

The younger of the shah's two surviving sons, Imam Quli, who was about seventeen, entered the pavilion with him and stood with his eyes lowered, never speaking and never spoken to: 'No one paid him any more attention than if he had been a page or some other servant.'[9] Destined to be blinded by his father, he was obviously in great fear after the assassination of his elder brother.

Guests were seated on carpets all around the pool, among them two new agents of the English East India Company, Thomas Barker and Edward Monnox. As night fell, candles and torches were lit, several great silver candelabra were placed by the pool and the whole of the surrounding garden was illuminated with lanterns. The shah joked with Figueroa about the Ottoman ambassador, speaking through the interpreter in Georgian so that the ambassador would not understand. It was a language he must have learnt from his many Georgian *ghulams* and concubines. Figueroa was convinced that the shah's outward display of friendliness towards him was all pretence, that 'his intention was to make the Ottoman ambassador jealous, to make him see that the King of Spain sought his friendship and sent him a very considerable present'.

Abbas spent most of the time in animated discussion with the Ottoman ambassador, whose country was once again preparing to invade Iran. Figueroa's interpreter, who overheard parts of the conversation, told him the shah sometimes got angry and said

> the Turks must not imagine they could govern him as they had governed his father, who was blind and had let it be known he had no guts, as he had left the Turks with the whole of Greater Armenia and Media [north-western Iran] ... he [Abbas] had conquered both and was now firmly resolved never to return them, nor to pay any tribute.

After it had been dark for two hours, several young boys appeared with long hair falling from their turbans to their necks and wearing jerkins and tight-fitting pantaloons, both of gold brocade, and laid down cloths of flowered silk on which dinner was served. This was a simple meal of rice with mutton and chicken as the main course, and with plums, cucumbers and celery to start and finish with. The shah continued talking to the Ottoman ambassador, but broke off in the middle to drink the health of the King of Spain and Figueroa. The latter had the interpreter whisper into the shah's ear in Georgian that he was drinking to the beard of the Ottoman ambassador. Abbas burst out laughing, knocking his forehead with delight. It was almost midnight by the time dinner was finished and Figueroa, by now very tired, withdrew with the shah's permission and returned to his lodging.

Figueroa met Abbas on two other occasions in Qazvin, but failed to close the widening gap between Spain-Portugal and Iran. Abbas wanted to see Spain engage the Ottomans seriously and was not impressed to learn of action being taken against Ottoman corsairs in the Mediterranean. He also firmly rejected Figueroa's demand that he hand back Gombroon and Bahrain.

The shah then left for the campaign against the invading Ottoman army, which ended in September 1618 with an Iranian victory and a renewed peace accord. He spent the winter at his new palace of Farahabad on the Caspian. Figueroa, meanwhile, went to Isfahan, where he received a letter from the King of Spain on the twin issues of the Iranian silk exports and the suggested Spanish blockade of the Red Sea, but tying them clearly to the return of the territories the shah had seized from Portuguese Hormuz. Figueroa dutifully gave the letter to the Carmelite friar Belchior dos Anjos to take to the shah at Farahabad, though he knew it was a waste of time. The shah refused to see the Carmelite and merely sent a message to say that he had no need for a naval force in the Red Sea or for a silk contract now that he had made peace with the Ottoman government. And he would not give back an inch of land he had conquered.

Figueroa was now anxious to return to Spain, but he could not leave without the shah's permission and this was not forthcoming. Doubtless the shah was influenced by a letter he received from Robert Sherley telling of his unfriendly reception in Lisbon and asking Abbas to detain Figueroa until he, Sherley, was able to report on his experience at the Spanish court. Figueroa's difficulties were compounded by the hostility he continued to meet from the local Portuguese. He was unable to communicate with Madrid because the governor of Hormuz would not let any couriers through and the Portuguese Augustinians apparently paid people in Baghdad and Aleppo to intercept any letters he tried to send overland. The Portuguese authorities on Hormuz would certainly not have wanted his critical views of them to get back to Madrid.

Abbas arrived in Isfahan in the spring of 1619 to receive a number of foreign embassies, including the magnificent Moghul embassy led by Khan Alam. A few days after his arrival, he turned up at Figueroa's house without any warning and accompanied only by his chief eunuch, Yusuf Agha, a companion called Iskandar Beg,[10] and a page who was carrying his bow and quiver. After surprising Figueroa while he was walking in his garden, he sat down and asked what he had been doing since Qazvin, how the King of Spain was and what news he had from Madrid. He left about half an hour later, promising to call again with the same familiarity and to give Figueroa an audience.

At a splendid reception for the Moghul ambassador, attended by several other foreign envoys, Figueroa handed the shah a new letter. The shah received it with satisfaction and informed the assembled company that it was from his brother, the King of Spain. He asked a Carmelite friar to read the letter and tell him the main points, which he repeated loudly. Figueroa left the reception early because he was again very tired and made his way home through the Royal Square, which was packed with soldiers. But he had no sooner gone to bed than he was summoned to join the shah and the ambassadors for a tour of the bazaar which had been specially illuminated for the occasion. This began with a visit to a louche coffee-house where boys performed lascivious dances to the accompaniment of drums and flutes, an entertainment that was not to the elderly Spanish ambassador's taste. A supper of roast chicken was served, which the shah tore apart with his hands and distributed to those around him. Standing at a little distance from Abbas were his two surviving sons, who appeared very submissive. Figueroa says the younger one, Imam Quli, held the shah's scimitar and shoes, and looked very sweet. The elder, Prince Muhammad, who was twenty-five or twenty-six, was strongly built, had a brown skin and black moustaches and a certain look of pride in his eyes. Figueroa again noted that no one paid them any respect. This was not surprising, in view of how easily and fatally Abbas's suspicions had been aroused against his eldest son. After supper, the shah led his guests through the bazaar, where the shopkeepers had put their finest goods on display. Figueroa found the heat and the press of people stifling and left as soon as he could.

One evening in July 1619, Shah Abbas asked Figueroa and the other ambassadors to join him on the new bridge which had been built over the Zayandeh River by Allahvirdi Khan. He wanted them to witness the celebrations for the ancient Iranian festival of *Abpashan*, or the Sprinkling of the Waters, which was clearly a favourite of his. Men were gathered by the river with copper or pewter jugs with which they scooped up the water and threw it over each other. This must have appealed to Abbas's slapstick sense of humour.

When Figueroa arrived, Abbas had two courtesans who were entertaining the ambassadors sent away, because, he said, the Spanish ambassador did not enjoy this kind of entertainment at his age. Abbas then made the other ambassadors laugh by asking Figueroa to admit that his attitude had more to do with impotence than with virtue. But Figueroa turned the tables by suggesting that the shah put him to the test by unveiling some of his own women, since the courtesans did not deserve that name. The shah was embarrassed and angry to find the ambassadors now laughing at him and quickly changed the subject.

After regaling the ambassadors with wine and pistachios, the shah dismissed them. He again promised to give an audience to Figueroa, who reminded him of the Spanish demand that he return the territories taken from Hormuz. Abbas pretended not to hear, but took Figueroa by the arm and, pointing to the Moghul ambassador, Khan Alam, said that if the Moghul emperor did not return Qandahar, he would take it from him by force. 'I do not want my children', he told Figueroa pointedly, 'to be able to reproach me for allowing an inch of land to be stolen from the crown of Persia.'[11]

There were more entertainments – ram and bull fights and illuminations – before Figueroa and the other ambassadors were summoned to a farewell audience[12] on the evening of 2 August 1619. Figueroa arrived in the Royal Square to find the ambassadors waiting on horseback at the gate of the harem.[13] To get away from the crowd he went into the middle of the square to talk to the Augustinian and Carmelite friars. Shortly afterwards the shah rode out of the palace accompanied by his courtiers and a great number of servants, some of them bearing flaming torches and great silver lamps. As soon as he saw Figueroa he cried out, 'Hispania! Hispania!' and rode straight over to him. 'I have come to see what I can do for you,' he said, and asked, 'What message do you bring from my brother, the King of Spain?' Figueroa said it was the same message he had already delivered. Otherwise all he asked was for permission to leave for Hormuz and for the Carmelites and Augustinians to be allowed to build churches. The shah said he wanted to hear more, and taking only his chief eunuch and his grand vizier with him led Figueroa, with the Carmelite friar and his interpreter, to the side of the square. There he dismounted and made Figueroa sit down on the ground next to him, with the others sitting opposite, except for the chief eunuch who stood six paces behind the shah holding his bow and arrows and his scimitar.

Abbas told Figueroa he wanted to satisfy him because he considered him like his own father. Seeing the shah apparently in such a receptive mood, Figueroa attempted to persuade him that now was the moment to resume the war with the Ottomans and recover his lost territories, including Baghdad. He cited the divisions at the Ottoman court and the rumours that European powers were preparing for war which, although they would come to nothing, would worry the Ottomans and act as a diversion. Abbas listened attentively, but was unmoved. He complained again that the Christian princes had failed to support him in the war against their common enemy – the emperor even making peace with them – and said that after God, he owed his victories to his sword. But if the Christian princes made war powerfully against the Ottomans in Europe, he would attack in Asia, march to Jerusalem and put it in their hands.

Figueroa then returned to the Spanish demands that Abbas keep the English out of Iran and hand back the territories he had taken from Spain's ally, the King of Hormuz. According to Figueroa, Abbas again listened patiently, but gave no ground. He said he could not see what difference it made to his brother, the King of Spain, whether he or the King of Hormuz owned these forts and islands, since they were both Muslims, but the King of Hormuz being a Sunni belonged to a religion that was more hostile to the Franks than his own Shi'ism. This reply struck Figueroa as absurd. He also says Abbas would not be drawn on trade with the English, although he raised the matter three or four times; each time the shah either cut him short or interjected something else. The Carmelite friar, who was present, had a different recollection. According to him, Figueroa told the shah that King Philip wanted him to be friendly to his Portuguese subjects 'and refrain from favouring the English corsairs'. Abbas replied that the Portuguese 'should change their methods' if they wanted his friendship, and that 'it did not please him to refuse access to anyone within his borders, least of all to the English who were useful in trade'.[14] The Carmelite friar found Figueroa rather tactless and says he made no special effort to improve relations between Iran and Spain.

When the audience was over, the shah held out his hands and helped Figueroa to his feet. He then mounted his horse and gave a brief farewell audience on horseback to each of the other ambassadors. He spoke angrily to the Ottoman ambassador, saying that he would not surrender a single stone of what he had won.

Figueroa left Isfahan for Hormuz around the end of August. On the way he met a soldier travelling in the opposite direction with a packet of papers for him from Madrid. These included the draft agreement that Figueroa knew was unacceptable because of the demands for territorial restitution and the exclusion of the English. There were also letters for the shah from the King of Spain and Robert Sherley, whom Figueroa blamed for misleading, as he saw it, the Spanish and Portuguese ministers. He saw no point in going back to Isfahan, so he sent the papers, with a letter of his own to the shah, to the Carmelite friar and asked him to continue the negotiations.

When the letters and the draft agreement were read to the shah, he was so angry that he tore them up and swore he would drive the Portuguese out of Hormuz. He had left Hormuz alone up till now because he was seeking Spanish co-operation against the Ottomans, and he anyway lacked the warships for a successful attack on the island fortress. But there was no longer any basis for co-operation with Spain, while the English East India Company was keen to do business and had the ships. The company had already successfully taken on the Portuguese in the Indian Ocean, and its factors in Surat and Iran expected to confront them before long in the Persian Gulf as well. Apart from anything else, they saw clearly that Hormuz was a much better place to trade from than Jask. The East India Company shipped its first consignment of Iranian silk in December 1618 and sold it to eager buyers in London nine months later. While Figueroa was in Iran, Abbas maintained an outward appearance of neutrality in his dealings with the English and the Portuguese. But in private he was already telling the company's factors that he would export all his silk to Europe through them, and 'sometymes he would seacretly whisper unto us that he had a resolution to take Ormus from the King of Spayne and deliver it unto the English nation, onely enjoyninge us to seacricie untill it were effected'.[15]

The Portuguese admiral, Ruy Freire, arrived at Hormuz from Lisbon with his squadron of five galleons in June 1620. Determined to drive the English from the gulf, Freire attacked four East India Company ships as they arrived at Jask at the end of December. The attack only served to demonstrate to the Iranians the naval superiority of the English, whose gunnery was far more accurate. The Portuguese were badly mauled. Freire rashly returned to the attack with the same lack of success when the English ships left Jask for Surat with more than 500 bales of silk on board.

Later that summer Shah Abbas fell ill with a feverish sickness that swept through his court at Farahabad on the Caspian. Some of his courtiers and many local people died, and for a time it appeared that the shah's life too was in danger. Fearing that he was being punished for his fondness for wine, Abbas issued an edict banning the sale or consumption of alcohol upon pain of the most savage sanctions. It was lifted the following spring after the shah recovered and found people had turned instead to an opium-based drink, which was much more harmful. A more serious consequence of his illness was that he became suspicious of his oldest surviving son, Prince Muhammad, and had him blinded. Abbas seems to have felt that, while he was ill, the prince became rather too enthusiastic about the prospect of succeeding him. A number of courtiers close to the prince were subsequently accused of plotting to help him escape from the court and were executed. It is impossible to know what truth there was in this charge, but it seems unlikely that any courtiers would have risked their lives in such a foolhardy way. Figueroa's comment that the courtiers showed the princes no respect suggests that they went out of their way to keep their distance from them lest they arouse the shah's suspicions.

Abbas's illness may also have been partly responsible for the severe persecution he unleashed on his Christian subjects in August 1621. It was instigated by some of the Shi'i clergy who may well have told the shah that his illness was the result not only of his drinking, but also of his tolerance of Christians. His anger and frustration with Spain and Portugal would have made him more inclined to listen to them. The persecution was initially directed against Armenian villages to the west of Isfahan, where strong pressure was put on the inhabitants to convert, their churches were turned into mosques and their bibles and other devotional material confiscated. Armenian men were forcibly circumcised, some of them dying in the process. The same harsh treatment was then extended to the Armenian and Georgian Christians who had been settled in Mazandaran. In September the Carmelite prior wrote to the pope denouncing Abbas as 'the greatest tyrant the Church has had since it began . . . for the methods he adopts are taken from hell'.[16] Interestingly, the prior cited the shah's 'Persian and Muslim legal luminaries' as saying that his actions were contrary to the Quran, indicating that the Shi'i clergy was divided on the issue. Once again the persecution did not last long. The shah ordered it to stop after the Armenian merchants in Isfahan responded by halting their caravans, which still carried the bulk of Iranian silk exports. As Abbas had made the silk a royal monopoly some two years before, this hit him where it hurt – in his pocket. By that time about 5,000 Christians are said to have suffered forced conversion.

Early the following year there was a further manifestation of strong anti-Christian sentiment among the Shi'i clergy after five Muslims who had been baptised by the Carmelites were caught trying to escape to Hormuz. Under Islamic law apostasy was punishable by death. Two of the converts suffered a cruel execution at the hands of the governor general of Fars, Imam Quli Khan, while the three others were stoned to death outside Isfahan on the orders of Abbas. More than 200 Shi'i clergy came to Abbas to demand that he have the Carmelite priors executed too. They accused them of ruining the Muslim religion and alleged that the Carmelites had secretly baptised more than 5,000 Muslims and sent them away to Christian lands. The Carmelite fathers were brought before the shah and their convent briefly surrounded by soldiers, but Abbas resisted the pressure from his clergy and refused to take any action against them. One of the Carmelite fathers, John Thaddeus, said afterwards that he thought Abbas only executed the converts because by then his alliance with the English for the capture of Hormuz was public knowledge, and he felt an anti-Christian gesture of this kind was necessary.

If the Portuguese had wanted Abbas to attack Hormuz with the help of the English, they could not have done more to provoke him. Ruy Freire carried out his instructions to build a fort on Qishm, the island which supplied Hormuz with most of its food and water and which had been captured by the Iranians in 1614. At this point, it appears to have been undefended. The Portuguese admiral also ravaged the neighbouring coast of Lar, killing any Qizilbash that were found and setting fire to villages where the Qizilbash had settled after the province's annexation by Shah Abbas. The Portuguese also burnt any boats that might be used to transport troops.

These actions are said to have had the support of the indigenous population of Lar, who had been ill-treated by the Qizilbash and remained as attached to their deposed and deceased ruler as they were hostile to the shah.

Abbas treated this as a declaration of war and ordered the governor general of Fars, Imam Quli Khan, to oppose the Portuguese. Imam Quli Khan sent a force to lay siege to Qishm, but was again hampered by a lack of ships. However, the Iranians knew that an East India Company fleet would be returning to Jask in December to fetch the annual consignment of silk. Sometime in the autumn the shah told the East India Company agent in Isfahan, Edward Monnox, that the silk would not be delivered unless the company provided naval support for the campaign against the Portuguese. Monnox reacted positively but said he would have to consult the ships' council when the fleet arrived. Abbas authorised Imam Quli Khan to negotiate the terms of an agreement.

The East India Company factors in Surat had sent a strong fleet of five ships and four pinnaces to Jask, because they anticipated further conflict with Ruy Freire and heard he was being reinforced from Goa. The fleet reached Jask on 14 December, where it received a message to meet Monnox and the other factors in Iran at a small port further up the coast towards Hormuz. Monnox had no easy task persuading the ships' council to fall in with the shah's wishes. It was one thing to fight the Portuguese when they tried to keep the English ships out of the Persian Gulf or the Indian Ocean. It was something else to join with a Muslim power in attacking fellow European Christians, albeit Catholics, with whom England was at peace. But Monnox was a forceful personality. After a long debate, he finally convinced the ships' council that the company's future in Iran was at stake and that they had no alternative but to do Shah Abbas's bidding and help him to expel the Portuguese from Qishm and Hormuz. On 18 January 1622 Monnox and his successor Bell concluded an agreement with Imam Quli Khan, but differences that emerged afterwards suggest that the terms were not spelt out clearly enough. In return for their assistance, the English were to have half the spoils of victory, a half share of all future customs receipts, and to be allowed to import and export goods duty-free. The Iranians also agreed to share the expenses incurred by the English ships in remaining in the Persian Gulf. The agreement brought protests from the crew of one of the English ships, the *London*. They had been hired for merchandising, they said, not for fighting, and an attack on the fortress of a friendly nation would be 'a breach of the peace'. Their opposition was overcome with a promise of a month's extra pay.

The ships were soon in action at Qishm, where Ruy Freire and a mixed Portuguese and Arab garrison numbering about 450 were holding out in the newly built fort against about 3,000 Iranian troops. The English bombarded the fort from the sea and from the land, where they set up a battery of five of their largest guns. The walls of the fort were not strong and were soon breached. Ruy Freire was faced with a mutinous garrison and surrendered. Many of the Portuguese prisoners were put ashore on Hormuz, where they added to the overcrowding in the citadel. Others were taken to the Portuguese territories of Muscat and Sohar on the other side of the gulf. Ruy Freire himself was taken to Surat, from where he managed to escape and return to the Persian Gulf to continue the fight, though with little success. Most of the Arab prisoners, having been previously subjects of the shah, were executed by the Iranians as rebels. Three Englishmen were killed in the action. One of them was the navigator and Arctic explorer William Baffin, who gave his name to Baffin Bay.

Two weeks later, on 10 February, a large Iranian force landed on Hormuz, rapidly overran the town and laid siege to the citadel, which is described by Iskandar Beg Munshi as 'an outstanding example of Frankish skill in the art of building forts'.[17] The English ships opened a bombardment from the sea, not only firing on the citadel but also on the Portuguese fleet that was sheltering under its walls. As at Qishm, the English set up a battery on the land as well. This time the Portuguese put up a stiff resistance. The Iranians blew up a section of the walls on 17 March and launched a full-scale assault, only to be repulsed. The garrison no doubt held out in the hope that a relief force would arrive from Goa. One was sent, but it was too small and arrived too late. On 23 April 1622, after enduring the siege for more than two months and fearing a massacre at the hands of the Iranians, the garrison surrendered to the English.

This ended a century of Portuguese hegemony in the Persian Gulf. For Figueroa it was a 'tragedy' brought about by a foolish Portuguese-Spanish strategy of aggression:

> I will not dare to say who obliged the Council to such a foolish enterprise as to make war against such a powerful King and to attack him in his own country, particularly being supported by a European nation as skilful as the English, although pirates and merchants, and that with the small forces available in the Indies, above all in this citadel and town of Hormuz, manifestly exposed to an inevitable loss, and at the mercy of the first enemy who attacked it.[18]

127

The Portuguese garrison and all the women and children were taken across the gulf to Muscat and Sohar. Muslims who had fought with the Portuguese were executed by the Iranians. Meanwhile, Hormuz, with its store of rich merchandise, was comprehensively looted, much to the dismay of Monnox: 'The Persians and the English began to pillage in such a sort that I was both grieved and ashamed to see it; but could devise no remedy at all for it.'[19] The Iranians were particularly impressed by the Portuguese cannons they captured, which were taken to Isfahan and placed in front of the royal palace. 'Each one was a masterpiece of the art of the Frankish cannon founders', writes Iskandar Beg Munshi admiringly.

Afterwards the English complained that the Iranians took more than their share of the loot. They were also annoyed at being presented with a bill for provisioning their ships during the siege and at not being allowed to share in the occupation of the fortress unless they left two warships to guard it on a permanent basis. So when the Iranians asked them for help in attacking Portuguese Muscat, they refused.

Once he had captured the island, Shah Abbas had no further use for Hormuz. He transferred its trade to Gombroon on the mainland, which he could better defend and which he renamed Bandar Abbas – 'the port of Abbas'. It grew rapidly into a sizeable town and immediately replaced Jask as the port of entry for the English East India Company. They were soon joined there by the Dutch East India Company, first as an ally, but before long as an aggressive rival. As for the Portuguese, they made a number of unsuccessful attempts to recapture the island, culminating in a great naval battle off Hormuz on 11 February 1625 between eight Portuguese galleons and an Anglo-Dutch fleet of similar strength. The Iranians watching from the shore are said to have been amazed at the sight of the ships belching fire and smoke. The battle was inconclusive, but was the last time the Portuguese threatened Hormuz. That year the Portuguese came to some accommodation with Abbas, who could see that competition between the Europeans could only be to his advantage and allowed them to establish a factory and build a fort further up the coast at Kong. They also strengthened their ties with the Ottoman Pasha of Basra, who regarded the Portuguese as useful allies in helping him to retain the virtual independence he had won from Istanbul.

The Spanish government protested in London over the action of the East India Company at Hormuz and asked for an explanation. It was told that the company had acted under Iranian duress. King James I and his favourite, the Duke of Buckingham, far from being embarrassed, were determined to get a share of the spoils. The Duke of Buckingham, as Lord High Admiral, claimed he was entitled to one-tenth of the value of whatever the East India Company ships had seized in recent years, both in the way of Portuguese prizes and the spoils of Hormuz. This was estimated at £100,000. He got his £10,000 after threatening to prosecute the company in the Admiralty Court and detain its ships. The king made it clear that he expected the same reward: 'Did I deliver you from the complaint of the Spaniard,' he asked, 'and do you return me nothing?'[20] He got his ten grand too.

Chapter 11

Final Triumphs: the Capture of Qandahar and Baghdad

The Anglo-Iranian victory at Hormuz was followed in a matter of weeks, on 11 June 1622, by another success for Iranian arms, when Qandahar was recaptured from the Moghuls. The recovery of this strategic city astride the trade route to India had been a fixed aim of Shah Abbas's ever since he lost it to the Moghul emperor, Akbar, in 1595, at a time when he was still fighting to impose his authority within Iran.

Shah Abbas tried repeatedly through diplomatic channels to persuade the Moghuls to return Qandahar. He resorted briefly to force when the Moghul Empire was weakened by internal conflicts at the end of Akbar's reign and the beginning of Jahangir's. Iranian forces captured the nearby town of Bust on the Helmand River, but their subsequent siege of Qandahar in February 1606 was unsuccessful. Abbas disowned the attack, telling Jahangir he had not authorised it, but continued to assert his claim with every envoy he sent or received. Zainal Beg, whom Abbas sent to India in response to the embassy of Khan Alam, had the specific task of negotiating over Qandahar. Jahangir wavered, but was warned by his advisers that surrendering Qandahar would be interpreted as weakness. Abbas then began to receive reports from Zainal Beg that Jahangir's health was declining and that the Moghul court was riven by rivalries over the succession. He decided the time had come to strike and set off from Isfahan at the head of his army in February 1622. Jahangir was unable to persuade his rebellious son, Shah Jahan, to come to the defence of Qandahar, which fell to the Iranians after a short siege. Abbas then set about repairing the damage done to bilateral relations by sending off conciliatory letters to Jahangir, Shah

Jahan and other prominent figures at the Moghul court. But Jahangir was enraged by Abbas's action and was corresponding with the Uzbeks and the Ottomans about an anti-Iranian alliance when he died in 1627.

Palace coups and rebellions in the Ottoman Empire also gave Shah Abbas the opportunity to recover Baghdad, which had been lost to the Ottomans by Shah Tahmasp in 1534. Abbas had implied that this was one of his war aims when he told the Ottomans after his victory over them at Sufiyan in 1605 that he would not lay down his arms until all the lands trodden by Shah Ismail I's horse had been restored to him. Since then, however, he had twice made peace, in 1612 and 1618, on the basis of the Treaty of Amasya of 1555 in which Shah Tahmasp had ceded Baghdad to the Ottomans.

But the prospect of capturing Baghdad was so enticing that Abbas was willing to break the peace he had made with the Ottomans in 1618. Possession of Baghdad would give him control of the shrines of the Shi'i Imams in Iraq, in particular the shrines of Imam Ali in Najaf and of his son, Imam Husain, in Karbala. This must have had a strong appeal to Abbas as a ruler who based much of his legitimacy on his claim to a close association with the Imams. It would be acclaimed by his Shi'i clergy, with whom he was keen to establish a strong bond. It would mean that his Shi'i subjects would be able to make their pilgrimages to the shrines without obstruction or harassment by the Ottomans. It would also bring a financial gain, since the pilgrims would no longer be taking gold coins out of the kingdom. To stem this drain on the country's very limited supply of gold and silver coin, Abbas had been promoting the shrine of the Eighth Imam, Ali ar-Riza, in Mashhad as an alternative pilgrimage centre inside Iran.

The latest bout of instability in the Ottoman Empire began in May 1622, when the sultan, Osman II, was garrotted following a revolt by the janissaries, who feared he planned to dissolve their corps. His feeble-minded uncle, Mustafa, who had already demonstrated his incompetence during a brief period of rule from 1617 to 1618, was installed on the throne once again, with no better result. A group of influential Sunni clerics had Mustafa deposed for good the following year, 1623, and replaced by his nephew, Murad. As Murad was only twelve, his mother, Kösem Sultan, ruled in his name.

Meanwhile, rebellions broke out in eastern Anatolia and other parts of the empire, including Baghdad, where the chief of police, Bakr al-Subashi, seized power with the support of the janissaries. The authorities in Istanbul sent the governor general of Diyarbakir, Hafiz Ahmad Pasha, at the head of a large army to restore order in Baghdad.

Bakr determined to resist and sent messages to the Safavid amirs on the frontier appealing for help and promising to recognise the authority of the shah. These messages were passed on to Abbas, who ordered his amirs to move their forces up to the frontier. Hafiz Ahmad was unwilling to confront the combined forces of Bakr and the Safavid amirs. In a rapid change of tactics, he decided to withdraw and told Bakr that if he kept the Safavid forces out of Baghdad he would be confirmed as governor of the province.

Bakr now backed away from the pledge he had made to the shah. When the Safavid amirs appeared before Baghdad, he first put off meeting them and then opened fire on their camp, forcing them to move. Abbas, who was on his way to Baghdad, sent an envoy to Bakr with a letter saying that if he recognised the shah's authority, as he had promised, he could remain as governor. Bakr refused to see the envoy, so Abbas ordered up more troops and finally arrived in front of the city towards the end of December 1623. There he issued an ultimatum, giving Bakr three days to submit and declare his allegiance. Bakr replied with more cannon-fire. When the ultimatum expired, Abbas began a siege. An assault force of *qurchis* managed to break into the city on the evening of 12 January 1624, and two days later Baghdad was in Safavid hands.

Much of the Sunni population was immediately put to the sword, as had happened when the city was first captured by the Safavids more than a hundred years earlier. Abbas also had the janissaries who had supported Bakr boiled in oil, saying that if they had betrayed the Ottoman sultan, they could just as easily betray him. On the other hand, Iskandar Beg Munshi says that Abbas took effective measures to deal with a famine that had been caused in the Baghdad region by a combination of a drought and Bakr's misrule. Abbas appointed a Safavid governor for Baghdad and devoted considerable attention to the Shi'i shrines, visiting them to engage in prayers and devotions, reordering their affairs and bestowing rich gifts on them. At Najaf he reopened a canal that had become silted up and planned the construction of cisterns to provide fresher water.

Meanwhile, Abbas's armies defeated an Ottoman relief force and rapidly overran most of Iraq north of Baghdad, as demoralised Ottoman garrisons abandoned their forts. They even penetrated into Anatolia, ravaging and plundering the region to the south of Diyarbakir. However, the governor general of Fars, Imam Quli Khan, failed to capture Basra to the south. The pasha of Basra repulsed the Iranian attack with help from the Portuguese, who sent five ships to relieve the city. Imam Quli Khan appealed in vain to the East India Company for support.

The news from Iraq caused uproar in Istanbul, where there were calls from the populace for the Iranians to be driven out of Baghdad. The governor general of Diyarbakir, Hafiz Ahmad Pasha, was appointed grand vizier and commander-in-chief, and given full powers to recover the city. Troops, provisions and siege equipment began to be assembled in Diyarbakir. When reports of this activity reached Abbas, he assumed the Ottomans were preparing for another invasion of Azerbaijan, and had all provisions and livestock removed from the route he expected them to take.

Abbas's position was made more difficult by reverses he now suffered in Georgia. Warned that a fresh revolt was brewing there, he despatched his commander-in-chief, Qarachaqay Khan, to deal with it. He sent with him a prominent Georgian convert, Morav Beg, who had experience of Georgian affairs and had become a favoured member of the court. However, when Qarachaqay Beg carried out a massacre of several thousand young Georgian men he suspected of being potential rebels, Morav Beg changed sides. He had Qarachaqay Khan and the Safavid commander-in-chief of Shirvan, Yusuf Khan, murdered – both of them Armenian Christians who had entered the service of the shah as *ghulams*. At the head of an army of Georgian rebels, Morav Beg scattered the Safavid forces and laid siege to the Georgian capital of Tbilisi, as well as to Ganja in neighbouring Qarabagh. He was joined by the Georgian prince, Taimuras, who had led the previous rebellion in 1616.

Abbas turned to the commander of his crack *qurchi* troops, Isa Khan, to save the situation. He made him commander of all Safavid forces in Georgia and ordered his governors in the Caucasus to join him with their troops. Isa Khan brought the rebels to battle on 30 June 1625. His army was nearly overwhelmed by a massive Georgian cavalry charge, but the arrival of the Safavid troops from Azerbaijan saved the day. The rebels were routed with heavy losses. However, they were not completely crushed. Shortly afterwards they ambushed and killed the governor general of Azerbaijan, Shahbanda Khan.

Through all their uprisings against Iranian rule the Georgians had appealed to Russia for help, and although no military assistance was forthcoming it was partly as a result of the intercession of Russia that Abbas finally recognised Taimuras as his viceroy, or *vali*, in eastern Georgia. In further moves to end the uprising, Abbas agreed that the viceroy should always be a member of the Georgian royal family, that the office of constable (*darugha*) of Isfahan should be reserved for one of the viceroy's sons who converted to Islam, that no further churches should be destroyed and that Georgia should not be burdened with taxation.

The Georgian rebellion encouraged insurrections elsewhere against Safavid rule, notably among the Kurds. The Ottoman grand vizier, Hafiz Ahmad Pasha, saw this as a favourable opportunity to recover Baghdad. That autumn he set out from Diyarbakir at the head of a large army, though some units, notably the janissaries, appear to have been reluctant to go. For some reason, he took no siege cannons. Perhaps he thought the shah had his hands full dealing with the various rebellions and that the garrison would surrender almost immediately. He reached Baghdad on 10 November 1625, meeting no opposition on the way, as all outlying Safavid garrisons had been ordered to fall back on the city. But he was too late to prevent the garrison being reinforced by 3,000 extra troops. These had been sent by Abbas as soon as he learnt that the Ottoman army was about to march on Baghdad. Despite his other distractions, Abbas also managed to assemble an army to relieve the city and put it under the command of Zainal Beg. This former ambassador to Europe and India was a Qizilbash amir of the Shamlu tribe and held the honorary court office of *tushmal-bashi* (superintendent of the royal kitchens). After sending the army on ahead, Abbas himself left Soltaniya, the assembly-point for the troops in north-west Iran, on 3 November.

The siege was a disaster for the Ottomans. Even after they had invested the city, the Iranians were able to slip in another thousand soldiers under cover of darkness – all of them experienced in siege warfare and carrying fresh supplies of ammunition. Hafiz Ahmad Pasha belatedly sent for cannons and gunpowder from Mosul and Basra. In the meantime, his forces were unable to prosecute the siege effectively, while constantly having to fend off attacks by the Iranians under Zainal Beg. He asked for negotiations, which Abbas agreed to, but they soon broke down. At one point the Ottoman troops succeeded in blowing a breach in the walls and stormed in, only to fall up to their necks in deep ditches filled with water and concealed with grass and straw.[1] The cannons finally arrived, but there was not enough powder, so the Ottomans built strong defences around their camp and settled down to try to starve the Safavid garrison into surrendering. But in the end it was the Ottomans who suffered most from hunger, after the Iranians cut their supply lines, and many of them fell sick. When their supplies were on the verge of running out completely, the janissaries mutinied and forced Hafiz Ahmad Pasha to lift the siege. Leaving behind large numbers of sick and dying and abandoning much of its equipment, the Ottoman army began an ignominious retreat early in July 1626. Although Abbas agreed not to attack them, the Ottoman troops were constantly harassed by Arab and Turkish tribesmen as they withdrew. According to some sources, less than half the army returned home.[2] The Ottomans made no further attempt to recover Baghdad during Abbas's lifetime.

Chapter 12

A Conflict of Envoys

Now that he was again at war with the Ottomans, Abbas was anxious to develop relations with his new European friends, the English and the Dutch, who were in a position to help divert at least part of the silk trade. The Dutch had opened a factory in Bandar Abbas in 1623 and were granted generous trading privileges shortly afterwards. In February 1625 Abbas despatched ambassadors to England and Holland on board ships of the English and Dutch East India companies. Each was accompanied by a suite of about a dozen persons, who included one or two merchants charged with selling silk on behalf of the shah.

Abbas's ambassador to Holland, Musa Beg, arrived there almost exactly a year later, the Dutch fleet having had to fight a battle with the Portuguese on the way. He had an audience with the States-General on 26 March 1626, at which he read a message from the shah to the King of Holland. In it, Abbas expressed his wish for friendly relations and said that Dutch merchants could trade in Iran without fear. Musa Beg had been instructed by the shah to pursue three demands and these became the subject of rather fruitless negotiations during the rest of his stay at The Hague, which lasted for more than a year.[1] He asked the Dutch to withdraw their consuls from Ottoman territory, especially from Aleppo which was the hub of the Levant silk trade; to engage in joint action against the Portuguese in Muscat and on the south coast of Arabia; and to permit the shah to despatch silk and other goods on Dutch ships, at his expense, for sale in Holland. The Dutch rejected the first and last of these demands and refused to make any commitment on military action against the Portuguese.

Musa Beg's personal behaviour while in Holland did not help his cause. He drank a lot, importuned women and resorted all too frequently to insults.[2]

He quarrelled publicly with other members of his mission and with the Dutch East India Company. The latter had agreed to pay his expenses, after unsuccessfully disputing the matter with the States-General, and was annoyed by his extravagance and his protracted stay. He finally left with a Dutch fleet on 14 March 1627, carrying presents and a letter for the shah from the States-General and the company.

Abbas's ambassador to England, Naqd Ali Beg, arrived at Portsmouth in February 1626, about the same time that Musa Beg arrived in Holland. There was, however, already an ambassador of the shah's in England – or at least one who claimed to be – in the person of Sir Robert Sherley. Naqd Ali Beg insisted that Sherley was no true ambassador and the dispute between them overshadowed his entire visit.

Sir Robert Sherley had come to London in December 1623 after spending nearly five years trying to bring Spain-Portugal into an anti-Ottoman alliance with Iran that would include the diversion of the Iranian silk exports to Lisbon through Hormuz. All his efforts foundered on Madrid's condition that the shah must first return the territories he had taken from Portugal in the Persian Gulf. After leaving Spain in March 1622, he had first travelled to Florence and then to Rome, where he and his wife Teresa were painted by the 23-year-old van Dyck.[3] From Italy he had gone on to Poland, and may perhaps have intended to return to Iran before changing his mind and going to England instead.

To begin with, his second embassy to England followed much the same pattern as his first in 1611. His proposals met with a positive reaction from the court, but with hostility from the Levant and East India companies. He told King James that Abbas had two requests.[4] The first was for help in building up a battle-fleet of galleys, by having every English ship bound for Iran carry a section of a galley, which would then be assembled at the Iranian port. In making his second request, Abbas drew attention to the restrictions on the export of bullion from England which limited the amount of goods the English could buy in Iran. He asked that Iranian merchants be allowed to bring their silk and other goods to England on English ships, paying appropriate freight charges and customs dues. They would either sell their goods in England or re-export them. As Abbas wished to deprive the Ottomans of the Iranian silk exports, he was willing to divert all these to London, which would then become the staple for Iranian silk. In return, the shah offered to provide King James with 25,000 troops for his use 'in these parts' – in other words, in the Persian Gulf region.

Later Robert Sherley drew up a report for the Duke of Buckingham giving more details of the proposals on the silk trade. He said the shah would sell as much silk as the English market could take at a fixed price and with no payment needing to be made until the English ships had brought the silk home. He estimated the likely annual shipment at around 5,000 bales, with a purchase price of a million pounds and a resale price in England of twice as much.

King James, who had tried to introduce the silkworm into England, was enthusiastic, as were Buckingham and other members of the court. They put pressure on the East India Company to take up the proposals, which it initially declined to do. It was already in an advantageous position in Iran, particularly after its collaboration over Hormuz, and had no interest in encouraging competition from Iranian merchants. It was also mistrustful of Sherley. It cast doubt on his credentials and pointed out that this was the second time he had come to England after acting against the English interest by trying to persuade the Spanish government to take over the silk trade. The Levant Company repeated its objection that diverting the Iranian silk exports would undermine its trade with Turkey. King James was preparing to trade with Iran on his own account when the governor of the East India Company, Sir Thomas Smythe, was finally won over. Under his influence the company agreed, in January 1625, to make London the staple for Iranian silk and, as a start, to take out to Iran four pinnaces and four galleys in sections. But Sherley's luck soon ran out again. King James died in March, followed by Sir Thomas Smythe in September, leaving the project dead in the water.

The situation got much worse for Sherley when Naqd Ali Beg arrived the following February. The East India Company, which had refused to pay for Sherley's upkeep, immediately treated Naqd Ali Beg as the true ambassador and accorded him full honours. It borrowed a royal coach drawn by eight horses to convey him on the last stage of his journey into London. Directors of the company and courtiers led by the master of ceremonies, the Earl of Warwick, escorted the coach.[5]

The Iranian ambassador's audience with the new king, Charles I, was fixed for an afternoon some days later. On the morning of the day in question Sir Robert Sherley went round to Naqd Ali Beg's lodgings to try to sort things out. He was accompanied by the Earl of Cleveland and a number of other courtier-friends. But when he produced his letter of accreditation, Naqd Ali Beg flew into a rage, tore it up and punched him in the face, while a young member of his suite rained further blows on the unfortunate Sherley, knocking him to the ground.[6] The courtiers dragged the young man away and Lord Cleveland told the ambassador that it was only their respect for his master that had allowed him to escape with his life. Naqd Ali Beg apologised, but said he had been unable to control himself when confronted with a man he believed had forged his letters of credence and who claimed to have married the shah's niece. He said Sherley's letter of accreditation carried the shah's seal on the back, whereas it should have been at the top. Sherley replied that the shah normally put his seal on the back when he employed a foreign envoy, and said he had only ever claimed to have married a kinswoman of the shah's wife.[7]

The incident was immediately reported to King Charles, who angrily postponed the ambassador's audience. When he did see Naqd Ali Beg, the ambassador again apologised. It is not clear exactly what Naqd Ali Beg's mission was, but the king was perplexed to find that his letters of credence made no reference to Sherley or to his proposals. He decided the only way to clarify the situation was to send Sherley back to Iran with an ambassador of his own. The man he chose for this post was Dodmore Cotton, a lawyer and a gentleman of his Privy Chamber. Cotton, who had been looking for employment in the East, was to be the first English ambassador to Iran since 1271.[8]

The East India Company was extremely reluctant to transport Cotton and Sherley to Iran and only agreed to do so when it was made clear that Cotton would conduct no negotiations on its behalf and would have no say in its affairs.[9] His instructions were to inform Shah Abbas of Naqd Ali Beg's behaviour in London, to ascertain whether Sherley was an officially accredited ambassador and whether the shah supported his proposals. If that was the case, Cotton was to give the rather non-committal assurance that King Charles would meet the shah's wishes as far as possible.

Cotton was given a final audience and knighted by the king at Whitehall on 12 April. A few days later he left for Dover accompanied by Sherley and other members of his suite, among them the young Thomas Herbert who was to write an informative and entertaining account of the mission. However, when they arrived at Dover they found that the East India Company fleet had taken advantage of a favourable wind and set sail. To their great chagrin, they had to wait another year, since the fleet had to sail in the spring in order to catch the monsoon winds.

Fresh tensions had meanwhile flared up between the company and Robert Sherley. This time, besides Naqd Ali Beg, an Iranian silk merchant called Khwaja Shahsavar was also involved. He had been sent by Shah Abbas on missions to Venice in 1613 and 1621, presumably mainly to sell silk for the shah. He had arrived in England with Naqd Ali Beg and fell out with the ambassador over the disposal of the fifty bales of silk he had brought to sell on the shah's behalf. He became friendly with Sherley and before long the company was accusing the two of them of conspiring to undermine its position in Iran. It accused them of writing to Shah Abbas, urging him to seize its goods and servants. There is no way of knowing what truth there was in the allegation, but the company complained to King Charles and asked to be excused from taking them to Iran. Khwaja Shahsavar died suddenly in August 1626 and became perhaps the first Iranian to be buried in London, being laid to rest in the churchyard of St Botolph's in Bishopsgate.[10] However, his son, Muhammad, who had accompanied him to England, continued the dispute, which was only ended by the intervention of the Privy Council. Muhammad also found time to fall madly in love with an English girl – a maid to Lady Cokayne, whose husband had been Lord Mayor of London. At one point he was offering her all his possessions and declaring his readiness to be baptised as a Christian. But for some reason nothing came of it, and he sailed for home with Cotton and Sherley.

The three ambassadors, together with Lady Sherley and their respective suites, went to join the East India Company fleet at Dover in mid-March 1627. The company gave Naqd Ali Beg his portrait in oils and fifty pounds-worth of silver plate as farewell gifts, while seven of its directors escorted him to the port. The fleet sailed on 23 March, with the Iranian and English envoys on separate ships. Cotton complained that Naqd Ali Beg was given every comfort, including 'two butts of Canary for his own mouth', while he and Sherley had to make do with 'kennels' for accommodation and no wine.[11]

The eight-month sea journey round the Cape to India must have been fairly typical. Many of the seamen died in an outbreak of scurvy; the ships got off course as they approached India, sailing too far south; were attacked by pirates as they beat their way north; and finally cast anchor in Swally Road near Surat on 30 November 1627. Muhammad, the son of Khwaja Shahsavar, and Naqd Ali Beg both died during the journey – Muhammad of a fever and Naqd Ali Beg apparently of an overdose of opium. Herbert believed Naqd Ali Beg became terrified at the prospect of having to answer to Shah Abbas for 'his abusive carriage in England' and other misdemeanours, and committed suicide. He died the day before they reached Swally Road and the East India Company honoured him to the end, giving his body an eleven-gun salute as it was borne ashore.

Cotton, the Sherleys and their companions resumed their journey to

Bandar Abbas on 18 December, sailing with a fleet of four East India Company ships, two of which carried more than 300 slaves bought by Iranian merchants in India. They reached Bandar Abbas on 10 January 1628.

Chapter 13

The English Embassy and the Death of Abbas

The English embassy was received with full honours in Bandar Abbas, after Sir Robert Sherley had gone ashore and shown a *farman* or order from Shah Abbas – probably an old one requesting Safavid officials to assist him. The ambassador was then rowed to the shore to a welcoming salute from the captured Portuguese guns on the citadel.

The governor of Bandar Abbas, who bore the title of sultan, and the chief customs officer, the *shahbandar*, handed Sir Dodmore Cotton out of his barge and 'mounted him upon a stately Arabian horse, whose saddle (being of the Morocco sort) was richly embroidered with silver and seed-pearl, and the stirrups of gold'.[1] Horses were also provided for the rest of the party and, accompanied by the agent of the East India Company, William Burt, and a 200-strong escort of Iranian cavalry, they rode to the governor's palace along a route lined with 'a double guard of archers and musketeers'. At the palace, which was in the bazaar, 'they were entertained with a very neat collation of sweetmeats and *pelo*, choice Shiraz wine, and music both of that country and from our ships'.

They remained fourteen days in Bandar Abbas, which Herbert found had become a bustling commercial centre with so many new buildings since the fall of Hormuz five years earlier 'that for grandeur it is now ranked with towns of best note in Persia'. The most impressive houses were those of the governor, the *shahbandar* and the English and Dutch East India companies. Only the English were allowed to fly their flag, because of the assistance they had given in the capture of Hormuz.

The embassy finally set off for Isfahan on 24 January 1628, in a caravan of twelve horses and twenty-nine camels. The English East India Company agent, Mr Burt, and several other English and Dutch factors rode with them for 3 miles, at which point the governor and the *shahbandar*, accompanied by a troop of cavalry, came to say their farewells. They now learnt that a much longer journey lay ahead, as Shah Abbas was not at Isfahan, but at his winter palace at Ashraf on the Caspian.

After a five-day journey to the north-west the embassy arrived at Lar, a busy commercial centre on the main trade route between the gulf and Isfahan. As was customary with distinguished visitors, they were met about 2 miles outside the city by the governor of the city, the chief magistrate, known as the *qazi*, and other leading citizens, who welcomed them 'with wine and other adjuncts of compliment'. A little further on they were greeted by a singer, dancers and musicians and a huge crowd of ordinary citizens who accompanied them into the city, 'shouting and whooping . . . all the way'.[2] Foreign visitors, especially foreign embassies, always attracted large crowds of curious spectators in the towns they passed through.

They were entertained with a banquet at the magistrate's house and remained in Lar for nearly a fortnight. When they left on 11 February, they were accompanied by an official known as a *mehmandar* or host, whose job was to look after foreign guests. On a journey, that meant finding food and lodging, although more often than not they camped with their tents. The Englishmen disliked his domineering manner with the peasants, 'for he would profer them a little money for what he liked', writes Herbert, 'which if they refused, then *nolens volens* he would have it, and *alla soldado* (soldier-like) paid them with big words and bastinados'.

When they reached Shiraz two weeks later, they had a much less friendly reception to begin with from the powerful governor general of Fars and Lar, Imam Quli Khan. No one came out to welcome them and for well over a week Imam Quli Khan ignored their presence. At one point he even went on an excursion out of the city for six days and when Sir Robert Sherley went to his camp to remonstrate with him, he answered arrogantly that, 'It was no dishonour for any man (his master excepted) to stay his leisure.'[3] Imam Quli Khan had undoubtedly been irritated by the refusal of the English East India Company to support him in attacking Muscat and Basra, but it is difficult to believe that he would have treated the English ambassador with such studied rudeness without some support from the shah's court.

After considerable diplomatic fencing on both sides, Sir Dodmore Cotton finally prevailed by announcing his intention of returning a visit paid to him by Imam Quli Khan's son. The latter had been sent by his father to offer his excuses for not coming to see the ambassador in person, as he had promised. For Cotton to visit the son first would have been an embarrassing snub to the father, so when the ambassador and his suite alighted near the palace, Imam Quli Khan had them led into his presence. He was sitting cross-legged at the end of a long gallery, 'not moving one jot till the ambassador was almost at him, and then (as one affrighted) skipped up, embraced, and bade him welcome'. There followed two hours of 'merriment', during which the whole party was regaled with wine and sweetmeats and entertained by 'dancing wenches'.

Imam Quli Khan now put behind him whatever reservations he had had and invited the embassy to a much grander banquet the following day. The splendour of the occasion illustrates Imam Quli Khan's regal lifestyle and his legendary extravagance. The banquet was held in a large room open on three sides, with crimson silk curtains that could be let down to provide shade from the sun. The ceiling, which was supported by twenty gilded pillars, was embossed with gold and, according to Herbert, exquisitely painted. The floor was covered with rich carpets of silk and gold. Against the back wall was the throne of the governor general, surmounted by a canopy of crimson satin embroidered with pearl and gold. On one side of this were paintings illustrating the victorious campaign against Hormuz. These showed the Iranian forces under Imam Quli Khan 'encamping upon the shore, their assaults, storms, batteries, entrance, plunder of the city, massacre of the Ormusians – some beheaded, some chained, some their heads serving for girdles; as also the English sea-fights and the like'. Sir Dodmore Cotton was seated on the left of the governor general's throne, and next to him were Imam Quli Khan's son and the former puppet king of Hormuz, who was held captive in Shiraz. To the right of the throne sat a 'discontented prince of Tartary', that is to say an Uzbek prince, and 'a disconsolate prince of Georgia'. Herbert says that Sir Robert Sherley 'seated himself' opposite the throne. Also in this part of the room were placed the gentlemen in the ambassador's suite, two princes of Hormuz, and leading provincial officials and military officers. The rest of the banqueting-room was filled with persons of note, including merchants and Qizilbash. The principal men of Shiraz sat around a great square court in front of the banqueting hall, while in an adjacent court were 500 'plebeians' – all these invited, according to Herbert, 'to aggrandise the invitation' and to illustrate the magnificence of Imam Quli Khan.

Fine-coloured pintado tablecloths were spread over the carpets for the feast. This consisted 'of several sorts of *pelo* of various colours, and store of candied dried fruits and meats; variety also of dates, pears and peaches, curiously conserved'. Youths, described by Herbert as 'young Ganymedes, arrayed in cloth of gold with long crisped locks of hairs', went around serving wine from flagons of gold.

Imam Quli Khan was absent until the end of the feast, when he made a spectacular entrance. He was preceded by thirty 'comely youths', dressed in crimson satin coats and wearing turbans of silk and silver, 'wreathed about with small links of gold' and, in some cases, adorned with pearls, rubies, turquoises and emeralds. They had 'rich hilted swords in embroidered scabbards' and hawks upon their fists, with hoods set with precious stones. Then came Imam Quli Khan. 'His coat was of blue satin, very richly embroidered with silver, upon which he wore a robe of extraordinary length; glorious to the eye, for it was so thick-powdered with Oriental pearl and glittering gems as made the ground of it imperspicable. His turban was of finest white silk interwoven with gold, bestudded with pearls and carbuncles; his scabbard was set all over with rubies, pearls and emeralds; his sandals had the like embroidery ... To this glorious idol the people offered their devotion in many tessalams, bowing and knocking their foreheads *à la mode* against the ground.'[4]

Sir Robert Sherley, who was dressed like an Iranian, greeted Imam Quli Khan in similar fashion. He then drank his health in a gold cup, which he afterwards put into his pocket, 'with this merry compliment, that after so unworthy a person as himself had breathed in it, it was some undignity to return it'. Only Sherley, with his familiarity with Iranian ways, would have dared to do such a thing. His English companions must have been astonished and rather shocked by his behaviour. Herbert says that Imam Quli Khan amiably accepted the compliment, 'but, perceiving our Ambassador not very merry, darted him a smile, then drank the King his master's health, and exceeding civilly bade him and his company heartily welcome; and so withdrew.' Cotton, Herbert says, was displeased by Imam Quli Khan's 'long absence and proud carriage'.

But Imam Quli Khan now seems to have been determined to make amends. Two days later, accompanied by a train of thirty followers, he came galloping up to the house where the English embassy was lodged. There he and his companions settled down with the members of the embassy to enjoy the heady wine of Shiraz. They stayed for three hours, during which time 'many bottles and flagons were emptied' and fresh supplies brought in from the governor general's cellars. By the time he left, Imam Quli Khan was so drunk that he nearly fell off his horse, but was fortunately caught and steadied in the saddle by Sir Dodmore Cotton, who was 'very abstemious'.

The next day Imam Quli Khan showed his appreciation by sending the embassy twelve good horses, with bridles and rich saddles. The ambassador, meanwhile, 'acquired the epithet of a generous and well-bred person'.

As a result of these warm relations, the embassy stayed nearly four weeks in Shiraz – a town, according to Herbert, 'defended by nature, enriched by trade, and by art made lovely, the vineyards, gardens, cypresses, sudatories, and temples ravishing the eye and smell'. In the end Imam Quli Khan was reluctant to see them go, but provided horses, camels and donkeys for the next stage of their journey, to Isfahan.

After visiting the ruins of the ancient palace of Persepolis on the way, they were met about 3 miles from Isfahan, on 10 April, by the East India Company agent, William Burt, and other European merchants who invited them to a collation in a royal garden by the roadside. A mile further on they found a huge reception party waiting for them, made up of royal and city officials 'in a cavalcade of about four thousand horse and innumerable foot'. The road all the way into Isfahan was crowded with men, women and children who welcomed them 'in a volley of acclamations'. There were also musicians, 'dancing-wenches' and jugglers. They crossed the Zayandeh River into the city by a bridge that 'was in like manner full of women on both sides', many of whom, 'equally coveting to see and to be seen, in a fair deportment unmasked their faces'. They were taken first to the Ali Qapu Palace in the Royal Square, 'where some of the Iranian noblemen kneeled down . . . three times kissing the King's threshold and as oft knocked their heads in a customary obeisance'. Robert Sherley, as always in Iranian costume, again played the native and prostrated himself on the ground, which, says Herbert, 'made him the more to be respected'. A Qizilbash then delivered an extravagant panegyric on how 'the excellency of Shah Abbas' had attracted them 'from the extremest angle of the world to see whether fame had been partial in the report of his magnificence; but no wonder, since his beams spread themselves over all the universe!' The welcoming ceremony ended with lavish quantities of wine being handed around, after which the ambassador and his companions were conducted to their lodgings.

They stayed three weeks in Isfahan, resuming their journey on 1 May. They crossed a part of the Dasht-e Kavir, the Great Salt Desert, travelling one night along the paved causeway laid down by Abbas, which Herbert said was 'broad enough for ten horses to go abreast'. But the journey through the desert was not one he was anxious to repeat. 'Those rolling sands, when agitated by the wind, move and remove more like sea than sand, and render the way very dreadful to passengers.' Continuing on their way north, they crossed the Alburz Mountains and descended onto the Caspian plain.

As, however, Shah Abbas regularly travelled this route to his palaces on the Caspian, there were caravanserais at frequent intervals offering decent accommodation, which did something to mitigate the hardship. The journey of about 400 miles took the best part of three weeks. The embassy reached Ashraf around 20 May and was escorted into the town at night by the governor and a detachment of fifty horsemen.

Sir Dodmore Cotton had an audience with Shah Abbas on 25 May, at which he was accompanied by Sir Robert Sherley, Thomas Herbert and seven or eight English gentlemen of his suite. He also had an English interpreter, by the name of Dick Williams, who was probably provided by the East India Company. They were escorted to the palace by a rather small cavalcade and few people turned out to watch. It seems that, contrary to normal practice, the time of the audience had not been generally made known. Herbert blamed this and the subsequent difficulties the embassy encountered on the shah's favourite, Muhammad Ali Beg, and his hostility to Sir Robert Sherley.

On alighting at the palace, they were ushered into a small building in the middle of a large courtyard. There they relaxed for two hours in a room furnished only with carpets spread around a white marble tank filled with water, while they were served refreshments in the form of *pelo* and wine, the cups and dishes being all of gold. They were then led through a spacious garden into another summer-house, which was 'rich in gold embossments and painting' and provided magnificent views from its terrace over the Caspian Sea to the north and to the Alburz Mountains in the distance to the south. The rooms on the ground floor were large and square, with a ceiling that was 'arched and richly gilded', and carpets of silk and gold. 'In the midst were tanks full of sweet water ... and round about the tanks were placed goblets, flagons, cisterns, and other standards of massive gold, some of which were filled with perfumes, others with rose-water, with wine some, and others with flowers'. They were conducted from there to an upper chamber where the carpets were richer, the tank larger and the gold vessels adorned with jewels. The ceiling was gilded with gold and decorated with finely painted scenes – the work of a Dutch painter employed by Shah Abbas. High-ranking courtiers and officials sat around the sides of the room, with their legs crossed, 'joining their bums to the ground, their backs to the wall, and their eyes to a constant object; to speak one to another, sneeze, cough, or spit in the Pot-shaw's [i.e. the shah's] presence being held no good breeding.'[5]

At the upper end of the room, cross-legged on a low throne, sat Shah Abbas: 'beloved at home, famous abroad, and formidable to his enemies', says Herbert, who was impressed by his unpretentious appearance. 'His grandeur was this: circled with such a world of wealth, he clothed himself that day in a plain red calico coat quilted with cotton, as if he should have said his dignity consisted rather in his parts and prudence . . . having no need to steal respect by borrowed colours or embroideries.' He wore a large white turban, and had a scimitar with a red scabbard and gold hilt.

Sir Dodmore Cotton addressed the shah, through his interpreter, on the purpose of his mission. He had undertaken a great journey, he said, at the command of his master, to congratulate the shah on his success against their common enemy, the Turk; to promote trade; to see Sir Robert Sherley vindicate himself from the imputations of Naqd Ali Beg; and to express the wish for 'a perpetual league of friendship' between 'the two powerful monarchs of Great Britain and Persia'.

Rising to his feet, the shah replied that 'the Turks were a mean people compared with the generous Persians, as appeared by several battles he had given them ample proof of'. But he wished the Christian princes would unite against the Turks, who profited from their discord to make their conquests. As for trade, he was ready to supply the King of Great Britain with 10,000 bales of silk a year, to be shipped from Gombroon, and would accept payment in English cloth. He knew this was more silk than the king could sell in his dominions, just as the cloth would be more than he could dispose of in Iran. But he would take the risk of having his merchants sell the surplus to his neighbours, so that neither of them 'should need to traffic or hold correspondence with Turkey'. He added that it would be a great satisfaction to him to deprive the Ottoman sultan of the revenue from the caravan trade, which he used to maintain his janissaries. 'What was this', he asked rhetorically, 'but to sharpen his enemies' sword to his destruction?'[6]

But Abbas avoided giving a straight answer on the question of Sir Robert Sherley's status when he was in England. He said he had known Sir Robert for a long time and had 'expressed as many considerable favours towards him (though a stranger and a Christian) as to any of his born subjects'. If Naqd Ali Beg had been unjust in his aspersions, Sir Robert should have satisfaction. The fact that Naqd Ali Beg had killed himself, Abbas went on, suggested he was guilty and feared to confront him: 'for had he come, and been found faulty, by my head he should have been cut in as many pieces as there are days in the year, and burnt in the open market with dogs' turds'.

Finally, Abbas said he cheerfully embraced a league of friendship with King Charles, and that the ambassador was truly welcome and the more deserving of respect as he was 'the first ambassador that ever came from Great Britain'. As he sat down, Abbas drew Sir Dodmore Cotton towards him and made him sit by his side, 'smiling that he could not sit cross-legged'. Later, in another room, he called for a bowl of wine and drank the health of King Charles, at which the ambassador stood up and took off his hat, and the shah, to oblige, lifted up his turban. After an hour's entertainment, he dismissed the ambassador, according to Herbert, 'with much satisfaction'.

Cotton too must have been reasonably satisfied with his audience, despite the shah's failure to give unequivocal support to Sir Robert Sherley. He certainly expected to see Abbas again. However, no further invitation of any kind came from the court, nor did any courtier or official come to see the ambassador for the rest of his stay in Ashraf, where the whole embassy had a fairly miserable time. They suffered torment from the humid heat during the day and from 'innumerable swarms of gnats, mosquitoes, and like vermin in the night'.

Abbas had other things on his mind than the English embassy. He was worried about the situation in Georgia where he feared another insurrection was brewing, and on 2 June he set off with the court for Qazvin to deal with it. The embassy followed, but by a different route. Cotton could not leave Iran without the shah's permission and had been led to believe he would have another audience in Qazvin. They stopped off first at Farahabad, 5 miles to the west of Ashraf, where Abbas had built another great palace, and after continuing a little further along the shore of the Caspian they turned inland, travelling by narrow and often precipitous tracks across the Alburz Mountains. Apart from the fear of falling into an abyss, they suffered from the sharp changes of temperature as they climbed and descended the mountains. One of the English gentlemen in the ambassador's suite died as a result, 'and myself', says Herbert, 'not minding to alter my thin habit, by the like cold I took upon the mountain, and in our descent into a very hot soil, fell into so violent a dysentery, as in eleven days gave me a thousand stools, most of blood'.

After crossing the mountains they reached the future capital of Tehran, which was then a medium-sized town with, according to Herbert, about

3,000 houses. The embassy was lodged in one of the tallest, from whose terrace, early one morning, Herbert saw most of the masters of families asleep with their seraglios on the flat roofs of their houses; some had three women with them, others six. He admits that his curiosity could have cost him an arrow in his brain.

The English ambassador was treated with marked coldness by the governor of Tehran, Zainal Khan. This soldier-cum-diplomat had been rewarded for his successful command of the Iranian troops in the defence of Baghdad by being promoted to the rank of khan and appointed to the court office of grand marshal (*ishik-aqasi-bashi*) – a post that carried with it the fiefdom of Tehran. 'Albeit our ambassador sent to visit him,' says Herbert, 'he returned a slight thanks without a re-visit; which we thought barbarous.' According to Herbert, Zainal Khan was a cousin of Naqd Ali Beg, which would explain his lack of enthusiasm for his English guests.

They arrived at Qazvin, 100 miles to the west of Tehran, two days after Shah Abbas and the court – 'unsaluted by all, not heeded by any', in the words of their chaplain, Dr Gooch. The hoped-for audience failed to materialise and Cotton was anxious to begin the journey home. So he went to see the favourite, Muhammad Ali Beg, to get a more explicit expression of support for Sherley and to hasten the process of departure. When Muhammad Ali Beg made clear that nothing more would be done for Sherley, Cotton protested that Sherley would not have dared to face Shah Abbas if he had been an impostor, and that he, Cotton, had Sherley's letters of credence stamped with the shah's seal. The favourite heard this with apparent sympathy and persuaded the ambassador to lend him the letter so that he could show it to the shah and see what he said. He promised to return it the next day. Three days later he came to the ambassador and told him that the shah had looked at the letter, denied that it was his and flown into such a rage that he had burnt it.

Cotton did not believe this story, but felt there was nothing more he could do. Herbert says further inquiry revealed that Muhammad Ali Beg had never shown the letter to the shah. He was convinced the favourite had been bribed by the East India Company to prevent Sherley recovering his former influence with Shah Abbas. This has long been discounted.[7] It has been suggested instead that during Sherley's long absence, a xenophobic faction at court had gained the shah's ear.[8] This faction, to which Muhammad Ali Beg belonged, disliked the 'foreign' and 'Christian' influence that Sherley represented. The *Carmelite Chronicles* may be referring to just such a faction in saying that some court grandees put it about that Sherley's

Circassian wife had been a Muslim, that she had been baptised by the Carmelite mission in Isfahan and that the shah intended to have her burnt for apostasy.

A xenophobic faction may have played a part in the shah's treatment of Sherley and the Cotton embassy, especially as Abbas's health was now failing and he was afflicted by recurrent bouts of fever. But it is equally likely that the shah simply became impatient with an embassy that appeared obsessed with salvaging Sherley's honour and had nothing concrete to offer, at a time when he was facing major challenges in Mesopotamia and Georgia. As soon as he arrived in Qazvin, Abbas issued orders for his troops to mobilise for a campaign in Georgia. In these circumstances, it is not so surprising that he failed to stir himself on Sherley's behalf and more or less forgot about the embassy.

Sherley too was now a sick man and his powers of resistance can only have been weakened by the attacks on his wife and the news that Abbas had disavowed him. He died on 13 July 1628, and was laid to rest 'under the threshold of his door without much noise or other ceremony'. Sir Dodmore Cotton, who had been suffering from dysentery, followed ten days later and was buried in the Armenian cemetery in Qazvin. Armenian priests and members of the Armenian community took part in the funeral ceremony. The ambassador's horse, with a velvet saddle on its back, was led before the coffin, on which were placed his Bible, sword and hat. The coffin itself was covered with a crimson satin quilt lined with purple taffeta.

Before he died, Cotton appointed the chaplain, Dr Gooch, to lead the embassy in his place. Gooch was summoned on 6 August by Muhammad Ali Beg, who gave him letters from the shah for Charles I and a safe-conduct out of the country. He seized this last opportunity to raise once again the issue of Sherley's letters of credence, which had, after all, been the main reason for the embassy. Pressed on the matter, Muhammad Ali Beg now admitted that they were genuine, but he insisted they had only been given to Sherley because he wanted to return home – which was patently untrue in 1615 – and conferred no authority on him to negotiate for the shah. He refused to discuss Sherley's proposals or to enter into matters of trade, saying only that Iran was an open country and the English could trade wherever they wished.

Not long afterwards, the embassy began the journey back to Bandar Abbas. More English gentlemen died on the way and Herbert himself suffered another severe attack of dysentery. 'In this sad condition and misery,' he says, 'I was forced to travel three hundred miles hanging upon the side of a camel in a cage resembling a cradle.' They sailed from Bandar Abbas for Surat on 19 December and arrived back in England almost exactly a year later, on 18 December 1629. Lady Sherley was allowed to leave Iran in September of that year, after resisting intense pressure on her to convert. She eventually settled in Rome, where she devoted herself to religion and good works. In 1658 she had her husband's bones brought to Rome and buried in the Carmelite church of Santa Maria della Scala. She died in 1668, at the age of seventy-nine, and was laid to rest beside him.

While the English embassy was on its way back to Bandar Abbas, two French Capuchin friars, Father Gabriel de Paris and Father Pacifique de Provins, arrived at the Safavid court.[9] Because of its close alliance with the Ottomans – born of a shared hostility to the Habsburgs – France was the only major European power which up to this point had not entered into direct relations with Safavid Iran. Pressed by the silk merchants of Marseilles, Louis XIII had attempted to send an ambassador to Iran in 1626, but the Ottomans had not allowed the envoy to proceed beyond Istanbul. The two Capuchin friars were not official envoys of the French government. They had been sent out by their order and by the Vatican Office for the Propagation of the Faith, but they had the backing of Louis XIII's powerful minister, Cardinal Richelieu.

Father Pacifique was received by Shah Abbas in Qazvin and immediately sent back to France by the shah charged with, among other things, obtaining cannons and a printing-press. Neither of these commissions was carried out. However, the shah had asked the Carmelites for a printing-press with Arabic characters as early as 1618, and as it happened they delivered one about this time – though presumably after Father Pacifique had left. It is not clear what use, if any, was made of it. Father Gabriel remained behind in Isfahan where he succeeded in establishing a Capuchin mission, which was henceforward regarded as representing the French government.

Shah Abbas had no sooner sent Father Pacifique on his way than he insisted on returning to his beloved Mazandaran for the winter of 1628-9, despite the fact that he was still suffering from recurrent fevers and his doctors advised against. He initially agreed to go by easy stages, riding at a gentle pace and taking twenty-four days instead of the usual twelve. 'But once in the saddle', writes Iskandar Beg Munshi, 'the shah could not wait to see the beautiful countryside of Mazandaran, and he covered the ground in eight or nine days!'

Back in his palace at Ashraf, he continued, in the intervals when the fever abated, to attend to state affairs and to go out hunting. He also had to consider the question of the succession. He now had no surviving son who could be considered for the sucession as he had blinded the youngest and last of his sons, Imam Quli, in 1627, in what appears to have been another fit of morbid and probably groundless suspicion. Iskandar Beg Munshi merely says that the shah regarded certain unwise actions by the prince as showing a lack of affection for his father and decided to have him blinded.[10] He then adds the curious comment that 'Although this was a terrible fate, it was the least of the calamities to which princes are exposed in this world.'

Sensing that his end was near, Abbas nominated his eighteen-year-old grandson, Prince Sam, the son of the murdered Prince Safi, as his heir apparent. The young man was in the palace harem in Isfahan and Abbas's first thought was to have him brought to Ashraf so that he would be under his personal supervision. But superstitious as ever, he took a prognostication from the Quran which caused him to delay sending the order.

On returning from hunting one day, Abbas was struck down by a renewed bout of fever, and his condition rapidly worsened. For three or four days he lay in his bed, afflicted by vomiting and diarrhoea, unable to stand up and his face swollen. He died on 19 January 1629, 'just as the sun was rising'. He was fifty-seven and had reigned for forty-two years. For Iskandar Beg Munshi, who had observed the shah closely throughout his reign, another sun had set, 'a radiant sun, in the shadow of whose justice men had lived in tranquillity'.

Shah Abbas's body was carried on the shoulders of Safavid Sufis, across the Alburz Mountains and by way of Tehran to the shrine outside Kashan of a descendant of the Shi'i Imams, Habib ibn Musa. There it lay in state for several days 'while teams of persons who knew the Quran by heart recited from the sacred text', before it was finally sealed up in a tomb.[11]

Chapter 14

Abbas, the Man and the King

There have been several descriptions of Abbas in previous chapters, but it is worth adding a word or two about some of his distinguishing features, beginning with his great moustache. Della Valle explains that the ends curled downwards 'for reasons of religion, as they say that moustaches which point upwards, as we wear them, show pride, and thus in a certain way they desire to fight with heaven'. According to Chardin, Abbas 'called moustaches the ornament of the face' and paid his soldiers according to the length of their moustaches. This was certainly a tall story, but it shows how famous Abbas's moustache had become some forty-odd years after his death.

His head on the other hand was completely shaven. As he grew older, he acquired a weather-beaten complexion burnt dark by constant exposure to the sun. He had great physical strength, as he demonstrated after the battle of Sufiyan when he wrestled to the ground a powerful and much taller Ottoman prisoner who tried to stab him. De Gouvea said that he had seen him 'slice a very big sheep in two with a single blow of his sword, and still cut through something that was on the ground'.[1] Later in life he became a little fat and lost some of his front teeth.

We can also look more closely at the kind of person he was and at his approach to government. Unlike most of his grandees who liked to wear expensive silks and brocades, Abbas preferred a simple costume of red, green or black cloth. He tried to get his subjects to follow his example and would sometimes rebuke a grandee if he thought him overdressed. In particular, he could not abide to see one of his soldiers indulging in rich clothing. When he was on campaign, according to the Carmelite, Father John Thaddeus, he wore 'red twill and cotton only, going poorly clad and wearing even rope shoes'.[2] He would dress more elaborately, however, on festivals and formal occasions, when he would also wear the distinctive Qizilbash headgear of a red felt bonnet with twelve folds (representing the Twelve Imams of Shi'ism) with a red stick emerging at the top and a long turban wrapped around it.[3] But he wore it back to front – something nobody else was allowed to do. At the banquet at Ashraf where Della Valle met him, his turban was red with silver stripes, and as soon as he sat down he took it off and placed it on the ground beside him.

He ate as simply as he dressed. The Carmelite, Father Paul Simon, says that in public he ate 'little else than rice, and that cooked in water only', but that in private he ate what he liked. He got more pleasure out of eating casually and informally. According to Father John Thaddeus, he was

> wont to go for a pastime to other places hardly respectable, such as to his kitchen, which is a house separate from the palace, and sit down there, eating whatever pleases him. Sometimes passing through the city on foot he will come to the shops of the greengrocers, fruiterers and those who sell preserves and sweetmeats: here he will take a mouthful, there another: in one place taste a preserve, in another some fruit.

He enjoyed preparing and cooking his own food, especially the fish and game he had caught or killed. Della Valle writes:

> On such occasions he will dissect the animal he has destroyed with the greatest nicety, separating with so much epicurism the daintiest morsels, as to collect no more from the carcase than a pound in small slices, which he seasons with different ingredients which are grateful to his palate, and makes of it when cooked a most hearty regale.[4]

If Abbas's eating was modest, his drinking was not. Almost without exception, the Europeans who visited his court were struck by the long bouts of drinking he indulged in with his courtiers. But none of them ever found him drunk, as was often the case with some of his successors. He seems to have been able to hold his drink and De Gouvea says he never lost his judgement.[5] Della Valle, who did not drink, accepted a cup or two of wine when pressed by Abbas. He says Abbas did not like people refusing to drink in his presence, 'because such people seem to him to be wanting to act hypocritically, reproving him as a transgressor of his own law'.[6] The Islamic ban on drinking alcohol clashed with a long-standing Iranian court culture in which drinking wine was regarded as normal, as well as with the culture of the Qizilbash Turkomans for whom wine had had a ritual significance. All the Safavid kings drank to a greater or lesser extent, although both Tahmasp, and even briefly Abbas himself, had bouts of repentence. Abbas was sensitive to any suggestion that he drank too much. When the Russian embassy of 1618-20 brought him a large number of casks of brandy as a present, he became angry, 'imagining that they tacitly thereby accused him of drunkenness', and gave most of it back, 'telling them at the same time that for his part he had no occasion for so much, and that as he knew they were used to drink deep he was unwilling to deprive them of what he was aware was so gratifying to themselves.'[7]

He was extremely restless and always had to be doing something. If there was nothing else to occupy him, he would busy himself with cleaning weapons or practising the various crafts which he had learnt as a prince in Khurasan. Equally, he disliked laziness in others and is said to have taken a particularly dim view of vagabonds and beggars.

An even more serious offence in his eyes was lying. De Gouvea says Abbas hated lies so much and was 'so rigorous in punishing those he finds to be lying that he has cut off the tongue of several for that'. He would certainly have approved of the three things the ancient Persians are said to have taught their young men above all else – to ride, to draw the bow and to speak the truth.

However deficient Abbas's formal education may have been, all who met him were impressed by his lively intelligence. 'He is very clear-sighted', reported Father Thaddeus, 'and it is sufficient when discussing business to drop a hint for him to understand everything; and he penetrates to the smallest niceties.' De Gouvea praises his 'very good judgement'. At the same time he was deeply superstitious. He was always accompanied by his astrologers, to whose readings of the heavenly bodies he paid the greatest attention. He also sought prognostications from randomly opening the Quran and lighting on a passage. But when he did this at the end of his life in Qazvin to discover whether it would be right for him to return to Mazandaran, which he dearly wanted to do against the advice of his doctors, he typically kept on opening the Quran until he got an answer that corresponded to his wishes.[8]

The people looked to the king to give them justice, which more often than not meant protecting them from oppressive officials. In this respect, Abbas had a reputation for being conscientious, impartial and very severe. Anthony Sherley witnessed how he dealt with the governor of Qazvin who had been accused of extortion. The shah's judgement was that he should 'goe, during his life, with a great yoke, like a Hogges-yoke, about his necke, have his Nose and Eares cut off, and have no charitable relief from any . . . This judgement strooke a mighty amazement into all the great men present and gave an infinite joy and comfort to the people.'[9] The Carmelite, Father Paul Simon, says that Abbas was even stricter with his own favourites in order to set an example to others, and that while the Portuguese embassy was at the court, 'he caused the bellies of two of his favourites to be ripped open, because they had behaved improperly to an ordinary woman'. He also describes how Abbas adjudicated on disputes and complaints at the gate of the palace, wasting no time and making sure he got through all the cases of the day. 'The parties stand present before him, the officers of justice and his own council, with whom he consults when it pleases him. The sentence which he gives is final and is immediately executed. If the guilty party deserves death, they kill him at once.' That is why, concludes the Carmelite friar, there are so few murderers and robbers in his country. And he adds that in all the four months that he was in Isfahan, there was not a single case of homicide.[10]

Abbas had to be ruthless to create, as he did, a well-ordered state out of the chaos he inherited. His court chronicler, Iskandar Beg Munshi, says that 'reports of his severity had a restraining influence on those who oppressed their subordinates, and meant that his orders were carried out without delay'. He goes on to give a chilling example of what was expected: 'If a father was commanded to slay his son, the order would be obeyed instantly; if the father procrastinated out of compassion, the order would be reversed; and if the son hesitated in his turn, another would be sent to put them both to death.' As a result, says Iskandar Beg, 'his writ became law, and no one dared to oppose his orders for an instant.'[11] One of the benefits this brought which would have been most appreciated by his subjects was the discipline he imposed on his troops, who no longer simply seized whatever they wanted from the local population. Abbas insisted that they respect people's property and pay a fair price for any supplies they obtained. As Pietro Della Valle points out, few European armies of the time behaved so well.

Iskandar Beg also draws attention to the conflicting aspects of Abbas's character:

The character of the Shah contains some contradictions; for instance, his fiery temper, his imperiousness, his majesty and regal splendour are

158

matched by his mildness, leniency, his ascetic way of life, and his informality. He is equally at home on the dervish's mat and the royal throne. When he is in a good temper, he mixes with the greatest informality with the members of his household, his close friends and retainers and others, and treats them like brothers. In contrast, when he is in a towering rage, his aspect is so terrifying that the same man who, shortly before, was his boon companion and was treated with all the informality of a close friend, dares not speak a word out of turn for fear of being accused of insolence or discourtesy.[12]

When he was angry, Abbas would sometimes behave with an impulsive and savage violence. Iskandar Beg says that from birth he was inclined to despotic behaviour and had a quick temper. One of the gentlemen in the suite of the Sherley brothers, George Manwaring, tells what happened during a mock battle in the main square in Qazvin, when Abbas became enraged by the poor performance of his officers and soldiers:

He presently ran in amongst them with his sword drawn, like to a Hercules and, upon a sudden, he gave four of them their death's wound. Then did he grow more into blood, and not sparing any, but cutting off the arms from divers of them and riding after. One gentleman which did but only smile the King never left, and, coming for succor into our company, the King gave him such a blow in the middle, that the one half of his body fell from the other.[13]

But when he was in a good mood, Abbas was a lively and engaging companion. He enjoyed banquets where the wine flowed, and talked and joked easily with those around him. His curiosity ensured a warm welcome for European visitors to his court, who could expect to be plied with questions. A good illustration of this is his conversation with Pietro Della Valle at the banquet in the royal palace at Ashraf on the Caspian in 1618. Abbas was delighted to learn that Della Valle spoke Turkish, and to begin with they conversed in this language, but after a while they had to use an interpreter because the shah, who spoke the Azeri Turkish dialect, had difficulty understanding Della Valle's Ottoman Turkish. Abbas himself translated everything Della Valle said into Persian for the benefit of those around him.

Why had he come to Iran? Abbas asked. What was Rome like? Was the pope well? How old was he? How was he elected? How were the cardinals created? Was Pietro a priest? What sort of a Christian Arab was Della Valle's wife?[14] On being told that she was a Chaldean and 'obedient to the Pope', Abbas launched into a disquisition on Christianity for the benefit of the courtiers present. He declared that the pope was the head of the Christians, and the vicar of Jesus Christ the Messiah, but that many Christians did not obey him, and that there were sixty-two sorts of Christians in the world, 'though I do not know where he got this from', comments Della Valle. Abbas was now in full flow as he recounted the ritual, ceremonial and other differences between the various Christian denominations, 'that he knew from some nations subject to him' – a reference to Georgia and Armenia. He then announced that the Christians regarded the first Shi'i Imam, Ali, as a saint, and that he was identical with both St James the Greater and St George. This was too much for Della Valle. 'For truth's sake I replied that these were three different persons and not one, and that St James was very different from St George . . . But the King, deceived either by false histories or by apparent similarities, insisted before all and everyone that they were one and the same, and that he knew this very well indeed.' Della Valle wisely decided not to press the point.

At this juncture Abbas questioned Della Valle about the Spanish ambassador, Don Garcia de Silva y Figueroa, who was on his way to the court, and gave advice on how the King of Spain should rule, and how he should deal with his enemies. He should combine all his forces and fall on them one by one, he said, 'starting first with the innermost: for it was madness to assault the enemies on the outside, before first having broken those at home, and that this was what he had done in Persia'.

Abbas next explained the reasons for his Georgian campaigns and became very worked up on the subject of the Crimean Tartars, whose help had been solicited by the Georgian king, Taimuras. 'What can they do with their arrows, which go *ter, ter?*' he demanded, imitating the sound they made, and then, putting his hand to his sword and looking fierce, he declared, 'Let them come! Let them come! I'll teach them a lesson!'

He was now onto his favourite subject of warfare and after discoursing on weapons and tactics, he gave a piece of advice on how to deal with an enemy horseman in battle. Never attack the rider, he said, aim at the horse, at its head not its neck, and when a man is down don't dismount to cut off his head – finish him off with a lance.

Della Valle says this was listened to 'with minute attention and much approbation' by the courtiers, while he himself tactfully remarked 'that it was only for masters to give such lessons, and that he was certainly qualified to teach from so much experience, and such great success as he had ever had. The King smiled at the compliment, modestly observing that what he had ever done was but of little value.'[15]

Abbas had an earthy and slapstick sense of humour. In the course of the same banquet he laughed heartily when a rather fat courtier, hurrying to fetch him some wine, fell into a fish-tank full of water and he was highly amused again when the same unfortunate courtier, as he was bringing the wine, collided with a pillar, sending the glass decanter crashing onto the floor and spilling the wine in front of the shah. Towards the end of the evening, as one of his khans[16] was leaving, he asked him laughingly whether he was going 'to serve that person?' – meaning a woman he had given him from the royal harem. The khan replied that he was 'and that he served her very well, as one needed to do with these women given by the King'.

Della Valle's conversation with Abbas at Ashraf again reveals the extent of his knowledge of and interest in Christianity. He much enjoyed discussions on the finer points of Christian theology. At an audience in Isfahan in June 1621 he quizzed the Carmelite friars and the representatives of the English East India Company, who were accompanied by an Anglican clergyman, on the differences between Roman Catholicism and Protestantism. He then arranged for the two sides to hold a disputation in his presence at which the main topics were fasting and good works; the Cross and the adoration of images; free will; the antiquity of the Roman Catholic religion and the primacy of the pope; and finally whether there was one wound or two in Christ's feet on the Cross. Much to the shah's delight, the discussion became quite heated, so much so that the English, as they were leaving, asked the Carmelite fathers' pardon for exceeding the limits of politeness.[17]

Informality was the hallmark of Abbas's style of government. His official chronicler, Iskandar Beg Munshi, comments that he mixed 'freely with all classes of society, and in most cases is able to converse with people in their own particular idiom'. Father Paul Simon says he was 'courteous in dealing with everyone', would 'speak at ease to the lower classes, cause his subjects to remain sitting while he himself is standing, or will sit down beside this man and that'. The Carmelite, Father John Thaddeus, says he gave audiences 'in all sorts of places and even in his shirt and drawers'. He told the Carmelites,'that is how to be a king, and that the king of Spain and other Christians do not get any pleasure out of ruling, because they are obliged to comport themselves with so much pomp and majesty as they do'.[18]

Whatever city he was in, Abbas would ride out into the town to talk to people, if he could, and to see what was going on. Almost every day in Isfahan he could be found exercising his horse in the Royal Square in front of the palace, riding up and down and stopping to listen to anyone who wanted to speak to him. However, when Figueroa saw him walk around Isfahan accompanied only by two or three servants, he says that no one dared to approach him. Instead they kept their distance and cried out 'Long Live the Shah!'[19] In the end it was through his servants that Abbas learnt of complaints against his grandees. Often Abbas would arrive unannounced at shops, coffee-houses and even private homes. But the sudden arrival of the shah was not exactly calculated to put people at ease. Abel Pinçon, a Frenchmen in the suite of the Sherley brothers, writes that 'although he is so familiar with his people that he makes no scruple about entering the booth of a merchant and drinking with him, yet he is so feared by them that as soon as they see him they bow their heads to the earth as if they saw some divinity, crying in their language "Long live Shah Abbas"'.[20] He especially loved going round the bazaars and would sometimes do so in disguise, both to hear what people were saying about him and to check on the goods offered for sale. One evening he went out dressed as a peasant and bought some bread and roast meat. He took them back to the palace and weighed them, to find that in both cases he had been sold short weight. He had the baker thrown into a hot oven and the meat-seller roasted alive.

This was not the only way Abbas kept himself informed about the state of his kingdom. Like most Iranian rulers and regimes, he had an army of spies. Although all regimes have used spies, their use in Iran was extensive and had long been regarded as an essential tool of government. It is strongly insisted on by the great Iranian vizier, Nizam al-Mulk, in his 'Book of Government or Rules for Kings' (the *Siyasat-nama* or *Siyar al-Muluk*), which he wrote at the end of the eleventh century for the Seljuq sultan, Malik Shah, and which would have been well known to Abbas. 'Spies', writes Nizam al-Mulk, 'must constantly go out to the limits of the kingdom in the guise of merchants, travellers, sufis, pedlars (of medicines), and mendicants, and bring back reports of everything they hear, so that no matters of any kind remain concealed, and if anything [untoward] happens it can in due course be remedied.'[21]

Iskandar Beg Munshi makes Abbas's intelligence system sound positively Stalinist. He says that Abbas had 'a well-developed intelligence system' and that even in the privacy of the home no one could 'express opinions which should not be expressed without running the risk of their being reported to the Shah'.[22] But this must have applied mainly to people of power and influence, people who could pose a threat to the shah, not to his more humble subjects. Nor even to the intellectuals who frequented the coffee-houses. When their criticisms of his government reached his ears, he merely sent mullas into the coffee-houses to preach edifying sermons. But the experiences of his childhood and youth made him liable to suspect plots against himself and he is said sometimes to have changed his bed for fear of an assassination attempt.

There seems little doubt that the great majority of his subjects regarded Abbas with awed admiration and affection. The Portuguese envoy, De Gouvea, was impressed by the enthusiastic crowds that turned out to greet Abbas as he travelled from place to place. The people also credited him, as they had his Safavid predecessors, with supernatural qualities, which derived originally from his position as a Sufi sheikh and his claim to be not merely a descendant of the Shi'i Imams, but the representative of the Hidden Imam. However, the popular belief that Abbas had magical powers must have been reinforced by his remarkable successes on the battlefield. The Spanish ambassador, Figueroa, recounts that when the wife of his next-door neighbour in Isfahan fell ill she sent her husband, a weaver, to beg one of Figueroa's servants for some of the sweetmeats the ambassador had been sent by Abbas. The servant obliged, and when she recovered three or four days later she was convinced it was because she had been touched, through the sweetmeats, by the shah's supernatural healing powers.

Shah Abbas was an absolute ruler, holding his position by divine right, as his use of the ancient Iranian title of 'Shadow of God on Earth' indicates. But he was not expected to exercise his power in an arbitrary manner. He had clearly recognised duties which had been laid down over centuries in manuals known as 'Mirrors for Princes', which had their origins in pre-Islamic Iran. Nizam al-Mulk's 'Book of Government' is the best-known of these. An idea of what Abbas considered his duties to be may be gained from a 'Mirror' which he had translated from Arabic into Persian. It is known as 'The Book of the Covenant', and ostensibly contains the instructions of the fourth Caliph and first Shi'i Imam, Ali ibn Abu Talib, to his governor of Egypt, although it is now thought to have been written much later. It was so highly regarded that several more translations were made in the later Safavid period.

'The Book of the Covenant' has been described as 'a good exposition of the duties of the ruler prior to the introduction of Western political thought and the closest Persian equivalent to a general theory of government'.[23] It 'made four tasks incumbent upon the ruler: equitable collection of taxes, defence of the community (*jihad*), welfare of the people, and improvement of the cities. It required the ruler to be forthright and god-fearing, to exercise self-control, and to display affection, forgiveness, and justice toward his subjects.' No blood should be shed without justification, as this would lower the ruler's authority. The ruler should avoid self-admiration and exaggerated praise, have control over his sense of prestige, and prevent outbusts of anger or sharpness of tongue. He should avoid haste by delaying severe action until his anger subsides.

'The Book of the Covenant' stressed that 'the government must take into account the interests of the common people more than those of the elite' and that the well-being of the merchants and craftsmen must not be compromised, 'since they are the sources of profit and provide society with useful articles'. The ruler 'should also keep an eye on the cultivation of the land more than on the cultivation of revenue', because revenue 'cannot be had without cultivation, and whoever asks for revenue without cultivation ruins the land and brings death to the people. His rule will not last even a moment.' A further very important piece of advice was that the ruler should be accessible to his subjects and ready to listen to their concerns. The shah might be an all-powerful and sacred figure, but he was not meant to be a remote one. His rule was very personal. 'The Book of the Covenant' warns the ruler not to seclude himself from the people lest he become divorced from reality. There was no danger of that with Abbas. Although it could certainly be argued that he sometimes shed blood unnecessarily and gave way to outbursts of anger, nonetheless he fulfilled most of these requirements to a remarkable extent.

Chapter 15

The Court of Shah Abbas

The court was a rich mix of peoples. Foremost among the courtiers were the old nobility of Turkoman Qizilbash amirs and their sons. Although no longer controlling the state, they continued to provide many of the senior army officers and to fill important administrative and ceremonial offices in the royal household. There were the Tajiks who still dominated the bureaucracy and under Abbas held the two highest government offices of Grand Vizier and Comptroller-General of the Revenues (*mostoufi-ye mamalek*), which was the nearest thing to a finance minister. There were also the *ghulams* or 'slaves of the shah', who were mainly Georgians, Armenians and Circassians. As a result of Abbas's reforms, they held high offices in the army, the administration and the royal household. Last but by no means least there were the palace eunuchs who were also *ghulams* – 'white' eunuchs largely from the Caucasus and 'black' eunuchs from India and Africa. Under Abbas, the eunuchs became an increasingly important element at the court.

The primary court language remained Turkish. But it was not the Turkish of Istanbul. It was a Turkish dialect, the dialect of the Qizilbash Turkomans, which is still spoken today in the province of Azerbaijan, in north-western Iran. This form of Turkish was also the mother-tongue of Shah Abbas, although he was equally at ease speaking Persian. It seems likely that most, if not all, of the Turkoman grandees at the court also spoke Persian, which was the language of the administration and of culture, as well as of the majority of the population. But the reverse seems not to have been true. When Abbas had a lively conversation in Turkish with the Italian traveller Pietro Della Valle, in front of his courtiers, he had to translate the conversation afterwards into Persian for the benefit of most of those present. Georgian and Armenian were also spoken, since these were the mother-tongues of many of the *ghulams*, as well as of a high proportion of the women of the harem. Figueroa heard Abbas speak Georgian,[1] which he no doubt acquired from his Georgian *ghulams* and concubines.

European visitors generally found the Safavid courtiers to be polite and pleasant company. Thomas Herbert, who accompanied the English embassy to Iran in 1628, must have based his opinion of the Iranians largely on members of the courtier class whom he met. He describes them as being 'of all men the most civil; which disposition they reserve unto this day, being generally of a very gentle and obliging nature – facetious, harmless in discourse, and little inquisitive after exotic news; seldom exceeding this demand: if such and such a country have good wine, fair women, serviceable horses, and well-tempered swords?'

Others were struck by their refinement. The sensibility of the courtiers is charmingly illustrated by the French merchant Jean Tavernier, who first visited Iran in 1632, three years after the death of Shah Abbas. He says they often paid homage to the shah – in this case, Abbas's grandson and successor, Shah Safi I – by gathering a bouquet of beautiful flowers and presenting it to him in a crystal vase. Tavernier was also clearly delighted that, whenever he left the court, 'four or five of the principal white eunuchs, each of whom has a little garden in front of his room' would ask him to bring back some flowers from France. He describes the Safavid court as the most polite and well-mannered in the entire Orient, where foreigners were made the most welcome and where they were cherished and protected – 'in a word,' he adds, 'Persia is in Asia what France is in Europe'.[2]

Court receptions were a colourful sight. Herbert was impressed by the large and valuable turbans worn by the grandees. They were woven, he writes, 'with silk and gold with a rich fringe or tassel of gold and silver at the end; but at feasts, entertainments, and gaudy-days I have seen them wreath their shashes [i.e. turbans] with ropes of Orient pearl and chains of gold set with precious stones of great value'.[3] Abbas also liked foreigners to wear the costume of their country. He said it added 'lustre to his Court, to behold exotics in their own country habit – so that the greater the variety appeared, he would say the more was his Court and country honoured at home and in estimation abroad'.[4] When he held a banquet in his palace at Ashraf on the Caspian, Abbas had the youthful pages who served the dinner dressed in the local costume of Mazandaran – stockings and a tight-fitting gown – but each of them in different colours. The pages brought the food – pilau rice with a variety of sauces – in great basins of gold and silver, and the guests were served on plates of the same metal, on cloths 'of gold brocade fringed with gold tassels of different shapes and colour'.[5] As the guests talked, seated all the while on beautiful carpets, the wine circulated in a little gold cup and musicians played quietly in the background. It was a charming and elegant reception, but relatively modest and informal compared with the extravagance and the elaborate ceremony that characterised Safavid court receptions later in the century.

The arrival of foreign embassies and the celebration of religious and secular festivals were the major events at the court and the occasion for grand receptions and colourful entertainments. These would often be celebrated with the illuminations so loved by Abbas, when the Royal Square in Isfahan was lit up with thousands of lamps and candles. They were inevitably particularly splendid during the ancient Iranian Festival of Lights (*Cheraghan*).

Abbas encouraged the celebration of ancient Iranian festivals as representing one side of the Iranian identity, the other being Shi'ism. These festivals which were celebrated by the court and the whole country included *Mehregan, Chaharshanbe Suri, Abpashan*[6] and the greatest and most important of them all, the festival of *Noruz*, which marks the arrival of the Iranian New Year on 21 March, the first day of spring.

The precise moment of the spring equinox was carefully calculated by the royal astrologers and greeted with salvos of artillery and musket fire and the drums and trumpets of the royal band. All the courtiers put on a fine set of new clothes and went to wish the shah a happy New Year and to give him their presents. If the court was in Isfahan all the presents received by the shah, including those sent by vassal rulers and provincial governors, would be paraded around the Royal Square. Typical gifts were purses of gold, jewellery and precious stones, expensive textiles, horses, camels and mules. The vassal king of Georgia used to send boy and girl slaves and wine. Among the costliest were those sent to Shah Abbas by his governor of Fars, Imam Quli Khan, who became a byword for wealth and extravagance. According to Sir Thomas Herbert, he 'presented the king in larrees the value of four hundred and sixty-five thousand florins, forty-nine goblets of gold, seventy-two of silver, and such other rarities, as in all burdened three hundred camels: a royal present from a subject.'[7] Della Valle, who was in Iran when Shah Abbas I was at war with the Uzbeks and the Ottomans, says that the governor of Khurasan included in his New Year presents nearly 300 heads of Uzbeks, while the governor of a province on the frontiers of Baghdad sent the heads of 600 Turks. He adds that 'the heads of those of distinction were enveloped in a silk turban, the others bare, and each thrust through with a lance'.

The court was wherever Abbas happened to be, and he was seldom in one place for very long. For much of his reign he was on the move, suppressing internal rebellions in the early years of his reign and later campaigning against the Uzbeks in the north-east and above all against the Ottomans in the west. The towns and cities where he established his court also changed. During the first decade of his reign Qazvin was the capital to which he regularly returned. It was then replaced by Isfahan, but from around 1612 he spent much more time in the new palaces he built at Ashraf and Farahabad on the south-east coast of the Caspian Sea.

His palaces are best described as palace complexes, because they did not consist of a single huge building which could be labelled 'the palace', but rather of a number of buildings in a park or garden setting. The palace complex in Qazvin was built by Shah Tahmasp and the building where Shah Abbas was crowned survives to this day. It is a small pavilion open on all sides and known as the Chehel Sutun, or Forty Columns, not to be confused with the more famous palace building of the same name in Isfahan.[8] Pietro Della Valle, who disliked almost everything else about Qazvin, was nonetheless impressed by the gateway to the palace. It is, he writes,

> very large with a most majestic view, and inside there is a beautiful tall and lofty atrium for the door-keepers; and beyond the entrance there is a large, beautiful courtyard, the former being completely shaded by a thicket of tall plane trees, in whose shade people wait comfortably in the open air of a morning, paying court and waiting to greet the King as he comes forth.

The palace complex in Isfahan was laid out by Abbas, although several buildings were added to it by his successors. The whole complex was surrounded by a high wall. It was entered through the palace building of five storeys on the west side of the Royal Square called the Ali Qapu – the Lofty Gate or Sublime Porte. It was from here that Abbas watched the various spectacles in the square – the polo matches, the archery competitions, the ram and bull fights and the ceremonies to commemorate the martyrdom of Imam Husain on Ashura, the tenth day of the Muslim month of Muharram, which was the most important date in the religious calendar. Women from the harem who enjoyed his favour were able to do the same through windows with slatted blinds on the top floor. The Italian traveller Pietro Della Valle says the beauty of the Ali Qapu lay in the walls of its rooms, 'which are enriched with gilding from the ceiling to the floor with excellent miniature paintings in various colours, with dark ornaments, which have a very fine effect, and the more so, the walls being of a shining white, resembling satin'. He adds that the vaulted ceilings 'likewise are loaded with decorations, gilding, rich colours, sculpture, and *alti-relievi*, in different compartments, and without confusion; and are well worthy our imitation in Italy'.[9] The building was used to house administrative offices and for official receptions, as well as for more intimate entertainments. A room on the top floor is known as the music-room, because it is thought probable that the variously shaped niches cut into a plaster outer-covering on the walls and ceilings were intended to improve the acoustic as well as to display glass, porcelain, pottery and other vessels. Abbas certainly had a great fondness for music. Iskandar Beg Munshi describes him as 'a skilled musician, an outstanding composer of rounds, rhapsodies and part-songs'. This is borne out by De Gouvea, who relates how, after the Augustinian fathers had sung a psalm for him, Abbas took up an instrument and sang a song of his own composition.

Under the gateway of the Ali Qapu was a semicircular stone of green porphyry which was regarded as a sacred object. Passers-by would show their love for the shah by stopping to kiss it, and anyone entering the gate had to be careful to step over it. If they stepped on it by mistake, they were liable to be beaten by the Sufi guards, who carried battle-axes on their shoulders.

But people could pass through the gateway fairly freely, as it gave access to a place where anyone being pursued for some alleged offence could take refuge, so long as they were unarmed and able to feed themselves. This sanctuary, or *bast* as it was called in Persian, was a short distance down an open paved passageway with whitewashed walls and through a door on the right, which opened onto a small garden, where there were rooms to sleep in, a pool to wash in and a domed shrine. So long as a person or persons were within the sanctuary they could not be touched, and while they were there they could usually negotiate a settlement of their dispute and a safe departure.

Further along the passageway was a door in the wall surrounding the rest of the palace complex, through which only government ministers, court officials, grandees and those with business at the court could pass. Beyond it, on the right, were storehouses and some of the workshops which provided the court with its necessities and its luxuries. On the left were the royal stables, which were later moved by Abbas's successor, Shah Safi I, to make way for a grand new reception hall, The Hall of the Stables.

Horses and riding were among Abbas's great passions. He knew just about everything there was to know about horses – how to break them in, shoe them and otherwise take care of them. And of course from the crafts he had learnt as a youth in Herat, he knew how to make bridles and saddles for them. He had a real love for his horses and often visited his stables just to look them over. The Portuguese envoy Antonio De Gouvea wrote that, 'He loves them so much that I have often seen him embrace them and kiss them, as if it had been some rational creature, and as one day he thought I noticed, he said, "Don't be astonished at what I am doing, because this horse has helped me kill many Turks", and in truth it seemed the horse recognised the caresses he made to it.'[10] Besides the horses in the royal stables, he is said to have had about 30,000 in studs around the country. A careful pedigree was kept of each of his horses. Abbas is generally acknowledged to have been an outstanding rider and perhaps the only occasion on which he refused a gift was in 1621 when the representatives of the English East India Company brought him a coach. He told them firmly that 'he was not a stone to be dragged from place to place in a cart, because he on his part preferred to go about on horseback as long as he lived'.

Beyond the stables, the storehouse and the workshops was another walled enclosure, containing the private area of the palace complex – the *anderoun* as it was called in Persian – which was guarded by eunuchs. The buildings of the royal harem were within this inner enclosure, where they were surrounded by a spacious garden with trees and flowers, pools, fountains and channels of running water. The harem was a self-contained community, with its own offices, kitchens, baths and workshops.

Shah Abbas had between 400 and 500 women in his harem, where they were looked after by black eunuchs and slave maidservants. Three or four were full wives who had undergone a marriage ceremony; the rest were concubines, mainly Georgian, Armenian and Circassian. These concubines were slaves either taken in war or purchased, or else sent as gifts by local governors and vassal rulers. The many Christians among them were not compelled to convert as male slaves were, and it is likely that Abbas acquired at least some of his knowledge of Christian teachings from them.

If Abbas felt the need for some fresh blood in the harem, he would sometimes issue a proclamation for all presentable young women in the city to be brought to the gates of a certain bazaar, where the royal eunuchs would admit the most beautiful among them for the inspection of the king. Failure to bring the women would result in loss of life and property. The Spanish ambassador, Figueroa, witnessed one such cull in Isfahan in the spring of 1619.[11] The women were brought shortly after midday by their mothers or another female relation to the Imperial Bazaar on the Royal Square, which was specially illuminated and decorated for the occasion and where the shopkeepers had been replaced by female relations. Large numbers of women arrived at the two gates of the bazaar, where five or six eunuchs dressed in gold and silver brocade with rich turbans on their heads and gold batons in their hands were waiting for them. The eunuchs lifted their veils and let in the most beautiful. Abbas then arrived and the gates were shut and guarded until early the following day when he emerged and the women were collected and taken home – except for some Armenian women whom Abbas chose to add to his harem.

To make way for younger blood, Abbas would periodically dispose of his longer-serving concubines by marrying them off to ambitious officials and courtiers who were keen to win his favour. But before he would let them go, they had to swear an oath not to reveal any of the secrets of the harem. Pietro Della Valle once saw thirty women leave Abbas's harem after he had found husbands for them. He describes how the shah sent them off:

> He gives each of them a camel to enable her to perform the journey she has to make; a covered litter, such as is used in this country to ride more conveniently, on the camel's ribs on one side, and on the other a coffer filled with her things, that is to say, a silk bed or rather mattress, a pillow and coverlid, dresses and linen, her gold, her jewels, and everything belonging to her; as all of them, according to their rank and birth, possess either less or more property. When she who leaves the harem happens to be in any esteem, her equipage and clothes, without which none are dismissed, are worth from one thousand to two thousand sequins, which in the East, where a woman brings nothing to her husband, is a handsome portion.[12]

The shah would sometimes arrange outings for the ladies of the harem. This might be a visit to the Isfahan bazaar, which would take place at night when the bazaar was specially illuminated for the occasion and the shopkeepers replaced by female relatives. Most of the inmates of the harem would be allowed out for this. However, a more select number would be chosen to join the shah for a picnic in the countryside or to accompany him on a hunting expedition. The shah would also take many of his women with him when he progressed around the country or went on a military campaign.

Whatever the occasion, all males over the age of seven had to keep well away when the harem passed. This was known as *quruq*, which literally means 'forbidden', and was enforced by eunuchs who rode on ahead and warned any males in their path to keep away. Anyone who ignored the warning was immediately put to death.

On short excursions, the women of the harem rode on horseback with their veils raised, while Abbas chatted and joked with them. But on any long journey they travelled in covered litters strapped to the side of camels. As in the account given above, the weight of the litter was balanced on the other side of the camel by a chest containing the bedding, clothes and jewels that the lady was taking with her. Pietro Della Valle says the women used to be helped into their litters by muleteers until Shah Abbas I had these replaced by eunuchs following an embarrassing incident that occurred when the harem was accompanying the army on campaign:

> The King travelling one night on horseback by himself with the army, incognito, as is usual with him, perceived the loading of one of the camels had slipped down on one side, whereupon calling the muleteer to set it to rights, and he not appearing, the King to ease the camel himself put his shoulder to the pannier, but finding it rather heavier than it should be, and seeking the cause, he discovered the muleteer comfortably reposed in the lady's arms, without any regard to the majesty of him he offended, or care for how the camel went. The King, upon this, immediately ordered the heads of the lady and her gallant to be severed, and since then eunuchs have been substituted for muleteers, in helping the ladies into their panniers.[13]

Abbas seems to have been bisexual. He was served at table by good-looking youths – the 'Ganymede boys' as Herbert calls them – and clearly enjoyed the lascivious dancing of the Georgian youths in the more louche coffee-houses of Isfahan, which so disgusted Figueroa. Provincial governors and vassal rulers sent him gifts of boys as well as young women. The Carmelite father, John Thaddeus, asserts that he kept 'more than two hundred boys' in his *anderoun* and was accompanied by thirty to forty naked boys when he went to the baths.[14] This sounds somewhat exaggerated. Nonetheless, bisexuality and pederasty were not uncommon among the Iranian elite in Safavid times – as indeed they were not in Elizabethan and Jacobean England.

For all that, Abbas clearly enjoyed the company of his women, if this account by Pietro Della Valle of his behaviour in the harem is anything to go by, although one wonders where Della Valle got these intimate details from. Perhaps he got to know one of the eunuchs.

When he retires to the harem among the women, if he is in a bad mood, no one speaks or goes to him, except for his principal wife, a Georgian and former Christian, who through the great authority she has over him, consoles him little by little, and brings him to a better temper. But when he sometimes relaxes cheerfully, all the women are around him, all speak to him, all joke with him, and, singing and playing, they eat and drink together. And he finds them excellent and numerous company, there being about a hundred all told, very beautiful young women, Georgian for the most part or Circassian, with whom he swops jokes in great good humour. He is given a tweak by one, and a pull by another, and swept off his feet by his legs, arms and head, to be whirled through the rooms, then thrown down on the carpets, while he calls out: 'you strumpets, ah you mad things.'[15]

There was always a matriarch who presided over the harem and during the reign of Shah Abbas it was his paternal aunt, Zainab Begum. It was she who strongly advised him to attack the Ottomans at Sufiyan in November 1605, which resulted in one of his greatest victories. Abbas is said to have greatly valued her advice and on occasion to have included her in his highest advisory body, the Council of State, where, according to De Gouvea, 'she made it very apparent that she deserved the honour'.[16]

It was under Abbas that the court eunuchs began to acquire real influence. Abbas increased their numbers and created new positions for them. He also introduced white eunuchs for the first time. Up till then, only black eunuchs had been employed in the palace. From the reign of Shah Abbas, an increasing number of key offices in the palace were given to eunuchs. But it was above all Abbas's decision to confine the royal princes to the harem that gave the eunuchs far greater influence than they had had before. All the Safavid rulers after Abbas would come to the throne having spent their life up till that point in the company of eunuchs and women.[17]

The eunuchs were slaves (*ghulams*) who had been purchased as young boys and castrated between the ages of seven and ten. Abbas liked to castrate many of them himself and is said to have done it with such care and precision that very few died under his hands.[18] Some of the black eunuchs came from Africa, but most came from India, from Malabar and the Gulf of Bengal. As the black eunuchs had exclusive charge of the shah's women, they suffered the most severe castration, having all their genitalia removed, which obliged them always to carry a quill to urinate through. The white eunuchs, who came mainly from the Caucasus, were more fortunate. As

173

they were employed outside the harem, they were only deprived of their testicles. The white eunuchs guarded the entrance to the harem. They also accompanied the shah when he left the palace.

The black and white eunuchs together were mainly responsible for the internal administration of the palace, which covered the entrance to the harem, the harem itself and the shah's private quarters. The chief eunuch, who held the office of Grand Chamberlain (*mehtar*), stood at the head of this administration and was a very influential figure. He always had the shah's ear because he was constantly with him. For most of Shah Abbas's reign this position was held by a white eunuch, Muhibb Ali Beg. Besides his palace responsibilities, he held a host of other important offices. He was tutor to the young slaves before they grew a beard, which was the sign of puberty. He was also head merchant and royal silk factor, controller of the assay (*mu'ayyir al mamalik*), head of the mint (*zarrabibashi*) and supervisor of the royal buildings in Isfahan (*sarkar-e imarat-e khassa-ye sharifa-ye Isfahan*). In all his various occupations he acquired considerable wealth, so that after supervising the construction of the Royal Mosque in Isfahan he was able to give it the second-largest endowment after the shah.[19]

Slaves who were not castrated were employed in the military corps of *ghulams*, in the administration or in the royal workshops. The 160,000 prisoners whom Shah Abbas brought back from his campaigns in Georgia in 1613–14 and 1616–17 greatly increased the supply of available slaves. According to the French merchant Chardin, who spent much time in Iran between 1664 and 1677, a reserve supply was housed in a building in the city called the Cow House (*khana-ye gav*). Either this or something similar may well have existed in Abbas's day. Many slaves of both sexes, of course, also joined the households of Iranian grandees.

The external administration of the palace – that is, everything outside the harem – remained under Abbas in the hands of the nobility, in other words the Qizilbash amirs, although the eunuchs were later to intrude into this sphere too. The most senior figure was the Chief Steward of the Royal Household who was better known under his title of Supervisor of the Royal Workshops (*nazir-e buyutat*). As this indicates, one of his main responsibilities was to oversee the thirty-three or so workshops that supplied the court with its necessities and its luxuries. He was also in charge of the Royal Treasury and responsible for the finances of the court. Second in importance was the Grand Marshal, known as the *ishik-aqasi-bashi*, which translates literally as 'head of the masters of the threshold'. His main responsibility was security and he had direct charge of the numerous ushers, porters, guards, doorkeepers

174

and gentlemen in waiting (*yasavolan-sohbat*). The latter were usually the sons of Qizilbash amirs.

Two important groups of Tajik officials at the court were the physicians and the astrologers. The shah was always accompanied by a number of them wherever he went. Towards the end of his stay in Iran, Thomas Herbert had a violent attack of dysentery and was treated by one of the shah's doctors. 'He did me little good', recalled Herbert, 'albeit I took what he prescribed (part of which I well remember were pomegranate pills, barberries, sloes in broth, rice and sundry other things) and returned what he expected: so that it was hard to judge whether my spirits or gold decayed faster.' Abbas himself seems to have had little confidence in his doctors, if De Gouvea is to be believed. He writes that when he took his leave of the shah, 'he asked me to do everything possible to bring a Christian doctor with me when I returned, because he did not dare entrust his life to Mahommedans'. This would not have been surprising since Europeans, whether they were doctors or not, were generally credited with superior medical knowledge. This was curious since European medicine was still largely based on the works of the great Iranian physician and philosopher Ibn Sina or Avicenna (980–1037), although that was about to change with Harvey's discovery of the circulation of the blood in 1628.

The shah's astrologers carried astrolabes attached to their belts so as to be able to take their celestial readings and make their predictions at a moment's notice. The astrologers on whom he relied most were the senior Shi'i cleric and polymath Sheikh Bahai, and, above all, his chief astrologer (*munajjim bashi*) Jalal al-Din Munajjim Yazdi. It was on the advice of the latter that Abbas stepped down from the throne for three days in 1593 in favour of a Nuqtavi dervish, whom he then had executed. Jalal al-Din Munajjim Yazdi also wrote an important historical chronicle entitled 'The History of Abbas' (*Tarikh-e Abbasi*) that begins with the reign of Shah Ismail II and covers the reign of Shah Abbas until around 1611.

The court officials with whom European visitors had most to do were the *mehmandars* or official 'hosts', who were appointed to look after them from the moment they crossed the frontier, taking care of all their needs and acting as their go-between with the provincial and royal courts. A new *mehmandar* would take over as they reached each province on their way to the court, wherever that might be. When they drew near to their destination, the 'chief host', the *mehmandar-bashi*, would ride out with an escort to meet them and would either take charge of them himself or appoint a subordinate to do so. Both Figueroa and Della Valle were looked after by the *mehmandar-*

bashi, Hasan or Husain Beg. Della Valle describes him as 'a person very high in esteem, not only on account of his high charge and the favour he enjoys, but also from his being the son-in-law of a Khan, who is one of the most considerable persons about the court, as well as being descended from the ancient nobles of Persia Proper, where he has very large estates in the neighbourhood of Shiraz . . .'[20]

The *mehmandar* was responsible for providing the guests with accommodation and with the supplies of food and drink and anything else ordered for them by the shah.[21] If they were travelling he would provide them with camels, horses and mules, and if they were merchants his presence would exempt them from tolls and other imposts. He would try to find out as much as he could about their business and inform the shah accordingly. He would carry messages to and from the shah and his ministers and might even play a part in negotiations. Foreign visitors were perfectly free to decline the services of a *mehmandar* if they so wished, but they can rarely have done so as it was invaluable to have someone who knew the Iranian court and was a direct channel of communication to the shah and his ministers. Ambassadors from the Ottoman sultan and the Moghul emperor were alone in not being assigned a *mehmandar*. They were considered to rank above all other foreign ambassadors, and in recognition of this one of the great amirs of the court was appointed to look after them.

Among the principal entertainments of the court were polo matches, archery contests and ram and bull fights which took place in the main square of Qazvin, when it was still the capital, and then later in the Royal Square of Isfahan. Abbas would watch these from the palace overlooking the square, if he was not taking part himself. European visitors were much impressed by the game of polo, which was new to them. Della Valle commented that it required 'great skill and agility', and that it trained both riders and horses 'in all the actions that are most necessary for war'. It was, he said, 'a very fine game, much more so than the carousels and suchlike put on among us; and if it were done with the displays of livery and devices that we Christians use, it would be worthy of the presence of the grandest ladies of Europe'.

Hunting was a major pastime of the court, as it was of courts everywhere. It was organised by the master of the hunt, the *amir shikar-bashi*, a high court office that was held by Abbas's general, Allahvirdi Khan. He was succeeded by another *ghulam*, this time from Armenia, Yusuf Khan. The best hunting grounds were in the Caspian province of Mazandaran, which was doubtless one reason why Abbas eventually chose to reside there for much of the year. In the most common form of hunt, thousands of peasants would be recruited to drive the game for miles around into a large area enclosed by nets, where it was then systematically slaughtered, with the king leading the attack and his courtiers following behind. In one such hunt in 1598 or 1599, Abbas killed 162 gazelles and other animals in the space of a morning.[22] Abbas also hunted with dogs and birds of prey – mainly falcons. Wherever he went, Abbas would always manage to take time off to go hunting. He left a grotesque monument to this sport of kings in the form of a tower in Isfahan composed of the skulls and bones of beasts, mainly deer, killed in the chase.

In about 1612 Abbas began the construction referred to earlier[23] of the two new palace complexes of Farahabad and Ashraf in Mazandaran at the south-eastern end of the Caspian Sea. But it was not just a question of building palaces. They were to be contained within entire new towns with all the normal amenities of a Muslim town – mosques, bazaars, caravanserais, baths and so forth. Abbas embarked on this huge project before he had even completed his plans for his capital of Isfahan. Besides the reasons already suggested for the move, Abbas was famously restless and an obsessive builder. The towns were built on the plain between the Caspian Sea and the densely wooded slopes of the Alburz Mountains. The most easterly of the two was Ashraf, known today as Behshahr, and about 26 miles to the north-west was the second town, which Abbas named Farahabad ('Abode of Joy'). It has been suggested that Farahabad was planned as the provincial capital and Ashraf as the royal retreat.[24] At all events, they quickly became his principal residences.

A few years after the construction work started, Abbas deported about 15,000 families from north-west Iran to populate and develop the towns and the surrounding area. They were mainly Armenians and Georgians. Many of these were peasant farmers, whom he encouraged to practise their traditional skills – the Armenians in cultivating the vine and the Georgians, among whom were Jews as well as Christians, in the gathering and manufacture of silk. He gave them land and whatever else they needed to get started, including large numbers of mulberry trees which he ordered to be planted around Farahabad to feed the silkworms.[25] He is quoted as saying that Mazandaran 'would be a paradise to Christians, as it abounded with wine and hogs', but the malarial environment claimed the lives of many of the new settlers. Despite this, when Della Valle rode from Farahabad to Ashraf in May 1618 he found 'the countryside through which we passed was all very fertile, and cultivated, especially near Farahabad, by the countless numbers of Christian Georgians and Armenians whom the king has brought there'.

Even by this early date, Farahabad was an impressive place. The circuit of its walls, says Della Valle, was at least equal to that of Rome or Constantinople. Its streets were more than a league[26] in length and were lined 'by rows of symmetrical houses, before which are canals to carry off the rain, with bridges in front of each house'.[27] The buildings were either of wood, or of earth mixed with straw, except for the royal palace which was not yet finished and was being built of brick. Della Valle was invited to a reception with the shah at Ashraf, who gave orders for him to be shown around the palace complex, which was also still under construction. He was escorted through the principal gate of the palace, which opened 'on a long and beautiful avenue of great breadth'. Beyond that, a garden had been laid out for the exclusive use of the ladies of the harem. It abounded 'in odoriforous plants and various fruits, but particularly oranges and lemons'. The alleys that traversed the garden had paved water channels in the middle and at the point where the four principal alleys crossed, there was an octagonal house several stories high. Its apartments were 'handsomely painted and gilt, but very small, and constructed only for sleeping rooms, or to rest in'. Della Valle was then shown the King's Garden, in the middle of which was the main palace building containing the audience hall (divan-khaneh). It was small, with an infinite number of apartments. The rooms were consequently very narrow, 'although well painted and gilt, and ornamented with exquisite miniatures of great cost'. There were numerous balconies on every side, 'with Venetian shutters and large curtains'. Della Valle adds that 'the floors of several of the most private rooms were strewed with mattresses of rich brocade, for convenience on being seated, or for sleeping on, and such as had not their mattresses were covered with carpets of great value'.

The towns and palaces were complete by the time Thomas Herbert saw them in 1628. He estimated that there were about 3,000 families in Farahabad and 2,000 in Ashraf. Among these were the many grandees, government and court officials who had established residences there. Herbert was enchanted by the main palace building at Farahabad with its view over the Caspian Sea and its gardens which extended to the shoreline. There were two large square courts within the palace, with grass plots and a variety of trees and flowers, including many tulips and roses. Plane trees, sycamores and chestnuts, he writes, 'surround the place with so much beauty, and every part of the house affords so amiable a prospect, as makes the eye and smell contend which shall surfeit soonest of variety'.[28]

Abbas built dams, canals and reservoirs to bring water to Ashraf from the nearby foothills of the Alburz Mountains. Because the almost continuous rain in winter made the roads virtually impassable, he built new improved highways, including two remarkable paved causeways – one extending for about 310 miles along the entire southern coast of the Caspian and the other connecting Farahabad with the interior. He also built residences and gardens at four other places in the region.

There are few traces today of all that Abbas laid out at Farahabad and Ashraf, or of any of his other residences in Mazandaran. Farahabad was destroyed in 1668, when it was sacked by the rebel Cossack leader Stenka Razin, who terrorised towns and settlements on the Caspian until he was captured and executed by the tsar in 1671. Ashraf was devastated in the Afghan invasion and the subsequent civil wars of the eighteenth century. The young George Nathaniel Curzon, the future Viceroy of India and British Foreign Secretary, visited the site of Ashraf during his tour of Iran in 1889. 'Terraces, and cascades, and halls have all gone to utter ruin,' he wrote, 'but the garden is still a glory, with its gigantic cypresses and orange trees.'[29]

Chapter 16

The Throne and Mosque Alliance

When Abbas came to the throne, he badly needed to bolster his legitimacy as ruler and to strengthen the ideological basis of his authority. The Shi'i basis of Safavid rule had been damaged by the pro-Sunni policy of Shah Ismail II, while its Sufi basis had collapsed altogether during the civil war that followed, when the Qizilbash tribal chiefs blithely ignored the duty of obedience which they owed to the shah as head of the Safavid Sufi order. Abbas's solution on the religious level was strongly to reaffirm and strengthen the bond with orthodox Twelver Shi'ism. This amounted effectively to the creation of a 'throne-and-altar' alliance in which the orthodox Shi'i clergy underwrote the shah's claim to a special Shi'i legitimacy and declared obedience to him to be ordained by God, while the shah in return did everything in his power to support and promote orthodox Shi'ism and the Shi'i clerical establishment. The clergy could not and did not, however, explicitly subscribe to the shah's claim to be the representative on earth of the Hidden Imam. This was a role which the clergy believed rightly belonged to them, or more accurately to the most learned and pious among them who had reached the high rank of *mujtahid*, and were able to make new legal rulings through rational inference. But challenges to the Safavid claim were few and far between, and there were none during the reign of Abbas.

Abbas's firm commitment to orthodox Twelver Shi'ism was the culmination of a development that had been going on ever since Shah Ismail I's divine aura was irretrievably damaged by his crushing defeat by the Ottomans at the battle of Chaldiran in 1514. That initiated a gradual shift away from the Shi'i-Sufi heterodoxy and mysticism which had invested him with this aura towards the orthodox Shi'ism of a growing clerical establishment, largely inspired and led by immigrant Shi'i clerics from Lebanon. This

181

development gained momentum during the long reign of Shah Tahmasp, but was interrupted by the brief reign of Shah Ismail II with his pro-Sunni policy and by the subsequent period of anarchy in which power lay in the hands of the Qizilbash with their heterodox beliefs. Once the Sufi bond between the shah and the Qizilbash had been found to be so disastrously wanting and Abbas had decided to use former Christian *ghulams* to break the power of the Qizilbash, it made absolute sense for him not only to renew and strengthen the Safavid dynasty's association with Twelver Shi'i orthodoxy, but to base his rule firmly upon it. In so far as the *ghulams* had undergone a genuine conversion and were not crypto-Christians, it was to orthodox Shi'ism that they were converted, not Qizilbash Sufi heterodoxy. A majority of the population of Iran had also by now been converted to orthodox Twelver Shi'ism as a result of the proselytising efforts under Shah Tahmasp. So whereas the Sufi basis of the shah's legitimacy had been important in the early years of the dynasty, when its power rested wholly on the Qizilbash, it was now the Shi'i basis that counted with a much broader 'national' constituency.

Abbas, however, continued to remind the Qizilbash of their duty of obedience to him as their hereditary sheikh and perfect Sufi guide. He did not hesitate to execute those who failed in this. As for the practising Safavid Sufis, the Safavid dervishes, some 200–300 of them guarded the entrance to the palace in Isfahan, provided a personal bodyguard for the shah and acted as his executioners. They wore long moustaches and carried battle-axes over their shoulder. These and other practising Safavid Sufis also continued to meet in the palace precincts every Thursday evening to perform the spiritual exercise known as *zikr*, the recitation of the name of Allah. But Abbas mistrusted the Safavid Sufis after he executed three of their leading members in 1592 or 1593 for conspiring against him with his deposed father, Muhammad Khodabanda, whom they still regarded as their Sufi master and rightful king. Thereafter he deprived the Safavid Sufi organisation of any meaningful role and the once-powerful position of the leader of the organisation, the *khalifat al-khulafa*, became purely ceremonial. From this point the Safavid Sufis steadily lost status until by the second half of the seventeenth century they were occupying such lowly positions as sweepers and porters in the palace.

On the other hand, Abbas continued to show devotion to the Safavid shrine at Ardabil. He valued it as a source of dynastic legitimisation, and no doubt as a useful symbol for the Qizilbash of his Sufi authority. He generously endowed it, repaired and renovated it, and made fairly frequent visits to it, usually to invoke the blessings of his ancestors before opening a new campaign against the Ottomans. There was a steady stream of pilgrims to this dynastic shrine from all over Iran. The Italian traveller, Pietro Della Valle, says that Abbas established a fund so that the large numbers of pilgrims and poor people who gathered at the shrine could be fed with good pilau rice twice a day, instead of just once, and that thirty-five large boilers were kept going all the time to cook the rice.[1]

Abbas also had the bones of his grandfather, Shah Tahmasp, interred within the shrine. Tahmasp, the pious Shi'a, who like himself had rescued Iran from anarchy and driven out the Ottoman and Uzbek invaders, was the Safavid ancestor Abbas most wished to be identified with. He promoted the association publicly by naming Tahmasp in the endowment inscriptions of a number of his buildings, the most notable being the inscription over the portal of the Royal Mosque in Isfahan, where Abbas states that he is dedicating the rewards accruing from his pious act in funding the building of the mosque to the soul of his grandfather.[2]

This public association with Tahmasp represented a further emphasis on Abbas's Shi'i credentials. Although a political calculation was present, it is very unlikely that that was the sum total of it. All the indications are that Abbas was sincere in his commitment to Shi'ism. Had he not been, it is unlikely that he would have made repeated pilgrimages to the shrine of the Eighth Imam, Ali ar-Riza, in Mashhad to invoke his aid before embarking on a military campaign – not to speak of the famous pilgrimage he made on foot all the way from Isfahan ahead of his campaign against Balkh. The Carmelite friar, Father John Thaddeus, concluded with exasperation that after all Abbas's expressions of sympathy for Christianity 'he is at heart a Muhammadan'.[3] The Portuguese envoy, Antonio De Gouvea, also notes that Abbas said his prayers five times a day and took his time about it.[4] But he was not such an observant Muslim in everything. He happily drank wine and sometimes went on a hunting expedition during Ramazan, so as not to be seen ignoring the fast.[5] He was much more tolerant of other religions than most of his Shi'i subjects, particularly if this served his political or economic interests, as in the case of the Christian Armenians he deported to Iran. But the vizier of Mazandaran, Saru Taqi, was certainly going too far when he told Pietro Della Valle 'that the King was wholly indifferent to what religion his subjects professed, holding all as good, either the Mahometan, the Christian or Jewish faith'.[6] This was clearly said for Della Valle's benefit in the hope that it would be reported to those Christian princes in Europe whose help Abbas was forever soliciting against the Ottomans.

Abbas's devotion to the shrine of the Eighth Imam at Mashhad was the most visible symbol of his commitment to Twelver Shi'ism. His devotion was probably genuine enough, but it also helped to identify him with the Imams in the eyes of his Shi'i subjects, thereby making more credible his theocratic claim to be the representative on earth of the Hidden Imam. He expressed his devotion in his pilgrimages, in the great endowment he made in 1607 in gratitude for his victories over the Ottomans, in embellishments and improvements to the buildings, and in the little acts of humility he performed, like sweeping the carpets in the shrine. He also encouraged his subjects to make pilgrimages to Mashhad as an alternative to the pilgrimage centres abroad – Mecca and the Shi'i shrines in Iraq – all of which were in the hands of his Ottoman enemy. This, however, was prompted as much by economic considerations because he was anxious to reduce the loss of valuable bullion in the form of gold and silver coins that the pilgrimages to Iraq and Arabia entailed.

Mashhad became Abbas's personal shrine and he did not show similar devotion to the other great Shi'i shrine in Iran – that of the Eighth Imam's sister, Fatima, in Qom. But he did not ignore it either. He built a theological college (*madrasa*) and a hostel for pilgrims in Qom, who visited the shrine of Fatima in increasing numbers, while many descendants of the Prophet, sayyids like the Safavids themselves, settled in the town.[7] But Qom became much more closely associated with the Safavids under Abbas's successors, all four of whom were buried there.

Abbas's attention to Twelver Shi'ism and his place in it was very much on display in his new capital of Isfahan. There he built new mosques and theological colleges and made Isfahan the main centre of Shi'i learning in the Islamic world, replacing the previously dominant Arab centres in Lebanon and Iraq. Just how dramatic an advance this was is illustrated by the story that when the Shi'i cleric Abdullah Shushtari (d.1612) began teaching in Isfahan shortly after Abbas transferred his capital there, there were only fifty theological students in the whole city. Shushtari himself had only just arrived in Isfahan after spending thirty years studying in the Shi'i shrine cities of Najaf and Kerbala in Iraq. Abbas put him in charge of one of the new colleges and by the time Shushtari died thirteen years later, the number of students is said to have risen to over 1,000.[8] Half a century later, according to the French jeweller Jean Chardin, there were forty-eight theological colleges and 162 mosques in Isfahan. This represented a huge increase in the numbers of the Shi'i clergy.

Abbas also made his new capital the principal arena for Shi'i religious festivals and commemorative ceremonies, which he turned into great public spectacles. The magnificent and spacious Royal Square, which contained the symbols of royalty and religion in the shape of the Ali Qapu palace and the Royal Mosque, provided the perfect setting for such spectacles. Apart from the fact that Abbas was fond of displays on a grand scale, his purpose seems to have been threefold: to encourage an emotional attachment to Shi'ism; to reinforce the image of Isfahan as the heart of the Shi'i world; and to provide a safety-valve that would allow a volatile urban population to let off steam. The main Shi'i festivals commemorated the martyrdom of the Third Shi'i Imam, Husain; the Prophet Muhammad's designation of Husain's father, Ali, the First Shi'i Imam, as his successor; and the death of Ali.

By far the most important of these was the commemoration over the first ten days of the Muslim month of Muharram of the martyrdom of the Imam Husain. This culminated in a highly theatrical procession of displays by the various quarters of the city which crossed the Royal Square and passed in front of the palace, from where it was viewed by Abbas. The processions included funeral biers draped in black velvet and accompanied by men dancing to the sound of cymbals and gongs, as well as more dramatic sights such as coffins with children inside simulating death and naked children with their heads and faces smeared with blood.

Abbas also introduced a new public ceremony to mark the Festival of the Sacrifice (*Eid-e Qurban*) – in this case a Muslim rather than a purely Shi'i festival commemorating Abraham's readiness to sacrifice his son Isaac. A female camel was decked out with flowers and garlands and led around the city for three days before being taken to a spot outside the city where it was ceremonially slaughtered before the shah, his courtiers and a great concourse of people.[9]

All these religious festivals usually ended with violent clashes between two age-old city factions, known as Haidaris and Nimatis. These 'were meant to represent the great turmoil in which Imam Husain perished'[10] and often resulted in fatalities. Indeed, some of the participants in the Muharram ceremonies actively sought death, because it was widely believed that anyone who died at this time would go straight to paradise. Abbas is also said to have encouraged these outbreaks of violence, while keeping them within limits, as a way of channelling popular frustration away from the government. As the seventeenth century progressed, the Muharram ceremonies became more and more elaborate and European visitors were often invited to watch them.

The support of the Shi'i clergy was also valuable to the shah in helping him to manage potential unrest in the urban population. The clergy had their main presence in the towns and cities and were particularly closely connected to the bazaar, where many of them had jobs. The bazaar, where commercial activity was concentrated, was a major source of revenue for the state, but it was also a potential focus of popular discontent over government policies – notably over government taxes and financial levies. The merchants, shopkeepers and artisans were the most pious section of the population and paid the largest share of the religious taxes which helped to support the clergy. In turn, they depended on the clergy to administer the Islamic law which largely regulated their business and they looked to them, as they always had, to defend them against government oppression and extortion. Shah Abbas sought to counteract the very free political discourse that went on in the new coffee-houses of Isfahan by sending in Shi'i clerics to preach edifying sermons. The clergy could also, of course, use their influence to stir up trouble for the government – for instance, fomenting anti-Christian sentiment as they sometimes did under Abbas. Generally speaking, however, this was much less of a problem for Shah Abbas and the Safavids than it was to be for the Qajar dynasty in the nineteenth century, when there was real interference in Iran by foreign 'Christian' powers. But as always in Iran, the clergy, or the mullas as they were popularly known, were mocked in the days of Shah Abbas as much as they were respected and listened to. They were often accused of hypocrisy and avarice. Chardin quotes an Iranian proverb current in his day, which went: 'Be careful of the front of a woman, the rear of a mule and all sides of a mulla'.

Just how concerned Abbas was to rally the clergy behind him may be gauged from the fact that whereas his predecessors had mostly married their daughters to Qizilbash tribal chiefs, Abbas married all but one of his six daughters to Shi'i clerics. He was often in the company of clerics and enjoyed listening to them discuss matters of religion. Those clerics who were closest to him accompanied him on military campaigns and hunting expeditions. During the fasting month of Ramazan, if he was not otherwise engaged, he entertained the clergy en masse. In 1595, on every one of the thirty evenings of Ramazan, he invited 366 clerics and theology students to the palace in Qazvin to break the fast with him.[11] They were served a sumptuous meal and each given a sum of money when they departed.

Many of Abbas's titles highlighted his special position within Twelver Shi'ism. He was 'The Promoter of the Doctrine of Twelver Shi'ism', 'The Dog of the Threshold of Ali' and 'The Viceroy of the True Lord'. When he introduced a new silver coinage at the beginning of his reign, Abbas replaced the secular titles of sultan and khan which had been used on the coinage for the past three centuries with an expression underlining his position as the representative of the Hidden Imam: 'Abbas servant of the ruler of the vicegerency' (*banda-ye shah-e velayat-e Abbas*). In this last capacity, he stood ready to hand over power to the Hidden Imam as soon as he should appear. This was symbolised by the stable in Isfahan and other cities, known as 'The Stable of the Lord of Time', where the finest horses were kept permanently saddled and harnessed for the Imam's use.

The belief in the imminent return of the Hidden Imam was one of the characteristics of Shi'i extremism that survived in an otherwise increasingly orthodox Shi'i state. So too was the employment of public cursers who went around with big axes over their shoulders. But under Abbas the cursing no longer embraced all the first three Caliphs of Islam. Instead it was concentrated on the second Caliph, Omar, during whose reign (634–44) the ancient empire of Iran with its Zoroastrian religion was overthrown by the Muslim Arabs. Omar was murdered by a Persian Christian captive and under Abbas the anniversary of his death became a festival, the Festival of the Killing of Omar (*Omar-Kushan*), which was an occasion for feasting and rejoicing. The French merchant Chardin says that in Abbas's day the cursing of Omar was the cause of frequent incidents with visiting Sunni Uzbeks. As soon as an Iranian crowd saw an Uzbek they would start chanting 'Cursed be Omar!', on hearing which the Uzbek would draw his dagger, hurl himself into the crowd and be cut to pieces. Chardin says that on one occasion the entire train of an Uzbek ambassador was killed in this way. After that, Abbas ordered that whenever an Uzbek embassy was approaching, a horn was to be blown and a proclamation made that there was to be no cursing of Omar within earshot of the Uzbeks.[12]

The continuing use of public cursers also reflected Abbas's undoubted wish to unite as far as possible the whole country around Shi'ism, to make it in a sense a national cause in the conflicts with the Sunni Uzbeks and Ottomans. There was still a considerable Sunni minority in Abbas's day. Then, as now, they were mostly found around the periphery of the Safavid kingdom – in eastern Khurasan, Qandahar, the northern Caucasus, Kurdistan and, in the south, in Laristan and along the coast of the Persian Gulf.

There was always the fear that the Sunnis might prove to be a fifth column, aiding and abetting their co-religionists, and Abbas put pressure on them to convert through discriminatory taxation. Sir Anthony Sherley identifies this motive behind Abbas's religious policy. He writes that,

187

the King knowing how potent a uniter of men's minds the selfsame Religion is for tranquility of a state: and the like dis-uniter several religions are for the disturbance of the peace of an Estate, he is exceeding curious and vigilant to suppress, through all his Dominions, that religion of Mahomet, which followeth the interpretation of Ussen [Uthman][13] and Omar, and to make his people cleave to that of Ali: not [as I judge] through any conscience which carrieth him more to the one than the other; but first to extirpate intrinsic factions, then to secure himself more firmly against the Turk, who being head of that part which followeth Omar and Ussen, should have too powerful sway into his Country, if his people's hearts were inclined unto him by the force of Religion. Therefore he doth not only strive to root it out, but to defile it, and make it odious; having in use, once a year, wth great solemnity, to burn publicly, as main Heretics, the Images of Ussen and Omar.[14]

The Shi'i clergy under Abbas were not a monolithic body. Some of those he was closest to had strong Sufi leanings, which were disliked and bitterly opposed by the majority of their fellow clerics. But this was not a popular Sufism nor did it have the political overtones of Nuqtavi Sufism. It was an intellectual Sufism, sometimes referred to nowadays as 'high Sufism', which won adherents and sympathisers at the court and in intellectual circles but was too rarified to appeal to the wider population. However, it was more than just another form of Sufism. It was a major philosophical-theological movement that has come to be known as the School of Isfahan.

The School of Isfahan[15] represented a new form of gnostic Shi'ism. It set out to uncover the path to true wisdom through a synthesis of the intuitive and rational traditions. It was mainly inspired by the concept of 'illuminative wisdom' developed by the Iranian Sufi mystic Shihab ud-Din Yahya Suhravardi, who was executed for heresy in 1191 and who drew many of his ideas from the pre-Islamic Zoroastrian religion of Iran, from Neo-Platonism and from earlier Islamic mystics. It was also influenced by Ibn Sina (d.1037), known in the West as Avicenna, and through him by Aristotle.

The founder of the school, Mir Damad (d.1631), was one of Abbas's close companions and spent much of his time at the court. He was so highly regarded that after his death he was accorded the title of 'the Third Teacher' after Aristotle and al-Farabi (d.950). Besides philosophy, he is said to have been skilled in most other sciences of his day, including mathematics and medicine. He also wrote poetry of some distinction in Persian and Arabic. Abbas is said to have been greatly in awe of him.

Mir Damad was the first to effect a synthesis between the rationalist philosophy of Avicenna and the intuitive or illuminationist philosophy of Suhravardi within the framework of Twelver Shi'ism. According to Andrew Newman, a modern authority on Safavid Shi'ism, Mir Damad's best-known philosophical achievement was his development of the concept of 'origination in perpetuity' (*hodut-e dahri*) as an expression of God's relation to the world.[16] He arrived at this in examining a question that preoccupied Muslim theologians, which was whether God created the world in time, or whether both God and the world were eternal. Mir Damad defined perpetuity as an intermediate category of time between eternity, where God exists, and earthly time in which the world exists.

But the Shi'i cleric who was closest of all to Shah Abbas and who was also one of the founders of the School of Isfahan was Sheikh Bahai (1546–1621). Abbas appointed him Sheikh ul-Islam of Isfahan in 1597, which made him the chief religious dignitary not merely of Isfahan but of the whole country. He mastered even more fields of knowledge than Mir Damad, including some that were of great practical use. The Iranian scholar Seyyed Hossein Nasr has described him as 'the last eminent representative of the Muslim *hakim* in the sense of being master of all the traditional sciences'.[17] In addition to a thorough knowledge of theology, philosophy and jurisprudence, Sheikh Bahai was an outstanding mathematician and astronomer as well as an architect and garden designer of rare ability. He was one of the principal astrologers at the court, which required him to be frequently in attendance of the shah. He played an important part in Abbas's development of Isfahan, helping with the plans for the Royal Square, the design of the Royal Mosque and the layout of the Chahar Bagh avenue. He also designed the Fin garden in Kashan, which is one of the finest surviving examples of a Persian garden. He applied his skills as a mathematician to a number of irrigation projects, including a bold but unsuccessful attempt by Shah Abbas to increase Isfahan's water supply by cutting a channel through the Zagros Mountains in order to divert water from a tributary of the Karun River into the Zayandeh River. When this project was finally brought to fruition in 1953, it was found that Sheikh Bahai's calculations for the alignment of the channel were out by only a fraction of a degree.

Sheikh Bahai was a great teacher and many of the leading clerics of the next generation were his pupils. He wrote in both Persian and Arabic on a wide range of religious and other topics, including a much-admired essay on the astrolabe, which he dedicated to the grand vizier, Hatim Beg. He also composed poems in Persian that are generally considered to be of a high order. These reveal his strong Sufi leanings, which brought vitriolic attacks upon him by a section of the clergy. Because of this, Sheikh Bahai resigned as Sheikh ul-Islam in 1606 and left for an extended period of travel abroad. When he returned to the Safavid court, he was commissioned by Shah Abbas to write a book on Shi'i law in Persian. He was still working on it when he died in 1621. The 'Abbasid Compilation' (*Jamii Abbasi*), which is named after Shah Abbas, is one of the most celebrated works on the subject and remains in use today. Despite the clerical attacks on him, Sheikh Bahai was a popular figure and an immense crowd of people from all classes turned out to pay their last respects as his coffin was carried through the Royal Square in Isfahan.

A third member of the School of Isfahan under Abbas who should be mentioned is Mulla Sadra, although he spent much of his life in Shiraz where his patron was Abbas's famous general, Allahvirdi Khan. Mulla Sadra is generally considered to be the most outstanding figure in the School of Isfahan in terms of pure philosophy. He was born in Shiraz in 1571/2, but pursued his higher studies in Isfahan, where he was a pupil of both Mir Damad and Sheikh Bahai. His gnostic doctrines, such as his conception of the resurrection as 'knowledge of the self' as opposed to an otherworldly physical resurrection, brought down upon him the full fury of the strictly orthodox clergy, who went so far as to excommunicate him. He responded with the only treatise he ever wrote in Persian, attacking their literalism, and retired to a village near Qom where he engaged in contemplative exercises. He was eventually persuaded to come out of retirement by Allahvirdi Khan, the governor general of Fars, who asked him to teach in the college he had just founded in Shiraz, called 'the Khan Madrasa'. While he was in Shiraz, Mulla Sadra wrote his most important work, which is a massive treatise known as the *Asfar* or 'Journeys'. Seyyed Hossein Nasr has described it as 'one of the greatest monuments of metaphysics in Islam', which 'deals with the origin and end of all cosmic manifestation and in particular the human soul'. Mulla Sadra remained in Shiraz, teaching and writing, for the rest of his life, only breaking off to make frequent pilgrimages to Mecca. It was while he was on his way to the holy city for the seventh time that he died in Basra in 1640. The *Asfar* has had a lasting influence. Among those who fell under its spell was the leader of the Islamic Revolution in Iran in 1978-9, Ayatollah Khomeini, who studied it in his youth and later taught it at his seminary in Qom, where he became 'the most respected teacher of the book'.[18]

Both Mir Damad and Sheikh Bahai were among the relatively few clerics in Abbas's day who held the high rank of *mujtahid*, entitling them to practise *ijtihad* or intellectual effort in order to resolve doubtful questions on which the Sharia provided no clear guidance. They were to rule on these questions by applying their reason to the general principles, or *usul*, of Islamic law. Those clerics who accepted the role of the *mujtahid* were called *Usulis*, but they were bitterly opposed by another clerical faction whose members were called *Akhbaris*. They held that the traditions or *akhbar* of the Imams provided a sufficient guidance and that the *mujtahids* had no right to make law themselves. During the reign of Shah Abbas and, indeed, throughout the Safavid period, the *Usulis* had the upper hand in Iran, but the *Akhbaris* were dominant in the Shi'i centres in Iraq as well as in Mecca and Medina. The dispute between the two factions went on until the early nineteenth century, when the *Usulis* finally won the day.

This was no arcane matter since the *Usuli mujtahids* had supported the Safavids with helpful rulings since the days of Shah Tahmasp and continued to do so under Shah Abbas. These rulings had greatly facilitated the business of government, which would otherwise have been virtually impossible in the absence of the Hidden Imam. The close association between the *Usulis* and the Safavid court was strongly criticised by the *Akhbaris*, who maintained the traditional Shi'i view that association with any government is necessarily corrupting, because legitimate government belongs to the Hidden Imam alone. On the other hand, the *Akhbaris* only wanted to keep their distance from government; they did not want to oppose or replace it. But that possibility existed with the *Usulis*, since in theory they were the true representatives of the Hidden Imam during his absence, not the Safavid shahs. This theory was never pushed very hard under the Safavids, although one Shi'i cleric, Sheikh Ahmad Ardabili, is on record as reminding Shah Abbas I that he was ruling over a 'borrowed kingdom' (*mulk-e ariya*). There was also a call by some clergy for a *mujtahid* to rule towards the end of the reign of Shah Abbas II (1642–66). They were angered by the shah's open flouting of the Islamic prohibition on wine. But the call received no serious support and clerical rule was not an issue until it was taken up and implemented in recent times by Ayatollah Khomeini.

Abbas was able to keep his Shi'i clergy under control through his innate authority, his promotion of the more liberal, Sufi-inclined clerics like Sheikh Bahai and through the obvious services he was rendering to Twelver Shi'ism. Apart from those services already mentioned, his conquest of Bahrain, with its predominantly Shi'i population, and of Iraq with its major shrines, greatly enhanced his prestige in the eyes of the Shi'a. But in much enlarging and strengthening the Shi'i clerical establishment and making the legitimacy of the monarchy to a large extent dependent on its endorsement, Abbas stored up problems for the future. By the end of the seventeenth century narrow-minded and legalistic clerics were able to impose their agenda on much weaker Safavid rulers, leading to the persecution of Sunnis and other religious minorities which eventually helped to bring about the downfall of the dynasty. Although this clerical establishment was pushed into the background during the upheavals of the eighteenth century, it re-emerged as a powerful political force under the Qajar dynasty (1796–1925) and finally succeeded in replacing the monarchy altogether in the Islamic Revolution of 1978–9.

Chapter 17

The City that was Half the World

With its central position on Iran's main north–south trade route, Isfahan was an important city long before the Safavids. Its history reaches back into pre-Islamic times and Shah Abbas I was not the first ruler to make it his capital. In the second half of the eleventh century it became the capital of the extensive Seljuq Empire. But thereafter its prosperity was undermined by wars and invasions. It was sacked in each of the three centuries preceeding its capture by the first of the Safavid rulers, Shah Ismail I, in 1504, who inflicted further suffering on the city by slaughtering some 5,000 of its Sunni inhabitants. Its population around this time is estimated to have been no more than 25,000. Thereafter there seems to have been a slow but steady recovery, but the population is unlikely to have much more than doubled to some 50,000 by the time Shah Abbas decided to transfer his capital there in 1597–8. It is a measure of the extent to which he transformed the city and its fortunes that during his reign the population is estimated to have risen to 200,000.[1] Over the next half century that figure would treble, making Isfahan one of the largest cities in the world – on a par with Istanbul, Paris or London.

It is often said that Isfahan is Shah Abbas. The city had some fine buildings before him and his Safavid successors added more. But his large-scale, planned development, carried through over many years, changed the whole appearance of the city, which has borne his imprint ever since. His aim was to convey an image of Safavid power and magnificence. Isfahan was to be as splendid as Istanbul, the capital of the Sunni Ottoman Empire that had never ceased to threaten Shi'i Iran. In this he succeeded, in the view of travellers who saw Abbas's Isfahan in all its glory. The epithet attached to Istanbul of 'the city of the world's desire' was matched by the saying that became current during Shah Abbas's reign that Isfahan was 'half the world' (*Isfahan, nesfe-e jahan*).

The city Abbas inherited was a typical medieval Muslim city of narrow, winding streets surrounded by an earthen wall and a fosse. He began working on its redevelopment very soon after he came to the throne. His first idea was to carry out a programme of repair and reconstruction within the existing city and focusing on the main market area. It was only when he ran into opposition from influential local figures, who feared he wanted to lay his hands on their businesses, that he switched the focus to the southern edge of the city,[2] which throws an interesting light on the effective limitations of the absolute power the shah wielded in theory. To have ridden roughshod over such opposition would have risked provoking disturbances, perhaps involving the Shi'i clergy he was so anxious to have on his side.

Abbas had already had some work done there on a large area known as 'The Garden of the Map of the World' (*Bagh-e Naqsh-e Jahan*), where there was a small royal palace overlooking a polo field. All he had intended to do at first was to create an impressive arena for sports and entertainments, such as the fireworks displays he so enjoyed. To this end, he had turned the polo field into a great enclosed square, 500 yards long and 160 yards wide, surrounded by a wall decorated with paintings.[3] But he now decided to create a new commercial centre in and around this square. The perimeter wall was refashioned to provide for two arcaded storeys with shops below and living accommodation above, all of which was rented out. A new Imperial Market was built off the north end of the square, and joined to the existing bazaars behind the square, which were rebuilt.

The small palace was in the middle of the west side of the square. Abbas had it enlarged and heightened, and painted in blue and gold. At some stage it came to be known as the Ali Qapu or 'lofty gate', just like the Sublime Porte or gate of the palace in Istanbul which became a synonym for the Ottoman government. Cannons captured from the Portuguese at Hormuz and from the Ottomans at Baghdad were displayed in front of it.

Abbas also built two magnificent new mosques on the south and east sides of the square and an imposing gateway to the Imperial Market on the north side. These three buildings were rich with colourful glazed tilework and relieved the otherwise perfect symmetry of the arcading around the square. Finally, Abbas had the square bordered on all four sides with a black marble water-channel, a paved walkway and a line of plane trees. As well as providing shade, the plane trees were believed to have a special health-giving quality that prevented the plague. The surface of the square was covered with fine sand from the Zayandeh River (the 'life-giving' river).

The smaller of the two mosques, on the east side of the square, was begun in 1603 and named after Shah Abbas's father-in-law, Sheikh Lutfallah, who was a famous Shi'i preacher. It was intended as a private mosque for the royal household. The much grander Royal Mosque on the south side, on the other hand, was a very public affirmation of Abbas's role as the guardian of Shi'ism. It was built several years later, when he again found his plans opposed - this time by very humble people who either lived or earned their living on the site. One account tells of an old man who refused to leave his house despite offers of gold and fine garments, another of an old woman determined to keep her melon stall. Again there was no question of using force. At the very least, that would have seriously damaged Abbas's reputation for justice, which he clearly took seriously. It would also have been quite contrary to what he regarded as one of his fundamental responsibilities, which was to protect the weak against the oppression of the strong. Instead, it was tact and ingenuity which eventually persuaded them to move. The mosque that was finally built was breathtaking in its scale, its design and its brilliant decoration of multi-coloured tilework.

The senior Shi'i cleric, Sheikh Bahai, a man of wide learning and many skills, who was a close companion of Shah Abbas, helped to draw up the plans for the Royal Mosque, while the construction work was supervised by the chief eunuch, Muhibb Ali Beg, whose name is on an inscription at the entrance to the mosque. The Shi'i cleric and the *ghulam* were representative of the two institutions which more than any other upheld the Safavid state under Abbas. Prominent *ghulams* were responsible for much of the construction work that was carried out all over Iran during his reign.[4]

The Royal Square was greatly admired by Europeans who visited Isfahan during the reign of Shah Abbas, and has never ceased to impress. Thomas Herbert wrote that it 'is without doubt as spacious, as pleasant and aromatic a market as any in the universe'[5] and Pietro Della Valle conceded that it outshone the Piazza Navona in his native Rome. During the day much of the square was occupied by the tents and stalls of tradesmen, who paid a weekly rental. Shah Abbas decreed that everyday necessities should be sold there, rather than luxury goods. There were also entertainers - storytellers, actors, puppeteers, tumblers, wrestlers and so forth - who sought to attract a crowd and collect money for their act. Anyone who felt hungry could buy cooked food or slices of melon, while cups of water were handed out free by water-carriers paid for by private individuals as an act of charity. In the rooms at the north end of the square, by the entrance to the Imperial Market, there were coffee-houses where men could relax over a cup of coffee and a water-pipe.

At dusk, the tradesmen packed up their goods in chests or tied them up in bundles and left them. They were perfectly safe because the captain of the watch and his guards patrolled the square at night, and he was answerable for anything that was stolen. After dark, the Royal Square was entirely given over to entertainers and prostitutes. The prostitutes sat around in tents, where they could be viewed, and would generally take their client to an upper room in the square which they had rented. Sunset and sunrise were heralded by the blast of trumpets and the beating of kettledrums by royal musicians positioned on balconies on either side of the entrance to the Imperial Market.

A wide area in front of the palace was always kept free, and the whole square was cleared periodically for sports and entertainments. Polo was often played and two marble columns at either end of the square were the goalposts. There was also a tall pillar in the middle of the square on the top of which a golden cup would be placed for contests of the famous 'Parthian shot'. Riders had to try to hit it with an arrow while galloping past at full tilt and shooting backwards over the croup of the horse. The prize was a golden quiver full of arrows. The Turkoman 'nobility of the sword' and very often the shah himself took part in these sports. The entertainments included combats between bulls, rams, lions and elephants, gladiatorial contests, wrestling matches and performances by rope-dancers and jugglers. At night, on festive occasions, there were fireworks displays and illuminations, when the whole square would be lit up by 50,000 lamps.

The entrance to the commercial world of Isfahan was through the great portal at the north end of the Royal Square. This led into the large domed hall of the *qaysariya* or Imperial Market, built by Shah Abbas to rival the old market area to the north-east and as a powerful symbol of his commitment to promoting trade and commerce. In line with Abbas's wishes, more luxurious and expensive goods were sold here. The shops were rented out to jewellers, goldsmiths, sellers of rich brocades and money-changers – the last of whom were all Indians. On the jewellers' benches were displayed rubies, emeralds, pearls and turquoises. Here too was the Isfahan mint, where Thomas Herbert, accompanying the English embassy in 1628, saw 'one day silver coined, gold the second, and next day brass'.

But he was relieved to find that not far away were the cooks' shops, 'to feed the helpful belly, after the busy eye and painful feet have sufficiently laboured'.[6]

The rest of the Imperial Market was laid out like other bazaars with each trade or craft grouped together on a particular lane, except that the lanes of the Imperial Market were more spacious. They were eight or nine feet wide and had high vaulted brick roofs with holes in the middle at intervals to let in light and air. The East India Company surgeon John Fryer, who visited Isfahan in 1677, wrote that the markets in London were but 'Snaps of Buildings' compared to these 'Lofty-Ceiled and Stately-Erected Buzzars.'[7]

The bazaar was the centre of public life. Besides shops, it contained caravanserais, public baths, coffee-houses, mosques and colleges. The caravanserais were inns for merchants and travellers. They usually consisted of two storeys of arcaded rooms built around a spacious courtyard and provided accommodation, warehousing facilities and stabling for horses and pack animals. The Carmelite friars reported that these new caravanserais built by Abbas were very large and 'constructed with royal magnificence and grandeur.'[8]

Within the bazaar area around the Royal Square, Shah Abbas also built a hospital and provided an adjoining caravanserai to support it financially. The hospital was a two-storey building around a garden with eighty small rooms. There was a doctor, an apothecary, a mulla, a cook, a porter and a sweeper. During the morning, the doctor sat at the gate of the hospital giving advice and making out prescriptions free of charge.[9]

Beyond the southern walls of the city, Abbas laid out spacious new suburbs with broad, tree-lined avenues. The centrepiece of this development was the great avenue known as the Chahar Bagh, or Four Gardens, which Sheikh Bahai also helped to design. It is said to have got its name from the four vineyards which originally covered the area. The Chahar Bagh, with its shady trees, terraces and fountains, was intended as a promenade, a place where people could take the air and enjoy themselves. It was not originally designed as a thoroughfare, although it eventually became one.

The avenue began at one of the gates of the city, the Imperial Gate, which was close to the royal palace. From there it extended in a straight line for about a mile and a half, crossing the Zayandeh River and continuing to the foot of the mountains to the south, where Shah Abbas created the largest of his parks, the Hazar Jarib. The Chahar Bagh was more than fifty yards wide, and for just under half its length, as far as the river, it consisted of gently descending terraces. A marble water-channel ran down the middle, and at each terrace the water cascaded down into square or octagonal marble basins, in which fountains played. There was a broad, raised stone surface on either side of the water-channel on which people could walk or put out carpets to sit on. Shading this on either side was a row of plane trees, followed by an open space for people on horseback, another row of plane trees, a paved walkway, and a perimeter wall. Abbas is said to have taken such pleasure in laying out the Chahar Bagh that he could not bear for a tree to be planted without him being there – and under each tree he is said to have placed a gold and silver coin.

The mud-brick walls along the Chahar Bagh were of an unusual latticework through which could be seen the gardens and pavilions that lined the avenue. From the Imperial Gate to the river these belonged to the shah, while on the other side they were owned by grandees, Shah Abbas having more or less ordered his nobles and senior court officials to build residences there. All adhered to a general plan laid down by Abbas, although they differed in points of detail. The royal gardens bore such names as the Octagon Garden, the Mulberry Garden, the Vineyard, the Garden of the Ass, the Garden of the Dervishes and the Garden of the Nightingale. They were open to the public, who were free to take away some of the fruit in return for a small gratuity to the gardener. Chardin says each garden had two pavilions. One, built over the entrance gate, was small and open at the front and on the sides, 'so that the coming and going in the avenue could be seen more easily'.[10] The other was set back and much larger. It had a main reception room that was open on all sides, with other rooms and cabinets at angles to it. All the pavilions were painted and gilded, 'presenting the most striking and agreeable sight'.

The northern section of the Chahar Bagh from the Imperial Gate to the river presented an animated scene at almost all hours of the day. Some of the pavilions were used as coffee-houses, and tents and stalls were set up in the avenue where all sorts of things were sold. People would spread out carpets by the fountains and sit and drink coffee, smoke tobacco and exchange news. When night fell, the avenue was lit up with torches and candles.

It was a diverting scene, and even more so when some magnificent foreign embassy made its way up the avenue into the city. Shah Abbas had a two-storey pavilion built at the top of the avenue, so that his wives and concubines could watch the spectacle through latticed windows. The pavilion was connected by a special corridor to the royal palace and the harem a short distance away. From 1609 the Chahar Bagh and its adjoining gardens were set aside every Wednesday until nightfall for the exclusive use of the women of the royal harem. The area was closed off and all the men who normally worked there were replaced by female relatives.

To the west of the Chahar Bagh, on this northern side of the river, was the new suburb of Abbasabad, where Shah Abbas settled refugees from Tabriz who had been uprooted by the fighting between Safavid and Ottoman forces in 1610. He built 500 houses to accommodate them and had the suburb laid out with broad, straight avenues, similar to the Chahar Bagh, with a water-channel in the middle and trees on either side. He encouraged people of rank and means to build houses there and it quickly became a fashionable place to live. Fifty years after its foundation, the number of houses had grown to 2,000.

The Chahar Bagh crosses the river at the Bridge of Thirty-Three Arches. This is also known as the Allahvirdi Khan Bridge, after Shah Abbas's famous general who oversaw its construction, and as the Julfa Bridge, because it led to the quarter of New Julfa. One of the chroniclers of the reign of Shah Abbas, Mirza Beg Junabadi, wrote that 'so long as the wheeling stars of the sky above circle this world, the like of this bridge will never come before their gaze'.[11] Many today would share the opinion of Lord Curzon, who saw it in 1889 and had no hesitation in calling it 'the stateliest bridge in the world'.[12] It is nearly a quarter of a mile long. The upper part is built of brick and has a covered arcade pierced with arches for pedestrians on either side. This opens up at intervals into larger chambers which in Abbas's day were adorned with what Lord Curzon calls 'not too proper pictures'. At either end of the bridge are round stone towers with staircases leading down to a vaulted passageway underneath. This leads through the broad arches cut into the stone piers and over stepping-stones placed on the river-bed in between them. Della Valle, who saw the bridge not long after it was completed in 1602, found its architecture 'most strange', but delighted in 'the promenades under the bridge, level with the water, on stepping-stones specially placed there, where in summer, the shade, the cool, and the murmuring of the waters must be absolutely delightful'.[13]

On the south side of the river the Chahar Bagh continued for another mile and a half to the royal park, known as Hazar Jarib or The Thousand Jarib Park. A *jarib* was a highly variable measurement of land and the figure of a thousand is probably not meant to be exact, but simply to indicate that it was a very big park.[14] The largest and most impressive of the royal parks, it was laid out by Shah Abbas in 1596 in the first phase of work on the Chahar Bagh. It consisted of a series of huge terraces and at least five pavilions on the lower slopes of a mountain called *Takht-e Rustam* (the

'Throne of Rustam,' the hero of Iranian legend). It was planted with several thousand plane trees, and innumerable fruit trees and vines which Shah Abbas had brought from many different places. The garden, which was irrigated by an underground channel from the river, was traversed by alleys and streams, and there were stone-lined basins of water of different shapes and sizes, many with little pipes around the edge throwing jets of water up into the air. It was tended by four gardeners and forty assistants. For a nominal payment anyone could go in and eat the fruit, but they were not allowed to take any of it away.

On the south bank of the river and immediately to the west of the Chahar Bagh was the suburb of Julfa, specially built by Abbas for the Armenians he had deported from their homeland. Like Abbasabad, it had a modern layout of broad, tree-lined avenues with water-channels running down them. The well-built houses, some of them palatial, reflected the prosperity of the Armenian community, which played such a prominent role in trade and commerce. Although Julfa had a bazaar and a caravanserai, many Armenians went into the city centre to carry on their business. Armenian shopkeepers and artisans had their businesses alongside their Muslim counterparts and were spread all over the central market area. The merchants, however, had a caravanserai of their own called the Julfa caravanserai, which was near the Ali Qapu palace.

The Spanish ambassador, Figueroa, says the Armenians brought all the rich ornaments of their churches with them when they left Julfa in Armenia.[15] A cathedral was built immediately after the first deportees arrived, in 1606, and was enlarged fifty years later, by which time there were plenty of rich merchants ready to make generous donations. By the end of the Safavid period there were about thirty churches, together with a monastery and a convent. A Muslim governor (darugha) and a vizier appointed by the shah were responsible for the overall administration of Julfa. But the assessment and collection of taxes was in the hands of an Armenian mayor or kalantar, who was chosen by the Julfans themselves and represented their interests with the Safavid authorities.

The Zoroastrian community – those Iranians who had remained faithful to the religion of pre-Islamic Iran – also lived south of the river. Their presence in Isfahan was increased by Shah Abbas, who brought in large numbers from the towns of Yazd and Kerman to work as labourers. They were known by the disparaging term of Gebr, which meant a pagan or infidel, and originally inhabited a suburb called Gebrabad on the river to the east of Julfa. They were generally poor, doing menial work as fullers, weavers, carpet-makers, grooms and gardeners, or as hired labourers on farms around Isfahan. Like the Armenians, they had a degree of self-government, but they suffered discrimination and persecution. After the death of Shah Abbas they began to return to their original homes, so that in Chardin's day only 300 families were left.

To the north of Shah Abbas's airy and spacious 'new city' – the Royal Square and the southern suburbs – was the old inner city. The heart of it was the square of Harun-e Velayat, near the Saljuq Friday Mosque, where Abbas had originally planned his redevelopment. It was dominated by the citadel on the northern wall, which was a massive fortress with accommodation for a garrison of several hundred soldiers. The dungeon of the citadel housed the royal treasury.

The narrow streets of the inner city were intersected by bazaars and crowded with people and animals during the day. There were unpleasant sights and smells – refuse, blood from slaughtered animals and even the odd carcass. There were also the cess-pits at the side of the street, down a hole below the wall of each house. These were emptied daily by peasants from nearby villages. After they had sold their fruit and vegetables, they loaded their asses with the contents of the cess-pits, which they used as fertiliser. Chardin, however, says that either because of this regular cleaning or the dryness of the air, the cess-pits did not stink as they might have been expected to.[16]

The streets were unpaved and in summer the slightest wind was liable to raise a blinding cloud of dust. To prevent this, people sprinkled water in front of their houses morning and evening, and in the Royal Square this was done three times a day. In winter, when the snow melted or it rained, the streets became a sea of mud. There were drains which carried some of the water into underground channels running down the middle of the street, but these were liable suddenly to cave in and cause a passing rider to be pitched from his horse.

In the inner city, splendour and sleaze, the sacred and the profane, coexisted side by side. Old Isfahan families, courtiers, government officials, wealthy merchants and prominent Shi'i divines continued to maintain fine residences here, despite the attractions of the more salubrious suburbs. The area was full of mosques, shrines and colleges. But cheek by jowl with these palaces and pious establishments were louche coffee-houses, opium and cannabis dens, and brothels.

There was also a potential for violence in the inner city, which was divided between two rival factions known as the Nimatis and the Haidaris, after two Sufi orders.[17] The Nimatis controlled the eastern wards of the city, the Haidaris those in the western half. Fights would often break out, particularly during festivals and emotive religious ceremonies, such as the mourning ceremonies for the martyrdom of the Imam Husain. Several hundred youths from the two factions would attack each other with clubs and stones, and invariably a number would be killed and many more injured by the time the authorities intervened to separate them. Conflicts between the same two factions were a feature of other towns and cities. Shah Abbas and his successors are said to have encouraged the rivalry because it divided the bazaar, whose shopkeepers and artisans might otherwise have made trouble for the government.

The English and Dutch East India companies, and the Roman Catholic missions of the Carmelites and Augustinians, all had establishments in the inner city, not far from the royal palace.[18] They were given properties that had been confiscated from disgraced officials. The Carmelite convent was the former palace of Abbas's artillery commander, who was a violently jealous man. He suspected his neighbours of trying to look into his harem when they came out onto their terraces to take the air, and stationed eunuchs in his garden with orders to shoot at them. As a result, twenty people were killed. When the shah heard of this he had the commander and his entire household executed and his property confiscated. Abbas gave the English East India Company a magnificent residence which he had confiscated from the head of the town criers' guild. It consisted of three richly decorated buildings and a fine garden with beautiful pools of water.

The ancient Jewish community of Isfahan had their quarter in the inner city, where there was a Street of the Jews and three small synagogues. This was a large and flourishing community at the beginning of the seventeenth century, but was subsequently much reduced in size and impoverished by successive waves of persecution. Many of the Jews were traders and craftsmen with their shops in the bazaar. Some were bankers and money-lenders – though this business was increasingly taken over by the Indians – and some were engaged in wine-making. There was also a tradition of Jewish scholarship.

Two popular establishments in Isfahan attracted particular attention from European visitors. One was the *hammam* or public bath, which was an essential amenity of any Muslim city, because of the need under Islamic law for ritual purification through washing. Shi'i law lays down twenty-eight instances where a total ablution is required before prayers can be said. But Iranians also went to the *hammam* for relaxation and for health reasons.

''Tis accounted a catholicon against most diseases, especially colds, catarrhs, phlegm, ache, agues, lues venera, and what not,' writes Herbert.[19]

The *hammams* in Isfahan were built of stone with vaulted ceilings and round windows of thick, coloured glass in the domes to let in the light. There were rooms of varying temperatures for sweating in, others where customers would have a bath and be vigorously scrubbed and massaged by an attendant, and a large room with a cistern of cold water in the middle where they left their clothes and where they would get together socially. All the floors were marble. In the morning, after the water had been heated, one of the attendants would let the neighbourhood know that the *hammam* was open for business by blowing a trumpet or horn. Men could then use the *hammam* until 2 p.m., after which it was reserved for women, and a linen cloth was hung on the door to warn men off. Charges were modest.

The other establishment, which was relatively new, was the coffee-house. These were scattered through the bazaars and wherever there was a busy concourse of people. The first coffee-houses probably appeared during the reign of Shah Tahmasp, but it was under Shah Abbas that they became an established part of everyday life.[20] The typical coffee-house consisted of a spacious vaulted room, with a pool of water in the middle. There were raised platforms around the sides, which were covered with carpets and cushions and on which customers could sit in comfort. Herbert describes the coffee as being 'black or somewhat bitter (or rather relished like burnt crusts), more wholesome than toothsome'.[21] It was served in small ceramic cups. Besides drinking coffee, customers smoked tobacco through water-pipes provided by the proprietor and played chess, backgammon and other games. To attract custom, the coffee-house owners encouraged recitals by poets and storytellers, who were sometimes seated for the occasion on high chairs in the middle of the room and who made a collection afterwards.

The coffee-houses were open from as early as seven in the morning, but the busiest time was in the evening when glass lamps were suspended in a circle from the ceiling. They were frequented by a broad cross-section of the better-off and better-educated members of society, including merchants, court officials, government ministers, and even the shah himself. But the real habitués were writers, artists and intellectuals who met there to discuss everything under the sun, including the actions of the government. Shah Abbas tried to counteract this by sending Shi'i clerics, or mullas, into the coffee-houses to preach edifying sermons. This only added to the general hubbub.

A number of coffee-houses employed good-looking Circassian and Georgian boys to attract customers. The boys, who were aged between ten and sixteen, dressed lasciviously, wore make-up and had long, curling locks of hair. They performed erotic dances and recited obscene stories to arouse the libido of the customers, who could then go off with them. These 'sodomy shops', as Chardin called them,[22] were closed down by Shah Abbas II in 1656.

Abbas enjoyed the coffee-houses, but he detested the growing habit of smoking and from time to time he imposed a ban on the trade in tobacco. One such ban was in force when Sir Dodmore Cotton's embassy was in Iran in 1628. Herbert reports that just before the embassy reached Qazvin a caravan of forty camels laden with tobacco from India arrived in the city, apparently in ignorance of the ban. Abbas ordered that the drivers of the caravan have their ears cropped and their noses snipped, and that the tobacco be placed in a pit and burnt. The 'black vapour' this gave off, writes Herbert, 'gave the citizens gratis for two whole days and nights an unpleasing incense'.[23]

Abbas greatly increased the presence of Shi'i clerics in Isfahan. He built new schools and colleges, which were run and staffed by clerics, although the curriculum was a broad one. Most children went to a primary school, called a *maktab*, from the age of six, and if Chardin is to be believed the lessons were a noisy and confusing affair. At the same moment, 'one is reciting the alphabet, one is spelling, another is reading Persian, another Arabic; one is translating from one language into another, one is repeating some verses, another some prose; one studies grammar, another syntax: but each is reading aloud, the teacher making them shout with all their force'.[24] After the *maktab* came the college or *madrasa*, where the students began by studying theology, philosophy and mathematics. But Chardin says they then moved on to astrology and medicine, 'which are the two professions in which they can make the most money'. The revenues from pious endowments financed the schools and colleges and even provided the *madrasa* students with a daily allowance to spend as they wished.

The houses in Isfahan were mostly built of sun-dried mud-brick and rarely exceeded a single storey. All that could be seen from the street was a mud-brick wall with an entrance gate, but no windows. The typical house of a moderately well-off family faced onto a courtyard and had a wide central portico, with a pool of water in the middle for religious ablutions. There were two rooms on either side of the portico and a large reception room behind. The house of a wealthier person would have porticoes like this on all four sides of a central reception room, with more rooms on either side of the porticoes, and marble basins of water in all the principal rooms. Much of Isfahan was supplied with water from the river through underground channels, although many houses also had their own wells. All the houses had gardens, except those of the poor, which were cramped and dark and had no courtyard.

An official called the *mirab*, or 'water amir', was responsible for distributing the water of the Zayandeh River to irrigate the surrounding agricultural land, water the parks and gardens and fill the pools in the palaces and private houses. Water has always been a scarce commodity in much of Iran. It was at a premium in Isfahan, despite the river, because of the rapidly expanding population and the many parks, gardens, ornamental pools, fountains and water-courses. The general population used the river water for washing and in particular for their ritual ablutions before saying their prayers. For drinking water they relied mainly on wells, springs and underground channels from the mountains. Each quarter of the city received water from the river on a specified day and a special water tax was levied on gardens according to their size. Tavernier described the office of *mirab* of Isfahan as the most profitable in the kingdom because of the 'sweeteners' people felt obliged to give him to maintain his goodwill, or in some cases to secure more than their fair share of water.

The rapid growth of the population put a strain on the city's water resources and Abbas turned to a bold scheme for increasing the water supply which Shah Tahmasp had attempted to carry out without success. The plan was to divert water into Isfahan's Zayandeh River from a tributary of the Karun, which also rises in the Zagros Mountains but flows in a south-westerly direction into the Shatt-al-Arab and the Persian Gulf. It was a massive undertaking, as a channel had to be cut through the mountain that separated the two rivers, while the water level on the tributary of the Karun had to be raised by building a dam. Skilled masons and engineers, among them Sheikh Bahai, together with a large number of labourers, were engaged on the project for many years.[25] However, the physical difficulties continued to defy them and the project was eventually abandoned by Abbas's successor, Shah Safi I.

Isfahan was the seat of the central government, but of course it also had a government of its own. The highest-ranking official was the *darugha*, who was mainly responsible for maintaining law and order. It was his men who patrolled the bazaar at night, led by the captain of the watch who bore the colourful title of 'king of the night'. Tradesmen and artisans paid the *darugha* a fee to protect their shops and he was entitled to a substantial share of the value of any stolen goods that were recovered; if they were not, compensation had to be paid. From the reign of Shah Abbas, the office of *darugha* was reserved for a Georgian prince who had converted to Islam.

The general administration was in the hands of a vizier, whose main task was to ensure that as much revenue as possible flowed into the royal coffers. He had to see that the rents and taxes were collected, that the land around Isfahan was well cultivated, and that shops and houses belonging to the Crown were kept in a good state of repair. He was assisted by a financial secretary or *mustowfi*. An official called the *kalantar* acted as the link between the government and the people and had the difficult task of trying to represent the interests of both. He dealt with the craft guilds of the bazaars and was responsible for assessing and collecting their taxes. He also appointed the heads of the various wards into which the city was divided, after they had been chosen by the inhabitants. Another official called the *muhtasib* was charged with the seemingly unrelated tasks of enforcing price controls and the prohibitions of the Sharia on drinking wine, gambling, prostitution and so forth – all of which were widely disregarded.

Under Abbas, Isfahan became a very cosmopolitan city – with a resident population of Turkomans, Georgians, Armenians, Circassians, Indians, Chinese and a small but growing number of Europeans, in addition to the native Persian-speakers, the Tajiks, who were in the majority. Shah Abbas brought in some 300 Chinese potters to work in the royal workshops and teach the art of porcelain-making. The Indians were present in very large numbers, mainly as merchants and money-changers. The Europeans were there as merchants, Roman Catholic missionaries, artists and craftsmen and even a few as soldiers, usually with expertise in artillery. Then there were other merchants who were constantly coming and going from the Arab world, Turkey, Russia, Central Asia, India and places even further afield. The Spanish ambassador, Figueroa, said that the people of Isfahan were 'very open in their dealings with foreigners, because of having to deal every day with people of several other nations.'[26]

This was despite the bad behaviour of some of the Europeans. The Carmelite, Father Paul Simon, reported that some of the Italians who came to Isfahan 'have caused no small scandal, and committed many follies, such as to get drunk and when drunk to dash about the main square (Maidan) at a gallop, striking this and that Persian, and killing one or other of them, of which the city of Isfahan made complaint to the king – all the same the king did not wish them to be condemned [to death] because they were Franks, although he is very severe with his own people, even when they be governors and nobles of the realm.'[27] *Plus ça change* . . .

Isfahan's period of glory came to an end with its capture by the invading Afghans in 1722. In the decades that followed, it was frequently fought over and ceased forever to be the capital of Iran. But although much damage was done during this period, many of the elegant Safavid palaces and pavilions survived until the late nineteenth century, when they were sadly pulled down by the Qajar ruler, Nasir ud-Din Shah, and his eldest son, the Zill-e Sultan, who was governor of Isfahan.[28] It was a tragic loss for Iran's cultural heritage.

Chapter 18

The Merchant King

Shah Abbas was acutely aware that a strong and productive economy, in which trade and commerce could thrive, was essential if he were to realise his ambitions for his country. The revenue of the state depended on it and without adequate revenue little could be achieved.

Economic activity was already at a low ebb at the end of the reign of Shah Tahmasp and since then it had suffered a further sharp decline as a result of civil war, foreign invasion and general insecurity. The Ottomans and Uzbeks between them had occupied some of Iran's richest revenue-bearing areas, including major centres of silk production. The funds available to the Crown were so reduced that Abbas's father, Sultan Muhammad Shah, had to ask the merchants for credit when supplying him with garments and cloth for his court, which they were most reluctant to agree to.[1] Sultan Muhammad Shah made the situation worse by giving in to pressure from the Qizilbash for lavish hand-outs which rapidly emptied the treasury.

A priority was to recover the occupied territories, which Shah Abbas succeeded in doing by 1607. He also took other steps from early in his reign to bring some order into the state finances and to revive the economy. These included a survey of the revenues and expenditure of each province, the introduction of a new silver coinage, and the re-establishment of security on the trade and pilgrim routes.[2] This last measure was so successful that Iran became famous for the safety of its roads. The armed guards or *rahdars* who were stationed along the roads charged merchants and travellers a modest toll for protecting them from thieves and robbers. Any traveller or merchant who had goods stolen was entitled to be reimbursed in full by the local governor, if they were not recovered within four months and ten days.[3] The Italian traveller Pietro Della Valle (1586–1652) was much impressed by an encounter with one of these road guards: 'He examined our baggage, but in the most obliging manner possible, not opening our trunks or packages, and was satisfied with a small tax, which was his due, amounting to four *abbassis* . . . For this small tribute he not only let us pass, but moreover sent a man forward to escort us part of the way, and direct us on our road.'[4]

Abbas also greatly improved the economic infrastructure by laying down new roads, building numerous hostelries, known as caravanserais, for merchants and travellers, and renovating the urban bazaars or markets and building new ones, notably in his new capital of Isfahan. Abbas set an example in this, which was dutifully followed by his chief officials. Apart from the usual pious foundations, extensive infrastructure work was carried out by Abbas's senior *ghulams*, notably the provincial governors Allahvirdi Khan and his son Imam Quli Khan in Fars and Ganj Ali Khan in Kerman.

The caravanserais were built in the towns and along the main trade and pilgrim routes.[5] They were rectangular, two-storeyed buildings around a central courtyard with a tank of water in the middle. They provided free accommodation for travellers or merchants and their servants as well as space or stabling for their animals. Most were plain and functional, with little ornamentation. Pietro Della Valle admired the new caravanserais in Isfahan and said that Abbas seemed to put 'all his zeal and talent for building into them'. But he confesses that when travelling, 'desirous of comfort and neatness, I always avoided them, lodging when possible in private houses, in which I was more at my ease, for a trifle of extra expense'.

Abbas's most famous roads are the ones already mentioned which he built in the Caspian region to serve his new palace complexes and towns at Ashraf and Farahabad – one extending along the entire length of the Caspian littoral, and the other running from Farahabad across the Alburz Mountains to just south of Tehran. Extensive sections of the road across the marshy Caspian plain were paved or at least had sloping banks of sand and gravel on either side and brick-lined water-channels to prevent them getting waterlogged during the severe rainy season. Abbas also built some paved causeways elsewhere, like the one the English embassy rode on in 1628 across a section of the Great Salt Desert. Abbas had ordered its construction during his pilgrimage on foot to Mashhad in 1601.

Abbas was actively engaged in trade in his own right. Indeed, Pietro Della Valle called him 'the greatest merchant in his kingdom'. He employed so-called 'royal merchants' to travel abroad and sell goods, mainly silk, on his behalf, and sometimes to buy particular items for him. Royal merchants accompanying a mission to Russia in 1594 carried some 450 lb of silk and bought weapons and sable fur for the shah.[6] The use of these merchants was noted by Thomas Herbert:

> He [Abbas] hath many factors abroad, whom he dispatches through the universe; some of which return in three, in five some, few pass seven years without giving an account to his commissioners: if they return empty they are rarely sent abroad again, for he is a strict auditor; but when they return full freight and to his liking, he rewards them considerably; further gratifying them with a woman out of his haram, a horse, a sword, a mandil or the like.

The ceremonial reception in Venice of one of these merchants, Fathi Beg, in 1603 is depicted in a great painting in the Sale delle Quattro Porte in the Doge's Palace.

The close interest which Abbas took in everything concerned with trade is well illustrated by an incident that was witnessed by the Spanish ambassador, Don Garcia de Silva y Figueroa. He relates that he was walking with Abbas one evening in the Royal Square in Isfahan, when the shah stopped to talk to five or six merchants from Bukhara and Samarqand. He says he learnt later that, among other things, Abbas 'asked them about the particularities of the journeys the caravans make every year from Balkh, Bukhara and Samarqand to Cambalu in Cathay [northern China], and how long it took them to go there and return'.[7]

Abbas also took measures to promote agriculture in which the overwhelming majority of the population was employed and which accounted for by far the largest share of the tax revenue, although much of this was paid in kind. He forcibly resettled large numbers of Georgians and Armenians in various parts of the countryside in order to populate and develop new areas, and also to take advantage of their particular skills. Della Valle writes that Abbas employed those he resettled in Mazandaran 'in breaking up the untilled lands, and thus introduced in the province culture unknown before, and arts and manufactures to which it was erst a stranger'. He says Abbas encouraged the Armenians to use their experience in cultivating the vine and rearing sheep, and the Georgians their experience in the production of silk – to which end Abbas had large numbers of mulberry trees planted around Farahabad.[8]

Government revenue grew as a result of these measures to promote trade and agriculture. More money also flowed into the government coffers from the provinces which Abbas had taken under direct government control and from the lands he recovered from the Uzbeks and the Ottomans. All this helped to provide the considerable resources needed to pay for his frequent campaigns, his greatly enlarged standing army, his court and his ambitious building programmes.

Nonetheless, Abbas was frequently short of ready money and in 1623, during his Baghdad campaign, he was forced to pay his troops with specially made leather coins which he later redeemed for copper coins.[9] His great problem was the shortage of gold and silver, which were not present naturally in Iran and which were needed for the coinage, to cover the trade deficit with India, and for such things as the gold dishes used at court banquets. Apart from silk, Iran had little to offer in return for the bullion it needed. Much of Abbas's cash revenue came not so much from what could be sold abroad as from the customs charges and transit dues he was able to levy on goods passing through the country, thanks to Iran's location on the crossroads between Asia and the Far East on the one side and the Middle East and Europe on the other. The French traveller Jean de Thévenot likened the country to a caravanserai 'that serves for passage to the money that goes out of *Europe* and *Turkey* to the *Indies*; and to the Stuffs and Spices that come from the *Indies*, into *Turkey* and *Europe*, whereof it makes some small profit in the passage'.[10]

Abbas tried in various ways to prevent bullion from leaving the country and to find new export opportunities. He promoted the manufacture in the royal workshops of carpets that were exported to Europe through the European trading companies. He also cleverly cashed in on the European demand for Chinese porcelain by bringing in 300 Chinese potters to pass on their skills, with the result that before long royal workshops in a number of cities were producing a very creditable imitation of Chinese porcelain. Indeed, it was so hard to tell the difference that the Dutch East India Company sold it as the genuine article. To prevent gold and silver coin leaving the country, Shah Abbas encouraged his Shi'i subjects to make pilgrimages to the shrine of Imam Riza in Mashhad rather than to Mecca or to the Shi'i shrines in Iraq, where they would be enriching the hostile Ottomans. In an attempt to cut the large import of Indian textiles, he encouraged the cultivation and use of Iranian cotton, wearing clothes of local cotton himself to set an example. He also explored the possibility of cultivating indigo, which was another Indian import used as for dyeing textiles. Then, in 1618, he banned the export of gold and silver altogether. A number of Indian merchants were executed for violating the ban. Despite this, it seems that the ban was not very effective and it was quietly forgotten after Abbas's death.

The one valuable item which Iran possessed and which could bring in silver in sufficient quantity was raw silk, which was produced by peasant farmers in the north and north-west of the country. It was as important to the government of seventeenth-century Iran as oil is today. The main export market was Europe, where there was such a demand for silk that, according to a merchant of the English Levant Company, as soon as the caravans arrived in Aleppo, the merchants were ready to pull the silk off the camels' backs and to buy without even opening the bales.[11]

To begin with, it was mainly Muslim merchants, Turkish and Iranian, who brought the silk overland to the Levantine marts of Bursa and Aleppo, where it was bought by European merchants, among whom were the English merchants of the Levant Company. During the latter part of the sixteenth century, however, Christian merchants from Julfa in Armenia became increasingly important as the middlemen in this overland trade, and before long they had houses not only in Bursa and Aleppo, but also in Europe itself, in Venice, Livorno, Marseilles and Amsterdam. The ability and success of the Julfa Armenians led Shah Abbas to resettle them in his new capital of Isfahan and to lend them money to maintain their dominant role in the overland silk trade. Abbas also gave them privileges not otherwise enjoyed by a Christian minority, such as the privilege of dressing as richly as the Iranians and of having gold and silver bridles on their horses.[12] Some of these Armenian merchant families of Isfahan became immensely wealthy and have been compared to the great merchant dynasties of Europe, like the Fuggers.[13] The preference given to the Armenians in the overland silk trade was understandably resented by Iranian Muslim merchants, but when the matter was raised with Abbas his blunt reply was that the Armenians were more competent. A large share of the silver which the Armenians brought back to Iran from their trading operations went directly into the royal coffers through taxes and the operations of the mints which turned the imported silver into local coin. This was so important to the shah in helping him to pay cash salaries to his soldiers and officials, that in 1621 Abbas immediately halted a persecution of the Armenian community in Isfahan after receiving news that this had caused an Armenian trading caravan on its way to the Levant to turn back.

The arrival on the scene of the English East India Company in 1616 and of its Dutch counterpart in 1623 was welcomed by Abbas for the opportunities it offered to diversify the export channels for silk and to obtain payments in cash. He granted both companies favourable conditions in which to trade, freeing them from customs duties and inland tolls and even granting them extra-territorial rights. Their factories or trading stations were declared inviolate and their employees, even if they were Iranians, were not to be subject to Iranian jurisdiction should they be suspected of involvement in a criminal matter. This was not dissimilar to the extra-territorial rights extended to European countries in the nineteenth century under the so-called 'capitulations', which caused so much resentment.

By making it a condition of trading in Iran, Abbas persuaded the English East India Company to give him the help he needed with ships and cannons to oust the Portuguese from Hormuz and to develop in its place his newly named port of Bandar Abbas on the mainland. For the first time in centuries Iran had a thriving Gulf port under its control. The customs receipts of Bandar Abbas soon became an important source of revenue for the shah. However, they were a bone of contention with the English East India Company, which was meant to receive half of them for the help it gave over Hormuz but never received anything like as much.

The strong interest of the two European companies in purchasing Iranian silk freed Abbas from complete dependence on exporting the silk through Ottoman territory to the Levant. But his talk of depriving the Ottomans of the overland transit dues was never likely to be more than that, because he had no wish to abandon his Armenian merchants, who were continuing to bring so much valuable silver into the country. Nor could the European companies really afford to take all of Iran's silk exports.

The arrival of the English East India Company is likely to have been a factor in Abbas's decision three years later, in 1619, to impose what is generally described as a royal monopoly on the purchase of raw silk from the farmers who produced it. In fact, it was not a real monopoly, because merchants were still permitted to buy raw silk directly from the farmers, only now they had to pay a substantial tax for the privilege of doing this. The tax was set at two levels, the higher rate being charged if the silk was for export.[14] Not surprisingly, this was very unpopular with both the silk farmers and the silk merchants, especially the Armenians who, as exporters, had to pay the higher rate.

The silk which the shah's officials had bought that year under the new monopoly was put up to auction by the royal factor, Muhibb Ali Beg, who invited the English East India Company and the Armenians to enter a bid. The Armenians put in the higher bid, so all the silk went to them. It seems, however, that the silk had already been set aside for them, besides which

214

they had the advantage over the English of being able to buy it on credit.[15] But the auction served the purpose of obtaining the best possible price for the shah's silk. Although the auction was not repeated, Abbas was able, through his factor, to continue to exploit the competition for Iranian silk, a competition that increased with the arrival of the Dutch East India Comany.

The royal factor, Muhibb Ali Beg, drove a hard bargain in negotiating the sale of silk to the European companies, compelling them to pay more than the market price. The agreements allowed the companies to pay for most of the silk they took with their own goods – cloth and tin in the case of the English, and in the case of the Dutch spices, in particular pepper, from south-east Asia. Abbas turned these imports into cash by selling them on to merchants and shopkeepers, forcing them, if necessary, to buy at a good price. But the English still had to pay in silver for a quarter of the value of the silk they bought and the Dutch for a third. Because of restrictions on the export of bullion from England, the Dutch were better able to meet this requirement. As there was also more demand in Iran for the Dutch spices, they became the principal European trading partners and remained so throughout the Safavid period.

The silk monopoly achieved its aim of giving Abbas an increased cash revenue, with both the Armenians and the European trading companies paying more for their silk than they would have done otherwise. But the monopoly began to cause unrest in the silk-producing province of Gilan towards the end of Abbas's reign and was so unpopular with the Armenian merchants as well as with the silk farmers that it was abolished immediately after Abbas's death by his successor, Shah Safi I.

Thomas Herbert describes a more disreputable method adopted by Abbas to make money for himself by interfering in the normal conduct of trade:

> ... from Hindustan, Tartary, and Arabia every year move towards Persia many caravans that import merchandise of several sorts (as China-ware, satins, silks, stones, drugs, tulipants [i.e.turbans], etc.), of whose approach he has early notice, and sometimes for reason of State prohibits his subjects to trade with them as contraband; whereupon none dare traffic, but by that artifice bringing them to his own price; or else his factors meet them upon entering his dominions with a report that the passage is not only long but dangerous, or that the late dearth makes the country incapable to buy – by such devices so startling them that, rather than run their risk, or incur his displeasure, they oft-times condescend to a reasonable mart, sometimes receiving money for goods, or by exchange

for what the Persian Emperor can best spare; to his own subjects and others his merchants then dispersing those new merchandises at good rates; and, having coin or bullion, to prevent its pilgrimage into other regions moulds it into plate of large assize, too heavy to go far – work, poor in show but not in value.

A report by staff of the English East India Company tells a similar story.

Despite such chicanery, the internal peace and good government which Abbas established, together with the measures he took to strengthen the economy, inaugurated a long period of relative prosperity. His improvement of the economic infrastructure, his establishment of security on the roads and the encouragement he gave to the experienced Armenian merchants, all contributed to a great expansion of trade. Forty years after his death, there were more than 1,800 caravanserais in Isfahan.[16] But there were also portents of difficulties that would arise in the future, long after the Safavids had gone, in the arrival of the English and Dutch East India companies. They represented a new and dynamic form of capitalist enterprise, eager for new markets, which was alien to Iran and would one day pose a serious challenge to its economy.

Chapter 19

Shah Abbas and the Arts

Abbas had a keen interest in the arts and a good understanding of them. This was only to be expected given his upbringing at a cultured provincial court and in a city, Herat, with a glorious artistic heritage. The Timurid achievement that was so visible in Herat made a strong impression on him, with the result that both politically and artistically he tended to hark back to it. On the political level, he sought to strengthen the secular legitimacy of the Safavid dynasty by associating it with Tamerlane. The story that Tamerlane had visited one of the early Safavid sheikhs was played up and expanded by contemporary chroniclers, notably Abbas's official chronicler, Iskandar Beg Munshi. On the artistic level, he showed a predilection for Timurid forms both in painting and in architecture, although it is just as likely that this was as much a political statement as an aesthetic one. Politics and art were always closely intertwined with Abbas and never more so than in his greatest artistic legacy of Isfahan, which is both a superb artistic achievement and an expression of his vision of a powerful, centralised state.

As in every other field, Abbas inherited a ravaged artistic environment. During the chaotic reign of his father, Muhammad Khodabanda, court patronage had virtually dried up, the royal library where the arts of the book were cultivated had to all intents and purposes ceased to function, and painters, calligraphers, poets and other artists had either retreated to provincial courts or emigrated to the rich pastures of Moghul India. Even in good times during the Safavid period, like the reign of Shah Abbas, Iranian artists and poets emigrated to India, where Persian was the language of the Muslim courts and where they could expect to find generous patronage and a relaxed political climate.

One of the first things Abbas did on coming to power was to revive the royal library and to put an accomplished and experienced artist in charge of it. The new chief librarian or *kitabdar* (literally 'keeper of books') was Sadiqi Beg, a distinguished painter who had helped to illustrate major manuscripts in the royal library for Shah Tahmasp and Shah Ismail II. Sadiqi Beg was unusual in coming from an aristocratic Qizilbash family with no artistic connections, whereas artists normally came from Tajik families with a tradition of working in this field. He had fought in the civil war alongside fellow Qizilbash tribesmen and is thought to have joined Abbas before he marched on the capital, Qazvin, with the king-maker, Murshid Quli Khan. Abbas immediately commissioned an illustrated manuscript of the *Shahnamah* or 'Book of Kings', the Iranian national epic composed by the poet Firdausi between 980 and 1010 CE, which had long been the work most favoured by rulers of Iran for richly illustrated manuscripts. Sadiqi Beg assembled an outstanding team of painters, calligraphers, gilders and bookbinders, some of whom had worked in the royal library in the past and others who were new, among them a young man in his early twenties known as Aqa Riza, who gave new life to Iranian painting.

The work that resulted introduced new elements into the Safavid style of painting, which was originally a blend of the elegant and balanced Timurid style of eastern Iran with the more exuberant Turkoman style of western Iran. Only sixteen illustrated folios of this *Shahnamah* have survived. A stylistic analysis has shown that four are by Aqa Riza and that most of the rest, including work by Sadiqi Beg himself, show the influence of the young artist's trademark characteristics of energy, psychological depth, rich and subtle use of colour and naturalistic line.

However, a number of illustrated manuscripts which Abbas commissioned later closely copy the Timurid style to which he was so attached. The most important work of this kind is another *Shahnamah*, produced this time in Isfahan in 1614. Its forty-four miniatures have been described as 'detailed restatements of Timurid painting' and the whole work as having a 'dazzling surface but little sense of vital strength beneath it'.[1]

Abbas in fact commissioned few illustrated manuscripts, preferring to ask his artists instead to produce single-page paintings or drawings. His main interest was in portraits of people from a wide range of backgrounds and occupations, from courtiers to dervishes. It has been suggested that this reflected that appreciation of men as individuals which Abbas showed by his forays into Isfahan to meet people and find out what was on their minds.[2]

These single-page works were produced by the artists not just for the shah, but for anyone who could afford to commission or buy them. This gave much greater importance to the artists, who increasingly signed their work. Wealthy connoisseurs eagerly bought paintings, drawings and fine samples of calligraphy by known and admired artists and assembled them in albums, called *muraqqas*. There were dealers in the Isfahan bazaar who specialised in such works of art and art lovers as far afield as India who were ready to pay large sums for them. But artistic work became heavily concentrated in Isfahan, which outstripped all other cities in wealth and population and where the rich patrons and buyers of art were to be found. Provincial capitals ceased to be important centres of art, as they had been in the past. So while the market for works of art broadened, the previous variety of provincial styles gave way to a dominant 'Isfahan' or national style. The political centralisation brought about by Abbas was thus paralleled by an artistic centralisation.

This 'Isfahan' style was largely shaped by Aqa Riza, who was highly esteemed by Shah Abbas. In 1603 the artist changed his name to Riza Abbasi to underline his association with the monarch. Shortly after that, however, he gave up court life altogether for several years and threw himself into the teeming 'low-life' of Isfahan, much to the horror of those who knew him. Among other things he took up wrestling. In his work during this period, he depicted many of the people he met who were barely eking out an existence, unlike the elegant dandies and fops whom he had often portrayed in his earlier works. Around 1610, however, he returned to the royal library, where he continued to work until his death in 1635 at the age of about seventy. Iskandar Beg Munshi says he was 'the marvel of the age in the art of painting and unequalled in portraying single features', but noted disapprovingly that there was 'a strain of independence in his character'.

Abbas would sometimes requisition artists whom he discovered working for some grandee. In 1593 he made the Qizilbash amir Farhad Khan Qaramanlu, whom he was shortly to appoint as his commander-in chief, surrender his highly talented calligrapher, Ali Riza Tabrizi. Ali Riza was put in charge of the calligraphers of the royal library and before long was calling himself Ali Riza Abbasi. He quickly won the shah's affection as well as his admiration and in 1596–7 Abbas dismissed Sadiqi Beg from his post of chief librarian and appointed Ali Riza in his place.

Sadiqi Beg was a person of many talents – he was a poet and writer as well as a painter – but he was not an easy person to work with. Iskandar Beg Munshi praises his skill as an artist, saying that 'with a brush as fine as a hair he painted thousands of marvellous portraits', but attributes his fall from favour to his 'surly, unpleasant character' and the way 'he always behaved towards his friends and associates with a discourtesy that went beyond bounds'. Abbas softened his dismissal by allowing him to keep both his title of chief librarian and his salary. The following year, however, Sadiqi Beg attempted to recover his office with an attack on Ali Riza's competence in carrying out an important commission. He made a formal complaint to the shah that Ali Riza was being dilatory in preparing a magnificent album containing the choicest samples of painting and calligraphy. Although Abbas was engaged in the vital task of driving the Uzbeks out of Khurasan, he summoned Ali Riza and his entire staff to his camp in Khurasan to answer the charge. That is a measure of the importance he attached to artistic matters. As it turned out, Ali Riza was quickly able to complete the work to the shah's satisfaction. Sadiqi mounted no further challenge to Ali Riza. He continued to work as a court artist, while also devoting much of his time to writing, until his death in 1610. But there was a scandal later when it was discovered that the Moghul ambassador Khan Alam, during his visit to Isfahan in 1618, had bought a fine Timurid painting which Sadiqi Beg had stolen from the royal library and sold to an Isfahan dealer. In the end Abbas decided not to ask for the return of the picture but to give it as a gift to the Moghul emperor, Jahangir.[3]

Of all the artists and calligraphers, Ali Riza was the one Abbas was most attached to. When he was working at night, Abbas would sometimes sit down beside him and hold a candle while he wrote. He was regarded as the supreme master of *nastaliq*, a curvilinear and sloping script which was used for fine manuscripts and for the calligraphic specimens that were collected in albums.[4] Abbas had the highest opinion of his work and charged him with the task of writing the inscriptions for his two great mosques on the Royal Square in Isfahan – the Royal Mosque and the Sheikh Lutfallah Mosque – as well as for the tomb of Imam Riza in Mashhad. He used *nastaliq* for the latter, but for the inscriptions on the tile mosaic of the Isfahan mosques he used another bolder script, known as *thuluth*, which was commonly used on buildings and is larger in size, with tall straight lines and rounded endings. In these lengthy inscriptions the shah's name as patron is always immediately over the entrance, so that 'anyone entering the building was literally under the ruler's sway'.[5] It is for these inscriptions, which bear his signature, that Ali Riza Abbasi is best known today.

But Ali Riza had a ruthless streak, which clearly played a part in the ousting of Sadiqi Beg. He showed it to fatal effect in his rivalry with another prominent calligrapher in the royal library, Mir Muhammad ibn Husain Qazvini, known as Mir Imad. The latter has been described as a high-minded, free-spirited type of person who paid little respect to rank. When Ali Riza was getting all the inscription commissions Mir Imad felt neglected and sent poems to the shah criticising him for this. The shah became angry and when Mir Imad persisted and his complaints became more outspoken the shah dismissed him. That still didn't silence Mir Imad. Ali Riza then fanned the shah's anger to the point where Abbas arranged for Mir Imad to be murdered. A band of ruffians fell on him one night and cut him to pieces. When the news was brought to Abbas he feigned sorrow and ordered his grandees to attend the obsequies. But Mir Imad's family fled.[6]

Abbas also employed one or two European artists. One was a Dutch artist by the name of Jan van Hasselt who accompanied the Italian traveller Pietro Della Valle to Iran in 1617, but then left him to enter the service of the shah. Abbas gave Van Hasselt the title of *ustad naqqash*, or 'master painter', and seems to have paid him a reasonably handsome salary.[7] We know from Thomas Herbert that he painted the room in the palace at Ashraf, where Abbas received the English embassy in 1629: 'The ceiling was garnished with gold, and pencill'd with Story in lively colours; all of which seemed to strive whether Art or nature to a judicious eye would be more acceptable. One John a Dutch-man (who had long served the King) celebrated his skill here to the admiration of the Persians and to his own advantage.'

The Spanish ambassador, Figueroa, also stayed in a small house in a royal garden between Isfahan and Kashan which he says was decorated with beautiful paintings by a Greek artist called Jules. He says Jules, who was trained in Italy, was employed by Abbas and had died recently in Qazvin. The paintings were in the Italian manner and depicted 'women, banquets, bottles of wine and dances of the country'.[8]

Through the presence of such artists and also through European pictures which began to be brought into the country, Iranian artists first began to become aware of European painting and to be influenced by it. That is one of the most important developments in Iranian painting during the Safavid period and it began under Shah Abbas.

The royal library where the painters and calligraphers worked was one of the royal workshops (*buyut-e saltanati*) which produced a huge range of goods for the court. They were overseen by the Supervisor of the Royal Workshops, the *nazir-e Buyutat*, who was also the Chief Steward of the Royal Household and one of the highest court officials. In Chardin's day, in the second half of the seventeenth century, there were approximately thirty-three workshops in Isfahan, some situated in the semi-public area of the palace precincts, others just outside. There were also royal workshops in other major cities. Each workshop employed on average as many as 150 people. In Chardin's day, in the 1660s and '70s, there were seventy-two painters working in the royal library, besides the calligraphers and other artist-craftsmen.[9] The conditions of employment were very attractive. The artists and craftsmen were well paid and every three years they were given either a wage rise or a present equal to one year's wages. They received free board, clothing and lodging, and could take cash equivalents if they preferred. If they fell ill, they received free treatment from one of the court physicians. The *nazir* carried out an annual review of the royal workshops in the summer, but instances of craftsmen or artists being sacked, like Sadiqi Beg, seem to have been very rare.

Hardly surprisingly, there were many applicants, but the standards were high and it was not easy to be taken on. An applicant had to show a sample of his work to the head of the relevant workshop, the *bashi*. If the *bashi* approved of it, he took the aspiring craftsman and his work to the *nazir*, who in most cases decided whether to employ him. But where the work was of a particularly artistic nature, as with painting and calligraphy, the sample was shown to the shah and it was he who had the final word.

Apart from the royal library, Abbas undoubtedly took a close interest in the workshops producing carpets, textiles and ceramics. Fine carpets were the essential furnishing of mosques, palaces and the houses of grandees and people of substance. But Abbas also promoted their export to Europe and sent them as gifts to European rulers. The outstanding carpet which first began to be produced early in his reign – probably with these purposes very much in mind – is known as the 'Polonaise' carpet. It was a silk knotted carpet brocaded with gold and silver which got its name from an incorrect attribution towards the end of the nineteenth century. Because it had the royal arms of Poland on it, it was thought to be of Polish origin. In fact it was one of a number of such carpets imported from Iran in 1602 by the Polish King Sigismund III (1587–1632) with the royal arms woven onto it. These 'Polonaise' carpets were made in the royal workshops in Isfahan and Kashan and proved so popular in Europe that some 230 examples survive in various collections today.

Carpet designs were no longer inspired by the work of miniaturists, as they had been earlier in the sixteenth century when they had included human figures. They were now entirely floral and were variations on a number of established patterns. On the other hand, luxury fabrics produced in the textile workshops often bore figural designs which imitated pictures by contemporary painters, notably Riza. This was the work of specialist textile designers. The most famous of these is Ghiyas ud-Din Ali-ye Naqshband, the word *naqshband* describing this skill of applying a design. Said to have been descended from the great Shirazi poet Saadi, he was born in Yazd where he became head of the Weavers' Guild and established such a reputation for his designed fabrics that his work was in great demand far beyond the borders of Iran. The Moghul historian Abu'l Fazl records that among the choice gifts Shah Abbas sent to the Emperor Akbar in 1598 were '300 pieces of brocade – all woven by the hands of noted weavers – and fifty masterpieces of Ghiyas Naqshband'.[10] Ghiyas became extremely wealthy and built himself a splendid residence in Yazd. He was also a poet and a principal figure at Abbas's court.

Just as Abbas had carpets made with an eye to export opportunities in Europe, so he did the same for ceramics by promoting the production of a blue-and-white porcelain similar to that made in China, which was so popular in Europe. Mention has already been made of the Chinese potters he brought in to teach the necessary techniques and of the very passable resemblance of the Iranian copy to the original. Much of this imitation Chinese porcelain was also sold in the domestic market, where it was much appreciated. Abbas himself was a keen collector of genuine Chinese porcelain and made a gift of more than 1,100 pieces to the Safavid shrine at Ardabil. It seems likely that he continued to collect afterwards and that choice pieces were displayed in the so-called 'Music Room' on the fifth floor of the Ali Qapu, in the variously shaped niches which were cut into the stucco on the walls and ceiling, many of them in the shape of flasks, bottles and jars.

But of all the arts, architecture was the one that benefited most from Abbas's patronage. Unlike his Safavid predecessors, who seem to have rather neglected architecture, Abbas had a passion for building, which extended right across the spectrum, from the grand and ornamental to the essentially utilitarian. Besides directly initiating new buildings himself, he put irresistible pressure on his officials and courtiers to follow his example, as in Isfahan where they were persuaded to build elegant garden palaces along his great new avenue of the Chahar Bagh. Political and economic motives played a large part in much of the building. Isfahan was intended to match the capitals of other great empires and to embody Abbas's vision of a powerful centralised state. The economic motive is equally apparent in the many utilitarian constructions, such as the port of Bandar Abbas on the Persian

Gulf, but above all in the large number of caravanserais that were built along the main trade routes.

The architectural form of the various buildings was not original, but echoed earlier Iranian models. The garden palaces, although not a conscious copy, nonetheless had precedents in ancient Iran. So too did one of the most characteristic features of palace buildings from Abbas onwards, which is the wooden flat-roofed verandah supported by columns, known as a *talar*. Many of the palace buildings that were set amid extensive gardens were delicate kiosks and pavilions, which were not built to last for any great length of time. Often the gardens themselves were the dominant feature. Inside the buildings there was much ornamentation in the form of frescoes, gilding and other paintwork, looking-glass veneer, niches and stalactite vaults made up of myriad small concave niches. There were also fountains of marble, jasper or porphyry, sometimes inlaid with precious stones. In the case of the Ali Qapu palace in Isfahan, the water was raised to an upper floor by hydraulic machines drawn by oxen.[11]

Similarly, the great Royal Square of Isfahan and its two mosques – the intimate Sheikh Lutfallah Mosque and the grandiose Royal Mosque – had their precedents in the Timurid architecture with which Abbas was so familiar from his early years in Herat and Mashhad.[12] The main difference lay in the much more extensive use of coloured tilework, to the point where it covered virtually the entire building. Nowadays, this is generally considered to be impressive when seen from a distance, but less so as one gets closer, and is sometimes labelled disparagingly 'façade architecture'. Part of the problem is that because Abbas was always in a hurry to see his buildings completed and because such vast surfaces had to be covered, an inferior kind of glazed tile was used. Previously, tiles had been painted with a single colour, fired at the temperature that was best for that colour, and then cut to fit into a real tile mosaic. But Abbas's builders used large, square tiles known as *haft-rangi* or 'seven colours', which could have two or more colours painted on them. That meant that they had to be fired at an average temperature which would do for all the colours, but was ideal for none of them. The result was, as one scholar has put it, that 'the deep, vibrant tones achieved in tile mosaic [gave] way to paler, even muddy, colours'.[13]

The construction of important buildings commissioned by Abbas was often supervised by senior *ghulams* like Muhibb Ali Beg Lala, who was the tutor of the *ghulams* and held the post of supervisor of the royal buildings in Isfahan. It was the job of the supervisor to assemble the craftsmen and the workmen and to provide whatever materials and equipment were

224

required. The buildings were designed by architects and, where necessary, by engineers as well, but both the supervisor of the works and the shah himself had an input into this. A decree (*farman*) of 1614 for the construction of a cathedral in the Armenian suburb of New Julfa in Isfahan requires that the design be drawn up jointly by Muhibb Ali Beg Lala, by the vizier of Isfahan and by the architects, and that the blueprints be sent to the shah for his approval, after which the work can begin.[14] In this, as in many other cases, the names of the architects are not recorded. Even where we do know their names from inscriptions on the buildings or from literary sources, we know nothing else about them. In this way they differed from the painters and calligraphers who threw off their earlier anonymity and became personages in their own right.

Thomas Herbert said of the Iranians that 'the women paint; the men love arms; all affect poetry'. Not only has poetry been the supreme literary achievement of Iran, but a love of poetry has traditionally been shared by all Iranians, regardless of their social background. It is typical that Sadiqi Beg the painter and Ghiyas al-Din the textile designer were both also poets, and that when the calligrapher Mir Imad wanted to express his discontent to the shah, he did so in the form of poems.

But no great poets were nurtured at the Safavid court – and the court of Shah Abbas is no exception. The best Iranian poets were to be found at the Moghul court in India where they developed a new poetic style known as the 'Indian style' (*sabk-e hindi*), which is characterised by a more colloquial language, a complex use of imagery and a tendency towards obscurity. Critics remain divided on its quality. Why so many poets chose to migrate to India also remains a much-debated question. But the generous patronage that was on offer at the wealthy Moghul court and the rather liberal intellectual climate that prevailed there must certainly have been important factors.

Iskandar Beg Munshi says that Abbas had a good understanding of poetry and sometimes composed verses himself. His favourite poets are said to have been Firdausi, who is famous for his great national epic the *Shahnamah* or 'Book of Kings', and Hafiz, who is the greatest lyric poet of Iran. Abbas is said to have always carried a volume of Hafiz with him. These choices are very conventional, but he obviously did have some poetic judgement. His principal court poet – and also his physician – was Sharafud-Din Hasan Shifai (d.1628), on whom he bestowed the official title of 'King of Poets' (*malik u-shuara*), equivalent to Poet Laureate. The great Czech scholar Jan Rypka, an acknowledged authority on Persian poetry, calls Shifai 'one of the best poets of the Safavid epoch'.[15] Iskandar Beg Munshi describes Shifai as 'a free-living, witty fellow' with 'a biting tongue' who 'delighted in sticking subtle barbs into people'. Despite his appreciation of Shifai, this was something that Abbas did not altogether approve of. He particularly disliked being satirised himself and is said to have imprisoned a number of poets on this account.[16] Equally, he was not immune to poetic flattery and had one poet who indulged in this weighed in gold, after which all the poets in the country are said to have deluged him with eulogies.[17]

With the exception of poetry, there can be no question that Abbas presided over a period of considerable artistic achievement. So many wonderful works of art from the paintings and drawings of Riza Abbasi to the great buildings of Isfahan are proof enough of that. It is a period that in some ways looks backwards, to Timurid models for instance, but which in other important ways is breaking new ground – in the assertion of the artist's individuality, in the opening up of art to a wider public of buyers and connoisseurs, in the first exposure of Iranian artists to European art and perhaps, above all, in Abbas's use of royal patronage, for better or worse, to serve political and economic ends rather than merely his own personal aesthetic.

Chapter 20

The Later Safavids

The Safavid dynasty continued to rule Iran for almost a hundred years after the death of Shah Abbas the Great. Historians used to regard this period as one of steady decline, taking their cue from Jean Chardin's famous comment that after the death of Shah Abbas, 'Persia ceased to prosper.'[1] But this view has been increasingly contested by historians, who have emphasised instead the stability and success of the Safavid state over at least a considerable part of this long period of time.[2] There remains a stronger case, in my view, for a weakening of the state under the last two rulers, Shah Sulaiman (1666-94) and Shah Sultan Husain (1694-1722). Almost to the end it continued to impress European visitors, including Chardin himself, whose detailed and often favourable account of the country persuaded Montesquieu to make two Iranians the amused observers of early eighteenth-century France in his satirical work 'Lettres Persanes'. Nonetheless, the reign of Shah Abbas the Great does clearly mark the apogee of Safavid power. Within ten years of his death, Baghdad was lost and by the middle of the century Iran had ceased to be the formidable military power it had been. All of Abbas's successors, with the exception of his namesake, Shah Abbas II, proved largely inadequate as rulers and what kept the whole show on the road so successfully for so long was the solid and relatively efficient bureaucracy he had established and a series of very able grand viziers. It also helped that there were no further civil wars, thanks to Abbas's reforms, and no serious external challenges until the Afghan invasion of 1722 which overthrew the Safavid state. The Afghans were not a great power like the Ottomans or the Uzbeks, and they owed their unexpected success less to their own military prowess than to the growing weakness of the Safavid state in the last few decades of its existence.

Paradoxically, some of this weakness sprang from the very reforms and practices Abbas had introduced in order to strengthen the state. The most damaging of these in the long run was the practice of immuring the royal princes in the harem. This prevented them from being a threat to the ruler. But it also meant that they came to the throne with no experience of government, trained only in indolence and self-gratification, and inclined to pay more attention to the eunuchs and the women they had grown up with than to their ministers. Shah Abbas II (1642–66) was an exception, because he came to the throne when he was only nine and was therefore too young for the life of the harem to have done lasting damage. It was all very well to have able grand viziers, but their efforts were often undermined by court cabals which succeeded in gaining the ear of a weak and capricious ruler.

Another reform which proved to have an adverse side over time was the weakening of the Qizilbash tribes. Abbas had reduced their importance in the army, but under his successors they became increasingly redundant.[3] As a result, the Safavid state lost a very effective fighting force and became dependent instead on a standing army which it lacked the financial means to maintain.

Abbas I's policy of imposing direct rule by the centre on provinces that had previously been administrative and military fiefs also proved to have its drawbacks. Chardin found that people regarded the viziers, or royal intendants as he called them, as 'insatiable leeches who suck their subjects dry to fill the royal treasury . . . and enrich themselves'.[4] He believed that the provinces fared better under a governor who held an administrative fief, because the latter tended to regard the province as his personal property and had an interest in its prosperity, which was not the case with the government viziers. Later in the seventeenth century, Uzbek attacks on Khurasan and Cossack plundering raids on the Caspian made it necessary to bring back some military fiefs that had been done away with.

The grandson whom Shah Abbas nominated as his successor on his deathbed, Prince Sam, had considerable support, but there were court factions which favoured two other candidates – Abbas's blinded youngest son, Prince Imam Quli, who claimed still to have some vision, and the son of one of his daughters. They were forestalled by supporters of Prince Sam who had him hurriedly crowned in Isfahan in a ceremony in which he took his father's name and ascended the throne as Shah Safi I. As a sign of the close association established by Abbas between the Safavid dynasty and the Shi'i establishment, the coronation ceremony was presided over for the first time by the most senior Shi'i cleric, the Sheikh ul-Islam of Isfahan. The place of dynastic legitimacy was highlighted as Safi was girded with the belt and sword of the dynasty's founder, Shah Ismail I.[5] The prayer mat of the Safavid Sufi sheikhs –'the rug of spiritual direction' – which had been used at previous coronations was again brought out, but for the last time. This symbol of the shah's Sufi heritage was banished from future coronation ceremonies, a move which reflected the Safavid dynasty's rejection of the Shi'i-Sufi blend of heterodoxy associated with the Qizilbash and its firm support for Twelver Shi'ism and its clerical representatives.

Shah Abbas's daughter, Zubaidah Begum, and her supporters refused to accept the *fait accompli* and Zubaidah Begum is alleged to have attempted to poison Shah Safi. It was this harem-based opposition to his rule that seems to have prompted Safi, in February 1632, to order the massacre of forty women of the harem and the killing or blinding of almost all the sons of Shah Abbas's daughters.[6] This ended any resort in the future to the Turco-Mongol tribal tradition which gave matrilineal descendants of the ruling family a claim to the throne and instead confined the succession to the Safavid male line. It also established the practice that was to be followed by the next two Safavid shahs, Shah Abbas II and Shah Sulaiman, of blinding all other Safavid princes on their accession.[7]

Shah Safi proved to be the most murderous ruler after Shah Ismail II. Besides the massacre of his own family, he also killed a number of high officials associated with his grandfather, including the commander-in-chief of the army, Zainal Khan, the grand vizier, Mirza Abu Taleb Ordubadi, and the governor general of Fars, Imam Quli Khan. The latter was executed together with his three sons on what was almost certainly an unjust charge of treason. When the executioners came for him, he is reported to have said simply, 'May the King's will be done'.

Before this, Safi had to put down a number of uprisings which broke out once the firm hand of Abbas was no longer there. The most serious was in Gilan and seems to have been caused by resentment over heavy taxation, the royal silk monopoly and the insensitive rule of the viziers appointed to govern the province. Several thousand people rallied around a man who claimed to belong to the former ruling dynasty of Gilan and who was crowned king with the title of Adil Shah, or 'the Just Shah', which has messianic overtones. The rebels captured and plundered the two principal towns of Rasht and Lahijan. They also broke open the warehouses where the royal stores of silk were kept and sold the contents. The rebel army was defeated in May 1629 and Adil Shah was sent as a prisoner to Isfahan, where he was executed. But the rebellion was not finally extinguished for another year. Shah Safi meanwhile ended the unpopular silk monopoly.

There was also an explicitly messianic uprising in Qazvin in July 1631, led by a militant Sufi known as Darvish Riza who declared himself to be 'the Mahdi of the Age'. The uprising was quickly crushed, but Darvish Riza succeeded in attracting the support of a number of senior Qizilbash, which reflected their discontent with Shah Abbas's reforms. For most of the rest of the century a form of 'popular' Sufism with messianic overtones was widespread, especially among the merchant, shopkeeper and artisan classes. Inevitably, it tended to gain more of a hearing in times of economic difficulty. This 'popular' Sufism, with its implicit threat to the established order, was vociferously attacked by prominent clerics. The Safavid court, however, attempted to keep in as far as possible with both sides and stay above the controversy.[8]

Shah Safi also faced renewed Uzbek attacks on Khurasan and a determined effort by the Ottomans to recover Baghdad, which they finally succeeded in doing in December 1638, despite fierce Iranian resistance. A peace treaty was signed the following spring known as the Treaty of Zuhab, under which Iran definitively ceded Baghdad and Mesopotamia to the Ottomans. This ended nearly a century and a half of bitter conflict and held for the rest of the Safavid period. Humiliating though the loss of this territory with the Shi'i shrines was, the establishment of peace with the Ottoman Empire gave a boost to trade, especially to the silk trade of the Armenian merchants with the Levant. The Persian Gulf became correspondingly less important as an export channel for Iranian silk.

Shortly before this, Safi lost Qandahar when his governor defected to the Moghuls. The governor had been summoned to Safi's court to answer accusations of financial impropriety and understandably interpreted this as a likely death sentence.

Shah Safi enjoyed hunting and heavy drinking. He was less interested in the business of government, which he preferred to leave to his grand vizier. For most of his reign this was a man of great ability by the name of Mirza Taqi, better known as Saru Taqi or Blond Taqi, on account of his fair hair. He had been appointed to high administrative positions in the northern provinces by Abbas, but in the middle of this career he had been castrated on the shah's orders for allegedly sodomising[9] a boy and then rehabilitated by Abbas when the accusation turned out to be false. Safi appointed him grand vizier in 1634, after executing the previous incumbent, Mirza Abu Taleb Ordubadi.

Saru Taqi remained grand vizier until 1645 and was the first of a succession of able grand viziers who made up for the incapacity of their royal masters. The challenge that faced all of them was to balance the books as the revenue fell short of what was needed to meet the cost of the administration, the standing army and, above all, the court. Saru Taqi extracted every last penny from the provincial governments, maximised the customs revenue, increased taxes, and drove a hard bargain with the English and Dutch East India companies, obliging them to buy silk above the market rate and to pay for more of it in coin. He also imposed direct rule on two more provinces – Fars and Lar – and waged a determined campaign against corruption.

Shah Safi had one undoubted success in the support he gave to a policy of reconciliation and reconstruction in the Christian principalities of eastern Georgia, which had been devastated by the brutal campaigns and deportations carried out by Shah Abbas I. The new policy was implemented by the Georgian prince, Khusraw Mirza, who was prefect (*darugha*) of Isfahan when Shah Abbas died and played an important part in securing Safi's accession. The shah rewarded him with the title of Rustam Khan and in 1632 he sent him to Tblisi as his viceroy (*vali*). Despite his advanced age of sixty-seven, Rustam Khan governed eastern Georgia with wisdom and energy for a quarter of a century, dying in 1658 at the age of ninety-two. He defeated those who still opposed Iranian rule and modelled his court and administration on Iranian lines, but at the same time set out to prove that Georgians could remain themselves and thrive as part of the Safavid realm. Although a Muslim convert himself, he saw to it that Christians and Muslims were treated absolutely equally and that Georgia's Christian identity was respected. He also persuaded Shah Safi to allow many of the Georgians deported by Shah Abbas to return to their homes. It was one of the happier periods in Georgia's often troubled history.[10]

Shah Safi shared his grandfather's tolerant attitude towards Christians and, like Abbas, he enjoyed attending Christian ceremonies. He corresponded with Pope Urban VIII, who in 1632 appointed the Carmelite Father John Thaddeus to be the first Bishop of Isfahan. Thaddeus's successor, Bishop Bernard Duval, bought a fine house in 1641 which he had refurbished as the episcopal residence and part of it turned into a church that functioned as the Roman Catholic cathedral. As Bishop Duval, a Frenchman, was a protégé of Cardinal Richelieu, the doors into the nave bore the cardinal's arms. The Carmelites were also able to build a larger church in Isfahan, with a campanile with two bells 'which were sounded day and night for the office'.[11] Such religious freedom was unheard of in Europe at that time and, it must be said, was not approved of by many Shi'i clerics.

Shah Safi fell ill of a fever and died on 12 May 1642, while on his way with an army to recover Qandahar. He was only thirty-one and had named none of his five sons as heir apparent. The campaign was abandoned and Saru Taqi moved swiftly to get the Council of State to proclaim the eldest son, Sultan Muhammad Mirza, as the new king, thereby ensuring an untroubled succession. The prince, who was not quite ten years old, took the throne name of his illustrious forebear when he was crowned in Qazvin later in the year as Shah Abbas II.

To begin with the grand vizier, Saru Taqi, acted effectively as regent for the young shah with the strong support of the deceased shah's mother. A Georgian concubine, she had become the influential matriarch of the harem after Shah Abbas I's aunt, Zainab Begum, was driven out of the harem in the events of 1632.

But Saru Taqi made many enemies through his insistence on financial rigour and his arrogant demeanour. In 1645, this sparked another palace bloodbath. Saru Taqi got on the wrong side of the *qurchi-bashi*, Jani Khan, and was murdered by him with the tacit support of the shah, who had grown tired of being treated as a cipher. But when Abbas learnt that Jani Khan and his fellow assassins were planning to abduct his grandmother from the harem and kill her too, after she expressed horror at what they had done, he had them killed in their turn by his *ghulams* and their mutilated bodies thrown into the Royal Square in Isfahan. He followed this up with a ruthless purge of all their associates. This was motivated by opportunism rather than any affection for his grandmother. He had her poisoned three years later, thereby freeing himself from any matriarchal interference from the harem, since his own mother had been stabbed to death by Shah Safi in a drunken frenzy.

Shah Abbas II replaced Saru Taqi with a cleric, Khalifeh Sultan, who had already held the post of grand vizier from 1624 to 1632. A son-in-law of Shah Abbas I, he was known for his unquestioning loyalty to the dynasty and for his piety. He sought to combat the moral laxity that had spread under Shah Safi, shutting down the coffee-houses where boys wearing make-up performed lascivious dances and attempting with less success to stamp out female prostitution. He also attached severe penalties to the sale of wine, but once again the Islamic prohibition was ignored by the court, where Shah Abbas II was soon drinking almost as heavily as his predecessor.

Khalifeh Sultan did little to resolve the government's financial problems and early in his viziership he was forced to concede a more generous trading contract to the Dutch after they blockaded Bandar Abbas and besieged the Iranian fort on the island of Qishm. The Dutch and English companies were now less interested in buying silk – the English bought none at all after 1642 – than in selling their own goods for gold and silver coin which they took out of the country, depleting Iran's always scarce supply. The shortage of these precious metals set in train a steady debasement of the coinage.

These problems were tackled more energetically by the man who replaced Khalifeh Sultan on his death in 1654, Muhammad Beg – an Armenian *ghulam* who had already been successful in a number of posts carrying financial responsibilities. Muhammad Beg continued Saru Taqi's policies of bringing more provinces under direct rule and reducing military expenditure. He had some success in enforcing a fresh ban on the export of gold and silver, but his search for new sources of wealth in mining and metallurgy proved fruitless. He was also quite unable to curb the extravagance of the court.

The more fanatical Shi'i clergy were always clamouring for a harsher line to be taken towards the religious minorities, and in 1656 Muhammad Beg and Shah Abbas gave in to this by instituting a severe persecution of the Jewish community. Violence or threats of violence and financial inducements were used to persuade them to convert to Islam. The persecution went on for a number of years, despite opposition from moderate Shi'i clerics and, in some places, from the local Muslim population. Even when it was eventually abandoned, Jews were compelled to give visible warning of their presence by wearing a piece of material sewn onto the front of their gown in a contrasting colour.

Some action was taken against the Armenian Christians as well, who were no longer allowed to live in Muslim quarters of Isfahan. But in general Shah Abbas II was well-disposed towards the Armenians and other Christians. He permitted six new Armenian churches, including a cathedral, to be built in the Julfa suburb of Isfahan between 1658 and 1666, which is evidence of the continuing prosperity of the Armenian merchant community.[12] He frequently attended Armenian church services and ceremonies, even if sometimes only to inspect an attractive Armenian girl he had heard of, with a view to taking her into his harem. He also gave permission for the Jesuits to establish a mission in Isfahan in 1653, making them the fourth Roman Catholic mission in the country after the Augustinians, the Carmelites and the Capuchins. He dismissed both the senior Shi'i cleric, the Sheikh ul-Islam of Isfahan, and the royal prayer-leader for preaching against Christians, and is even said to have threatened the former with impalement. Chardin says Abbas II regarded such clerics 'as either carried away by a false zeal which made them incapable of fair reasoning, or as interested parties who, under the specious pretext of religion, wanted to gain popularity with the masses and perhaps use that to form parties in the state and shake the government'.[13]

The shah himself came under attack at the end of his reign from a small group of clergy who denounced him as 'an impious wine-bibber'[14] and challenged his claim to be the legitimate representative of the Hidden Imam. Some said this role belonged by right to a *mujtahid*, others that it could be filled by a Safavid, but only by one who possessed the piety and religious knowledge required of a *mujtahid*. Much of the agitation was carried on by a certain Mulla Qasim from a hermitage in Isfahan. It was an indication of the apprehension felt by the authorities where the clergy were concerned, that they hesitated for six months before quietly arresting and killing him, and took no action against his followers. Nonetheless, the clerical leadership and the great majority of the Shi'i clergy remained firmly supportive of the Safavid monarchy.

Early in his reign, in 1649, when he was sixteen, Shah Abbas II enhanced his reputation by recovering Qandahar from the Moghuls after a two-month siege. It was to remain in Safavid hands until the fall of the dynasty. He also responded forcefully and successfully in 1653 to a Cossack attempt, apparently with Russian support, to encroach on Safavid territory in the Caucasus. But he was free of any threat from the Uzbeks until the end of his reign in 1665, when they descended on a whole series of towns in Khurasan and Mazandaran, leaving a trail of devastation behind them. He was preparing a major counterattack when he died in September 1666, probably of syphilis. He was the last strong Safavid ruler and has been compared in some ways to the first Abbas. Like him, he made a habit of meeting ordinary people and listening to their concerns. He also shared the passion for building of his forebear. Two of his creations – the Chehel Sutun Palace and the Khwaju Bridge – remain among the most beautiful monuments of Isfahan. He was an enthusiastic patron of artists, a talented artist himself, and a great lover of music.

Up to this point the Safavid state remained generally well-ordered, peaceful and prosperous. The situation began to deteriorate, however, under Shah Abbas II's successor, Shah Sulaiman, who was chosen by the Council of State over his younger brother after some debate.[15] A good-looking if somewhat effeminate nineteen-year-old, whose mother was a Circassian slave, he was initially crowned in Isfahan with the throne name of Shah Safi II. But over the next eighteen months the country was afflicted by plague, earthquakes, poor harvests and more Uzbek raids. In addition, the shah's health began to deteriorate through overindulgence in wine and women. It was eventually decided that this run of ill-fortune was due to an error on the part of the court astrologers in calculating an appropriate date for the coronation. So fresh calculations were made and the shah crowned again on 20 March 1668 in the Chehel Sutun Palace of Isfahan, with a new throne name of Shah Sulaiman to reinforce the sense of a new beginning.

But things did not improve. The coronation was barely over when Cossack rebels led by Stenka Razin began plundering towns on the Iranian Caspian coast from a flotilla of boats armed with cannons. In the course of this, they destroyed the beautiful palace of Shah Abbas I at Farahabad. An Iranian fleet was hastily assembled, but was annihilated by the Cossacks, as the Iranians had no experience of naval warfare. The Cossack menace was only finally removed when Stenka Razin was captured and executed by the Russians in 1671. But the Iranians also suffered further Uzbek attacks on Khurasan for much of the reign of Shah Sulaiman. The Uzbeks were egged on on sectarian grounds by the Ottomans and by the new Moghul emperor, Aurengzeb, who had abandoned the religious tolerance of his predecessors in favour of a narrow Sunni fanaticism.

Shah Sulaiman had all the defects of a harem upbringing of softness, indolence and self-indulgence. He was frequently drunk and had an insatiable lust for young women, sending out his eunuchs to search for pretty girls to add to his well-populated harem. That was where he spent much of his time. He left local forces to deal with the Cossacks and the Uzbeks as best they could and was the first Safavid shah never to go on a campaign. The pursuit of peace with his neighbours was the guiding principle of his foreign policy. He is quoted as saying that he preferred to ignore minor provocations rather than undertake a retaliatory campaign, the outcome of which was always uncertain.

Shah Sulaiman left the tedious business of government to his grand vizier, but undermined him by frequently taking advice from the principal women and eunuchs of the harem. For most of his reign his grand vizier was a Kurdish tribal chief, Sheikh Ali Khan Zangana, who had gained a reputation for administrative and military ability under Shah Abbas II. Like his predecessors, Sheikh Ali Khan worked hard but unavailingly to improve the Crown's finances. He was rigorous in securing the provincial revenues in full and on time, increased taxes and introduced new ones, including a tax on the Armenian churches. He also drove the hardest possible bargain with the English and Dutch East India companies. But he was quite unable to reduce the cost of the court, which had become much more grandiose than in the days of Shah Abbas I and where the ever-expanding harem was a growing burden.

Sheikh Ali Khan was a pious Muslim who was sometimes cruelly abused by his master for his refusal to drink wine at court assemblies. He was also sympathetic to the dogmatic and intolerant party among the Shi'i clergy which now began to gain the upper hand over the more liberal, Sufi-minded and philosophical clergy who had dominated the court since the reign of Shah Abbas I. He put pressure on the Armenian Christians and the Zoroastrians to convert and tried to gain a tighter control over eastern Georgia in order to pursue a similar policy there. It is more than likely, as has been suggested, that the religious minorities were made scapegoats at a time when natural disasters and a worsening economic climate were making life hard for ordinary people. The new Sheikh ul-Islam of Isfahan and therefore the country's senior religious figure, Muhammad Baqir Majlisi, called for the destruction of the idols of Isfahan's large Indian Hindu community, whose activities as financiers and money-changers made them obvious targets of resentment. All this, it is argued, was part of the struggle with 'popular' Sufism for the hearts and minds of the 'popular' classes.[16]

Shah Sulaiman died in 1694 at the age of forty-six, possibly as the result of a stroke after a heavy drinking bout. He left Iran in a far worse condition than he found it. All classes had suffered from heavy increases in taxation and Chardin observed a sharp decline in the wealth of country.[17] The coinage had been substantially debased, damaging trade and causing inflation. The army was starved of funds and neglected, and the famed security on the roads was now a thing of the past, with caravans being attacked even within sight of the capital.

The Council of State was again left to choose between two sons of the deceased ruler and opted for the eldest, Prince Husain, who had the overwhelming support of the harem. Crowned as Shah Sultan Husain, he was to preside over the overthrow of the Safavid kingdom. He was humane, pious and very weak-willed. He showed his humanity at the outset by refusing to have his younger brothers blinded. His piety was such that he quickly earned the nickname of 'Mulla' Husain. He was under the influence of the Sheikh ul-Islam of Isfahan, Muhammad Baqir Majlisi, who was a dogmatic, legalistic cleric and the author of a vast collection of Shi'i *hadith* or traditions of the Imams, known as the *Bihar ul-Anwar* ('the Spring of

Lights'). Shah Sultan Husain affirmed Majlisi's dominant position by giving him the new title of 'Head Mulla' (*mulla-bashi*). For his part, Majlisi gave strong support to the Safavid monarchy, declaring that 'one that does not obey the kings, has not in fact obeyed God'. It was a powerful affirmation of the throne-and-mosque alliance forged by Shah Abbas I, except that the mosque was now dictating events, something that Abbas would not have countenanced.

At Majlisi's request, Shah Sultan Husain issued a number of decrees. One of these banned the sale and consumption of wine but came to little as the shah was soon drinking like his predecessors. Another, however, expelling all Sufis from Isfahan was rigorously enforced. Majlisi was determined to purge Twelver Shi'ism of the Sufism that had crept into it through the influence of gnostic Shi'ism. In the following years Sufism was vigorously suppressed throughout Iran. Only the Safavid Sufi order survived within the precincts of the palace, but by now that was little more than a historical relic.

Majlisi was equally determined to root out the other component of gnostic Shi'ism, which was philosophy. He denounced its practitioners as 'followers of an infidel Greek', a reference to Aristotle, and succeeded in having it virtually eliminated from the syllabus of the religious colleges, the *madrasas*, which provided most of the higher education.

Majlisi's vision of Iran was of a unified society in which all members confessed his orthodox version of Twelver Shi'ism. In his eyes, that meant converting the religious minorities, by force if necessary. Previous attempts at conversion had been short-lived and focused on particular communities. Majlisi's approach, which had the full support of the shah, was more comprehensive, more determined and harsher. Sunni Muslims, Christians, Jews and Zoroastrians all suffered. But instead of absorbing the religious minorities into Shi'ism, this conversion drive merely alienated them and left Iran more divided than before.

Shah Sultan Husain's two principal preoccupations were the enjoyment of his harem and a passion for building – both of which placed a heavy burden on the finances of the state. He continued his father's unpopular practice of dispatching his eunuchs to find attractive young women. So many were added to the harem that an extra building had to be provided for them. The Carmelites estimated that the cost of the harem increased threefold under Shah Sultan Husain.[18] His building mania proved, if anything, even more ruinous. The project which absorbed him for most of his reign and consumed vast sums of money was the construction of a huge palace complex just outside Isfahan known, like Shah Abbas I's resort on the Caspian, as 'Farahabad'. Barely a trace of it remains today. The last of the significant grand viziers, Fath Ali Daghestani, struggled in vain like his predecessors to make up for this drain on the state finances. He halved the salaries paid to court officials and *ghulams*, imposed a special levy on the Muslim merchants and raised extra taxes from the religious minorities.

Shah Sultan Husain's preoccupation with his harem handed a further large measure of power to the eunuchs. They took over key court offices and had more influence on the shah than his ministers. But there was bitter rivalry between the black and white eunuchs and other members of the court attached themselves to one or other of the factions.[19] Provincial governors installed by one faction extorted all they could before they were ousted by the rival faction, forgetting other responsibilities like maintaining troops or ensuring security on the roads. Corruption grew unchecked and living conditions for the urban population deteriorated. In 1715 there were bread riots in Isfahan after a cabal of courtiers and *ghulams* cornered the wheat supply. Angry crowds denounced the shah and his ministers and threw stones at the palace.

None of the great powers on Iran's borders was in a position to take advantage of Iran's weakness. But there was a series of internal rebellions and tribal raids, as well as attacks in the Persian Gulf by Muscat Arabs, which exposed the weakened state of the army and the paralysis of power at the centre. Decisive and consistent action was rendered impossible by factionalism at the court and the shah's weakness and lethargy. The most serious of these challenges came from the Ghalzai Afghan tribesmen of Qandahar, who rebelled against the rapacious rule of the Safavid governor of the province. As Sunni Muslims, they had also been alienated by Majlisi's drive to convert the religious minorities. The shah's government, weak and divided, made one error after another and in the autumn of 1721 some 20,000 tribesmen under the Ghalzai chief Mir Mahmud set off from Qandahar, defeated a much larger Safavid army and laid siege to Isfahan. Eight months later the city was starved into surrender and a humiliated Shah Sultan Husain handed sovereignty over his people to the Afghan chief. It was the end of the Safavid kingdom, but the belief in the unique legitimacy of the Safavids as rulers of Iran took much longer to die. The warlords who fought for power in the turmoil that followed frequently used Safavid puppets as cover for their ambitions and no subsequent dynasty was to enjoy the same degree of support from the Iranian people as a whole.

Conclusion

So what in the end were Abbas's achievements, where did he fail and what was his legacy? He rescued Iran from the selfish dominance of the Qizilbash tribes whose rivalries were fatally weakening the country, created a strong central government with an effective bureaucracy, liberated those areas that had come under Ottoman and Uzbek occupation, greatly improved the economic infrastructure and promoted trade and agriculture. In doing this, he gave Iran an internal peace and prosperity that lasted for nearly a hundred years after his death. In the cultural field, he presided over a period of great artistic achievement, especially in architecture and painting. Some would say that Isfahan is his greatest legacy. He also consolidated a new Iranian national identity based on the twin pillars of pre-Islamic traditions and Shi'ism, reflected in the two great festivals of Noruz and Ashura. Abbas intentionally revived memories of Iran's ancient past by introducing the old Persian word *sipahsalar* for army commander in place of the Arabic term *amir al-umara*. It has also been pointed out that there was a greater use of the word 'Iran' during his reign. In the early Safavid period the country is usually referred to as 'the God-protected country' (*mamlekat-e mahrousa*), but under Abbas it is more frequently referred to as Iran and Abbas himself as the ruler of Iran (*farmanrava-ye Iran, shahryar-e Iran*).[1]

All these must be counted as important achievements. On the other hand, some of Abbas's reforms stored up problems for the future. The drawbacks of confining the royal princes to the harem, of governing provinces through centrally appointed viziers and of undermining the military capacity of the Qizilbash tribes as a component of the army – all these have already been mentioned as contributing over time to the weakening of the Safavid state and its eventual downfall. But Abbas also created a new dependence of the monarchy on a greatly strengthened Shi'i clergy for its legitimacy – a development which could be said to have led eventually to the overthrow of the monarchy in the Islamic revolution of 1978–9. It has also been noted that his promotion of Shi'i orthodoxy resulted in the greater seclusion of the women and sons of the ruling classes.[2] European visitors to the Safavid court in the sixteenth century often saw both of these, but by the end of Abbas's reign this was much less common. The practice of *quruq*, whereby men were not allowed so much as to catch a glimpse of the women of the royal harem on pain of death, seems to have been introduced at this time.

So great was the impression Abbas made on his countrymen that before long he became a legendary figure. The East India Company surgeon, John Fryer, who visited Iran fifty years later, found that he was idolised, 'his Name being invoked when any Commendable or Famous Action is performed; saying "Shaw Abas", or "Shabas", as we are wont to say, "Well done"'.[3] He was held in just as high esteem in the popular memory when Sir John Malcolm visited Iran as a British envoy in the early nineteenth century. 'The modern traveller', writes Malcolm, 'who inquires the name of the founder of any ancient building, receives the ready answer, "Shah Abbas the Great", not from an exact knowledge that he was the founder, but from the habit of considering him the author of every improvement.' Malcolm also relates a delightful story which was circulating in his day and which reflected the popular conviction that Abbas was no ordinary mortal:

> We are gravely told that on Abbas entering his kitchen at Ardabil, the lid of one of the pots which he approached raised itself twice, four inches each time, as if in respect to his royal person; and this wonder or miracle was attested not only by all the cooks, but by several officers of the court, who were in attendance on the king when it occurred.[4]

The reason for this profound attachment to the memory of Abbas is evident in Chardin's assessment of him, which it is fair to assume is based on his conversations with Iranians forty or so years after Abbas's death: 'He was a fair-minded prince whose only concern was to make his kingdom flourishing and his people happy. He found his empire usurped and in ruins and, for the most part, impoverished and devastated, but it would be hard to believe what his good government did everywhere.'[5]

Malcolm's comment that he was considered 'the author of every improvement' is also instructive. He was seen as a king who was not merely interested in power for its own sake, but for how it could be used for the good of the country as a whole. It is symbolically significant that in the field of construction he is at least as well known as a builder of things that were useful to his people, like caravanserais, roads and hospitals, as of palaces. Even his palaces were not grandiose or pompous affairs, and for the most part they did not exist in isolation from the urban amenities he provided alongside them. His secret forays into the bazaar to check on whether the butchers and the bakers were selling short weight showed his concern for ordinary people, as did his insistence that his soldiers pay a fair price for whatever they obtained from the peasantry and his refusal to remove by force people living or earning their livelihood on the ground where he wanted to build his Royal Mosque in Isfahan. Such instances reflect a genuine belief on Abbas's part that this is what it meant to be a king. They go far beyond any careful cultivation of an image, although there was certainly an element of that, particularly in his rather ostentatious demonstrations of religious piety and humility. He was in many ways the embodiment of the ruler as a strong father figure – accessible to his people, listening to their concerns, caring for their well-being, protecting them from enemies abroad and from injustice at home.

After the fall of the Safavids in 1722, Abbas's legendary status was enhanced by comparison with what followed. For most of the rest of the eighteenth century the lives of Iranians were blighted by chaos and war, oppression and extortion. The Qajar dynasty which ruled Iran from 1794 to 1925 brought peace and stability, but its governance was poor and corrupt and it was humiliated by the dominance and interference of the rival imperial powers of Russia and Britain. This made the reign of Shah Abbas appear like a lost Golden Age.

Interestingly, when the Qajars came to power, they deliberately sought to portray themselves as reviving the Safavid state, because they knew how much this resonated with the Iranian people. They cultivated the Shi'i clergy in an attempt to revive the throne-and-mosque alliance, set up an administration on the Safavid pattern and introduced Safavid court ceremonial. They also tried to restore the boundaries of the Safavid Empire and made repeated attempts to take back Herat from the Afghans, largely because of its symbolic importance as the former seat of the young Abbas and other Safavid princes. They were thwarted over Herat by the British and actually lost most of the former Safavid territory in the Caucasus to the Russians.

An amusing illustration of the Qajar attempt to emulate the Safavids is provided by Malcolm in his account of his diplomatic mission to the court of the second Qajar ruler, Fath Ali Shah, in 1800–1. He describes how shortly after his arrival in the Qajar capital of Tehran, the grand vizier sent a government official, known as a *mirza*, to instruct him on how he was to dress for the royal audience. The official 'produced a parcel; and after opening a number of envelopes, he showed several small pictures of ambassadors who had visited Persia two centuries ago. One, which was called the painting of the English representative, and believed to be Sir Anthony Sherley, was dressed in the full costume of the time of Queen Elizabeth. "This", said the Meerza, "is the pattern which it is hoped you will adopt, as His Majesty desires to follow in all points the usages of the Seffavean kings, since they well understood what was due to the dignity of the throne of Persia."' Malcolm had tactfully to explain that fashions had changed since then.[6]

In modern times, Shah Abbas has perhaps become less of a legendary figure in Iran. As a result of the increasing academic work that has been done on the whole Safavid period both in Iran and in the West, he is better understood as a historical figure with all his strengths and weaknesses, his failures as well as his successes. Nonetheless, he continues to exercise a hold on the public imagination, as is shown by the publication of at least two popular books on him by Iranian writers in recent years.[7] The achievements of the reign of Shah Abbas are an understandable source of national pride. The Shi'i Muslim clerics who have governed Iran since the Islamic revolution of 1978-9 have had to take account of this and have softened their original blanket hostility to the country's monarchs. In the early years of the revolution the Royal Square and the Royal Mosque in Isfahan – two of Abbas's greatest creations – were renamed the Square of the Imam and the Mosque of the Imam in honour of the leader of the revolution, Ayatollah Khomeini. But attempts by zealots to remove the frescoes from the Ali Qapu as un-Islamic were thankfully stopped and the frescoes are now being carefully restored. The clerical leadership has also given its support to international conferences and seminars on the Safavids. They in fact owe a debt to the Safavids who brought Shi'ism to Iran in the first place, and to Shah Abbas for the way in which he supported and promoted the Shi'i clergy. It was one of the greatest propaganda mistakes of the last shah, Muhammad Reza Pahlavi, to associate his monarchy with the Achaemenid kings of ancient Iran, most of whom were Zoroastrians and were long forgotten by the Iranians, rather than with Abbas and the strongly Shi'i monarchy of the Safavids, who meant so much more to them.

Notes

Introduction

1 Some might say that this honour belongs to the Medes, who were also an Iranian people. But their empire, which preceded the Achaemenid empire of Cyrus, was short-lived and much smaller.

2 To the best of my knowledge, there have only been two biographies of Shah Abbas in any European language and they have both been in French, one published in 1932 and the other, more recently, in 1998.

Chapter 1

1 Minorsky, V., *Persia in AD 1478–1490*, an abridged translation of Fazlullah G. Ruzbihan Khunji's *Tarikh-e Alamara-ye Amini*, Royal Asiatic Society Monographs, Vol. XXVI, 1957, p.63.

2 Sohrweide, Hanna, 'Der Sieg der Safawiden in Persien und seine Rückwirkungen auf die Shi'iten Anatoliens in 16 Jahrhundert', *Der Islam* (1965).

3 The caliphs were the successors to Muhammad, not in his prophetic function, but as leaders of the Islamic community. Sunnis recognise all the caliphs as legitimate, but the Shi'a only recognise the Fourth Caliph, Ali, because they believe that the rightful successors to the Prophet were the Imams, of whom Ali is the first.

4 Madelung, Wilfred, 'Al-Mahdi', *Encyclopaedia of Islam*. An eighth-century Shi'i hadith quotes the Prophet Muhammad as saying that a Man of his Family will come one day and 'will fill the world with justice', after it has been filled with injustice.

5 The first four caliphs, the 'rightly guided caliphs', were Abu Bakr, Omar, Uthman and Ali.

6 For an overview of the Safavid rise to power, see Aubin, Jean, 'L'Avènement des Safavides Reconsidéré', *Moyen Orient et Océan Indien*, 5 (1988); Glassen, Erika, 'Die frühen Safawiden nach Qazi Ahmad Qumi's Khulasat-at-Tawarikh' (Islamkundliche Untersuchungen 5, Freiburg, Klaus Schwarz, 1970).

7 This was the Bayandur clan of the Aq-qoyunlu, or White Sheep, a Turkoman tribal

confederation which ruled western Iran from 1468 until overthrown by Shah Ismail during the first decade of the sixteenth century.

8 Aubin, 'L'Avènement des Safavides Reconsidéré'.

9 Aubin, Jean, 'Chiffres de Population Urbaine en Iran Occidental autour de 1500', *Moyen Orient et Océan Indien* (1986).

10 Barbaro, Josafa and Contarini, Ambrogio, *Travels to Tana and Persia*, edited by Lord Stanley of Alderley (Hakluyt Society, 1873), pp.115, 206.

11 Families from the Afshar and the Qajar tribes ruled Persia after the Safavids. The Afshar dynasty came to power under the great conqueror Nadir Shah (1736-47), although the last of the Afsharids, his grandson Shah Rukh (1748-96), was confined to Khurasan. The Qajars ruled the whole country from 1796 to 1925.

12 The total population of Iran in Safavid times has been put at 'not more than nine million' (Floor, Willem, *The Economy of Safavid Persia*, Wiesbaden, 2000, p.2).

13 On Safavid provincial government, see Röhrborn, Klaus Michael, *Provinzen und Zentralgewalt Persiens im 16 und 17 Jahrhundert* (Berlin, 1966).

14 Floor, Willem, *Safavid Government Institutions* (California, 2001), p.159.

15 Aubin, Jean, 'Révolution chi'ite et conservatisme: Les Soufis de Lahejan, 1500-1514', *Études Safavides II, Moyen Orient et Océan Indien*, 1 (1984).

16 Savory, Roger, 'The Principal Offices of the Safavid State during the Reign of Isma'il I (907-30/1501-24)', *BSOAS*, XXIII (London, 1960).

17 *The Book of Duarte Barbosa: An Account of the Countries Bordering on the Indian Ocean and their Inhabitants*, written by Duarte Barbosa, and completed about AD 1518. Translated from the Portuguese by Mansel Longworth Dames, Vol. I (Hakluyt Society, 1918), p.84.

18 On Safavid Qizilbash in Anatolia, see Sohrweide, 'Der Sieg der Safawiden in Persien'.

19 On the First Safavid Civil War and the Uzbek challenge, see Dickson, Martin, *Shah Tahmasb and the Uzbeks: The Duel for Khurasan with Ubayd Khan, 930–946/1524–1540* (PhD thesis, Princeton University, 1958).

20 Membré, Michele, *Mission to the Lord Sophy of Persia (1539–1542)*, translated with an introduction and notes by A.H. Morton (SOAS, 1993), p.x.

21 The slaves of Safavid Persia had nothing in common with the later plantation slaves in the Americas. Essentially household or military slaves, they were not used as a large and anonymous labour force. They were generally far better treated and could expect to be appointed to responsible positions, some rising to high office. See Babaie, Sussan, Babayan, Kathryn, Baghdiantz-MacCabe, Ina and Farhad, Massumeh, *Slaves of the Shah: New Elites of Safavid Iran* (I.B.Tauris, London, 2004), pp.21-2.

22 Babaie et al., *Slaves of the Shah*, p.26.

23 Morgan, E. Delmar and Coote, C.H. (eds), *Early Voyages and Travels to Russia and Persia by Anthony Jenkinson and other Englishmen* (New York, 1963), pp.144-7.

24 Willan, T.S., *The Early History of the Russia Company 1553-1603* (Manchester, 1956).

25 On the role of al-Karaki and the Lebanese clerics under Shah Ismail I and Shah Tahmasp, see Abisaab, Rula Jurdi, *Converting Persia: Religion and Power in the Safavid Empire* (I.B.Tauris, London, 2004), pp.4-50.

26 Algar, Hamid, 'Nuktawiyya', *Encyclopaedia of Islam*; also Arjomand, Said Amir, *The Shadow of God and the Hidden Imam* (Chicago, 1984), pp.198-9.

27 Grey, Charles (ed.), *A Narrative of Italian Travels in Persia in the 15th and 16th centuries* (Hakluyt Society, 1873), p.215.

28 Grey, Charles (ed.), *A Narrative of Italian Travels in Persia*, p.225; Eskandar Beg Munshi,

Tarikh-e Alam-Ara-ye Abbasi, translated by Roger M. Savory (*The History of Shah Abbas the Great*), Boulder, CO, Vol. I, p.195.

Chapter 2

1 Gouvea, Anthoine Di (Antonio De Gouvea), *Relation des Grandes Guerres et Victoires Obtenues par Le Roy de Perse Chah Abbas contre Les Empereurs de Turquie Mahomet Et Achmet son Fils En Suite du Voyage de Quelques Religieux de l'Ordre des Hermites de S. Augustin envoyez en Perse par le Roy Catholique Dom Philippe Second Roy de Portugal* (Rouen, 1646), p.94.

2 Floor, Willem, *The Economy of Safavid Persia* (Wiesbaden, 2000), p.264.

3 To these were added, during the reign of Shah Abbas, his new capital of Isfahan and the resort of Farahabad with its palace complex which he built on the Caspian, in Mazandaran, and where he frequently spent the winter.

4 The argument was that a ruler's responsibility was to protect and defend the community. He was the head of the army. These tasks were thought to be impossible for a blind person to perform.

5 *TAAA*, trans. Savory, Vol. 2, p.1232.

6 Keyvani, Mehdi, *Artisans and Guild Life in the later Safavid period* (Klaus Schwarz Verlag, Berlin, 1982), p.40.

7 *A Chronicle of the Carmelites in Persia* (London, 1939), Vol. 1, p.286.

8 Babaie et al., *Slaves of the Shah*, p.115; also Reid, James J., *Tribalism and Society in Islamic Iran: 1500–1629* (California, 1983), pp.52–3.

9 Quinn, Sholeh, *Historical Writing during the Reign of Shah Abbas* (University of Utah Press, 2000), pp.86–9.

10 Bomati, Yves and Nahavandi, Houchang, *Shah Abbas: Empereur de Perse 1587–1629* (Paris, 1998), p.28.

11 *TAAA*, trans. Savory, Vol. 1, p.298.

12 *Don Juan of Persia: A Shi'ah Catholic 1560–1604*, translated and edited with an introduction by G. Le Strange, The Broadway Travellers, Routledge (London, 1926), p.135.

13 *TAAA*, trans. Savory, Vol. 1, p.369.

14 Minadoi, Giovanni, *The History of the Wars between the Turks and the Persians*, translated into English by Abraham Hartwell (London, 1595), pp.122–3.

15 Palombini, Barbara von, *Bündniswerben Abendländischer Mächte um Persien 1453–1600* (Freiburger Islamstudien, Wiesbaden, 1968), p.110.

16 *TAAA*, trans. Savory, Vol. 1, p.420.

17 *Don Juan of Persia*, p.204.

18 *Don Juan of Persia*, p.205.

19 *TAAA*, trans. Savory, Vol. 1, p.483.

20 *TAAA*, trans. Savory, Vol. 1, p.511.

21 *TAAA*, trans. Savory, Vol. 1, p.513.

22 *Don Juan of Persia*, p.210.

Chapter 3

1 Falsafi, Nasrullah, *Zendegani-ye Shah Abbas-e Avval* (Tehran, 1984), Vol. 2, p.569.
2 Röhrborn, Klaus Michael, *Provinzen*, p.59.
3 Falsafi, *Zendegani*, Vol. 1, p.182.
4 Falsafi, *Zendegani*, Vol. 1, p.183.
5 *TAAA*, trans. Savory, Vol. 2, p.551.
6 Falsafi, *Zendegani*, Vol. 1, pp.185–9.
7 Falsafi, *Zendegani*, Vol. 2, pp.515–17.
8 On the cursing of the first three caliphs, see Chapter 1, p.4.
9 Floor, *Safavid Government Institutions*, p.152.
10 Haneda, M., 'Army', *Encyclopaedia Iranica*.
11 The use of military slaves in the Islamic world goes back to at least the ninth century CE, when captured Turks from Central Asia were used in this way by the caliph in Baghdad. Military slaves also began to feature from about this time in Iran, where captured and enslaved Turks were employed in the armies of the first Iranian dynasties which began to assert their independence of the caliph, like the Saffarids (867–971 CE) and the Samanids (819–1005 CE).
12 See the earlier discussion of the *ghulams* in Chapter 1.
14 Pinkerton, John, 'Extracts from the Travels of Pietro Della Valle in Persia' in *A General Collection of the best and most interesting Voyages and Travels in all parts of the World* (London, 1811), Vol. IX, p.79.
14 For the Safavid attitude to artillery, see the essay by Rudi Matthee, 'Unwalled Cities and Restless Nomads: Firearms and Artillery in Safavid Iran', in *Safavid Persia: The History and Politics of an Islamic Society*, ed. C. Melville (I.B.Tauris, London, 1996).
15 Herbert, Thomas, *Travels in Persia 1627–29* (London, 1928), p.243.
16 This is based on the example of the Prophet Muhammad himself, who was so moved by the loyalty of his young slave-boy, Zaid, that he gave him his freedom and adopted him as his son. The Quran requires the master of a slave to treat him like a brother, effectively as a member of the family, especially where the slave has converted to Islam, and it makes the emancipation of slaves a meritorious act. But it also obliges the slave to give his master loyal service, promising him a reward in paradise. See Babaie et al., *Slaves of the Shah*, Chapter 1; and the article *abd* (slavery) in the *Encyclopaedia of Islam* (new edition, 1960).
17 Röhrborn, *Provinzen*, p.33.
18 It is known both as the Allahvirdi Khan Bridge and the Bridge of the Thirty-Three Arches.
19 Di Gouvea, *Relation des Grandes Guerres et Victoires Obtenues par Le Roy de Perse Chah Abbas*, p.68.
20 Savory, Roger, 'Qizilbash', *Encyclopaedia of Islam*. 2nd edition.
21 Babaie et al., *Slaves of the Shah*, p.17.
22 Melville, Charles, 'From Qars to Qandahar: the itineraries of Shah Abbas I (993–1038/1587–1629)', in *Études Safavides*, ed. Jean Calmard (Paris/Tehran, 1993).
23 McChesney, R.D., 'Four Sources on Shah Abbas's Building of Isfahan', *Muqarnas*, 5 (1988). For a contrary view of what this early construction work involved, now, it seems, largely rejected by other scholars, see Blake, Stephen P., 'Shah Abbas and the Transfer of the Safavid Capital from Qazvin to Isfahan', in *Society and Culture in the*

early modern Middle East: Studies on Iran in the Safavid Period, ed. Andrew J. Newman (Leiden/Boston, 2003).

24 Melville, 'From Qars to Qandahar'. Melville calculated that travelling with a small escort Abbas covered the 365 kilometres between Shiraz and Yazd at an average speed of about 13 kph (8 mph), which he describes as 'very good going for a party of horsemen'.

25 Thévenot, Jean de, The Travels of Monsieur Jean de Thévenot, Newly done out of the French (London, 1687), p.89.

26 Kaempfer, Engelbert, Am Hofe des Persischen Grosskönigs, ed. Walther Hinz (Horst Erdmann Verlag, 1977), p.81.

27 TAAA, trans. Savory, Vol. 2, p.912.

28 A Chronicle of the Carmelites in Persia, Vol. 1, p.159.

29 Sherley, Anthony, 'A brief Compendium of the History of Sir Anthony Sherley's Travels into Persia: And employed thence Ambassador to the Christian Princes; penned by himself, and recommended to his brother Sir Robert Sherley, since that sent on like Ambassage by the King of Persia', in Purchas His Pilgrimes, The Second Part (London, 1625), p.1393.

30 Floor, Safavid Government Institutions, p.202.

31 The Iranians had then, and still have today, two calendars – a lunar calendar and a solar calendar. The ancient Iranians had used a solar calendar, but this was replaced by the Muslim lunar calendar after the Arab Muslim conquest of the country in the mid-seventh century CE. However, a new solar calendar, which was worked out with great accuracy by the astronomer-poet Omar Khayyam, was introduced in 1079 CE, after which the lunar calendar was only used in Iran for Muslim religious purposes. For a recent account of how Khayyam went about his work, see Teimourian, Hazhir, Omar Khayyam (Sutton Publishing, 2007), pp.131–55.

32 Babayan, Kathryn, The Waning of the Qizilbash: The Spiritual and the Temporal in Seventeenth-Century Iran, PhD thesis (Princeton, 1993), p.64.

33 Babayan, The Waning of the Qizilbash, p.55.

34 Babayan, The Waning of the Qizilbash, p.57.

35 TAAA, trans. Savory, Vol. 2, p.649.

36 Arjomand, The Shadow of God and the Hidden Imam, p.199.

Chapter 4

1 Rabino di Borgomale, H.L., 'Les Dynasties Locales du Gilan et du Daylam', Journal Astatique (1949).

2 Don Juan of Persia, p.215.

3 TAAA, trans. Savory, Vol. 2, p.668.

4 Röhrborn, Provinzen, p.80-1.

5 'Farhad Khan', Encyclopaedia Iranica.

6 Don Juan of Persia, p.222.

7 TAAA, trans. Savory, Vol. 2, p.614.

8 According to the Portuguese envoy who was shortly to visit Abbas in Mashhad, Antonio De Gouvea, a thousand clerics usually resided in the precincts of the shrine.

9 Röhrborn, Provinzen, p.60; Floor, Willem, A Fiscal History of Iran in the Safavid and Qajar Periods 1500–1925 (Bibliotheca Persica Press, New York, 1998), pp.223-4; Burton, Audrey, The Bukharans (London, 1997), p.105.

Chapter 5

1 Sir Anthony Sherley had recently received his knighthood from Henry IV of France (1553–1610) as a reward for fighting for him in his struggle for the throne. Queen Elizabeth I took a dim view of his accepting a foreign knighthood without asking her permission and briefly imprisoned him.

2 Ross, Sir E. Denison, *Sir Anthony Sherley and His Persian Adventure* (London, 1933), p.177.

3 Ross, *Sir Anthony Sherley and His Persian Adventure*, p.205.

4 Penrose, Boies, *The Sherleian Odyssey* (Taunton, 1938), p.66.

5 Ross, *Sir Anthony Sherley and His Persian Adventure*, p.118.

6 Ross, *Sir Anthony Sherley and His Persian Adventure*, p.207.

7 Ross, *Sir Anthony Sherley and His Persian Adventure*, p.210.

8 Penrose, *The Sherleian Odyssey*, p.68.

9 Penrose, *The Sherleian Odyssey*, p.73.

10 *Don Juan of Persia*, p.232.

11 *Don Juan of Persia*, p.232.

12 Ross, *Sir Anthony Sherley and His Persian Adventure*, p.223.

13 For the English text of the decree, see Hurewitz, J.C., *Diplomacy in the Near and Middle East: A Documentary Record* (New York, 1956), pp.15–16.

14 Penrose, *The Sherleian Odyssey*, p.76.

15 Ross, *Sir Anthony Sherley and His Persian Adventure*, p.225

16 *A Chronicle of the Carmelites in Persia*, Vol. 1, p.88.

17 Davies, D.W., *Elizabethans Errant. The Strange Fortunes of Sir Thomas Sherley and His Three Sons as well in the Dutch Wars as in Muscovy, Morocco, Persia, Spain, and the Indies* (New York, 1967), p.134.

18 Davies, *Elizabethans Errant*, p.133.

Chapter 6

1 Savory, R., 'The Sherley Myth', *Iran, Journal of the British Institute of Persian Studies*, V (London, 1967).

2 Melville, Charles, 'Shah Abbas: the Pilgrimage to Mashhad', in C. Melville (ed.), *Safavid Persia: The History and Politics of an Islamic Society* (London/New York, 1996).

3 Herbert, Thomas, *Travels in Persia 1627–29* (London, 1928), p.143.

4 Melville, 'Shah Abbas: the Pilgrimage to Mashhad'.

5 Burton, *The Bukharans*, p.118.

6 Di Gouvea, *Relation des Grandes Guerres et Victoires Obtenues par Le Roy de Perse Chah Abbas*, p.91.

7 Di Gouvea, *Relation des Grandes Guerres et Victoires Obtenues par Le Roy de Perse Chah Abbas*, p.118.

8 *A Chronicle of the Carmelites*, Vol. 1, p.91.

9 Malcolm, Sir John, *The History of Persia* (London, 1829), p.382.

Chapter 7

1 A phrase used by historians. See Imber, Colin, *The Ottoman Empire, 1300–1650: the structure of power* (London, 2002), p.66.

2 *TAAA*, trans. Savory, Vol. 2, p.826.

3 Tectander, Georg, *Eine Abenteuerliche Reise Durch Russland Nach Persien 1602–1604* (Herausgegeben von Dorothea Mueller-Ott, Tulln, 1978), p.59. See also Matthee, 'Unwalled Cities and Restless Nomads'.

4 Cartwright, John, *The Preachers Travels* (London, 1611), p.46.

5 *TAAA*, trans. Savory, Vol. 2, p.833.

6 Tectander, *Eine Abenteuerliche Reise*, p.58

7 Tectander, *Eine Abenteuerliche Reise*, p.61.

8 Di Gouvea, *Relation des Grandes Guerres et Victoires Obtenues par Le Roy de Perse Chah Abbas*, p.224.

9 Islam, Riazul, *Indo-Persian Relations* (Tehran, 1970), p.65-6; *TAAA*, trans. Savory, Vol. 2, p.237.

10 Di Gouvea, *Relation des Grandes Guerres et Victoires Obtenues par Le Roy de Perse Chah Abbas*, p.239; *TAAA*, trans. Savory, Vol. 2, p.838.

11 Di Gouvea, *Relation des Grandes Guerres et Victoires Obtenues par Le Roy de Perse Chah Abbas*, pp.237-45; *TAAA*, trans. Savory, Vol. 2, pp.844-6.

12 Steensgaard, Niels, *Carracks, Caravans and Companies. The Structural Crisis in the European-Asian Trade in the Early 17th Century* (Scandinavian Institute of Asian Studies, Monograph Series No. 17, 1973), p.242.

13 Herzig, Edmund, 'The Deportation of the Armenians in 1604-1605 and Europe's Myth of Shah Abbas I', *Pembroke Papers*, 1 (1990).

14 Herzig, Edmund, 'The Rise of the Julfa Merchants in the Late Sixteenth Century', in C. Melville (ed.), *Safavid Persia: The History and Politics of an Islamic Society* (Pembroke Persian Papers 4, London, 1996).

15 Penrose, *The Sherleian Odyssey*, p.163.

16 Herzig, Edmund, 'The Deportation of the Armenians'.

17 Imber, *The Ottoman Empire, 1300-1650*, p.72.

18 Di Gouvea, *Relation des Grandes Guerres et Victoires Obtenues par Le Roy de Perse Chah Abbas*, p.286.

19 *TAAA*, trans. Savory, Vol. 2, p.893.

20 Di Gouvea, *Relation des Grandes Guerres et Victoires Obtenues par Le Roy de Perse Chah Abbas*, p.312.

21 *TAAA*, trans. Savory, Vol. 2, p.953.

22 Sadly, the shrine library was plundered by Russian forces in 1827 and many of the rare manuscripts removed to St Petersburg.

23 This was an amazing collection of 1,162 pieces of Chinese porcelain, some of which Abbas inherited and some of which he purchased or received as gifts. A special room, known as the Porcelain Room (*Chini-Khaneh*), was built at Ardabil to house some of the finest pieces. These were placed in plasterwork niches around the sides of the room.

Chapter 8

1 Di Gouvea, *Relation des Grandes Guerres et Victoires Obtenues par Le Roy de Perse Chah Abbas*, p.424.
2 Di Gouvea, *Relation des Grandes Guerres et Victoires Obtenues par Le Roy de Perse Chah Abbas*, p.424.
3 *A Chronicle of the Carmelites*, Vol. 1, p.119.
4 *A Chronicle of the Carmelites*, Vol. 1, p.123.
5 Steensgaard, *Carracks, Caravans and Companies*, p.257.
6 Steensgaard, *Carracks, Caravans and Companies*, p.262.
7 Steensgaard, *Carracks, Caravans and Companies*, p.269.
8 See the previous chapter on the settlement of the Armenians in Isfahan and Chapter 18 'The Merchant King' for a fuller discussion of the role of the Armenian merchants.
9 Di Gouvea, *Relation des Grandes Guerres et Victoires Obtenues par Le Roy de Perse Chah Abbas*, p.453.
10 Di Gouvea, *Relation des Grandes Guerres et Victoires Obtenues par Le Roy de Perse Chah Abbas*, p.498.
11 It was undoubtedly exaggerated reports of Abbas's generosity towards Robert Sherley that prompted Shakespeare to have Fabian say in *Twelfth Night*, 'I will not give my part of this sport for a pension of thousands to be paid from the Sophy!'
12 Davies, *Elizabethans Errant*, p.225.
13 *A Chronicle of the Carmelites*, Vol. 1, p.203.
14 *A Chronicle of the Carmelites*, Vol. 1, p.169.
15 *A Chronicle of the Carmelites*, Vol. 1, p.178.
16 *A Chronicle of the Carmelites*, Vol. 1, p.187.
17 *TAAA*, trans. Savory p.986.
18 *TAAA*, trans. Savory p.987.
19 On the peace treaty between Sulaiman and Tahmasp, see Chapter 1, p.9.

Chapter 9

1 The Zoroastrian festival of *Abpashan* or *Abrizagan* was held on 21 June, the first day of summer. It was originally instituted by the Sasanian shah, Peroz (459–84 CE), when the rains finally came after a long drought, apparently answering his prayers to God.
2 *TAAA*, trans. Savory, Vol. 2, p.1084.
3 Babaie et al., *Slaves of the Shah*, pp.94–5.
4 *A Chronicle of the Carmelites*, Vol. 1, p.201.
5 Steensgard, *Carracks, Caravans and Companies*, p.294.
6 Steensgard, *Carracks, Caravans and Companies*, p.295.
7 *A Chronicle of the Carmelites*, Vol. 1, p.207.
8 One of the principal modern historians of Safavid Persia, Hans Roemer, says, 'All the evidence suggests that the prince was innocent.' Roemer, Hans, *Persien auf dem Weg in die Neuzeit: Iranische Geschichte von 1350-1750* (Beirut, 1989).
9 Krusinski, Judas Thaddaeus, *The History of the Late Revolutions of Persia* (London, 1733), Vol. 1, p.69.

10 *TAAA*, trans. Savory, Vol. 2, p.1114.

11 *TAAA*, trans. Savory, Vol. 2, p.1116.

12 Pinkerton, 'Extracts from the Travels of Pietro Della Valle in Persia', p.132.

13 Pinkerton, 'Extracts from the Travels of Pietro Della Valle in Persia', p.75.

14 Pinkerton, 'Extracts from the Travels of Pietro Della Valle in Persia', p.88.

15 Quinn, Sholeh, *Historical Writing During the Reign of Abbas: Ideology, Imitation and Legitimacy in Safavid Chronicles* (University of Utah Press, 2000), pp.91, 142.

16 Islam, *Indo-Persian Relations*, p.76.

17 Figueroa, Don Garcia, *L'Ambassade de D. Garcias de Silva Figueroa en Perse* (Paris, 1667), pp.296–320.

18 *TAAA*, trans. Savory, Vol. 2, p.1193.

19 *TAAA*, trans. Savory, Vol. 2, p.1215.

20 Matthee, Rudi, 'Anti-Ottoman Concerns and Caucasian Interests: Diplomatic Relations between Iran and Russia, 1587–1639', in Michel Mazzaoui (ed.), *Safavid Iran and her Neighbours* (University of Utah Press, 2003).

Chapter 10

1 *A Chronicle of the Carmelites*, Vol. 1, p.215.

2 Davies, *Elizabethans Errant*, p.251.

3 Ferrier, R.W., 'An English View of Persian Trade in 1618', *Journal of the Economic and Social History of the Orient*, Vol. XIX, Part II (1976).

4 Boxer, C.R., *The Portuguese Seaborne Empire 1415–1825* (London, 1969), p.124.

5 Figueroa, *L'Ambassade de D. Garcias de Silva Figueroa en Perse*, p.199.

6 Bull, George, *Travels of Pietro Della Valle* (Hutchinson, London, 1989), p.167.

7 Figueroa, *L'Ambassade de D. Garcias de Silva Figueroa en Perse*, pp.231–2.

8 It was called 'the crown of Haydar' because it was believed to have been designed by Shah Ismail I's father, Sheikh Haydar, for his Turkoman followers, who were known thereafter as Qizilbash or 'red-heads'. The folds symbolised the Twelve Shi'i Imams. See Chapter 1, pp.2–3.

9 Figueroa, *L'Ambassade de D. Garcias de Silva Figueroa en Perse*, p.237.

10 This could well be Iskandar Beg Munshi, Abbas's official chronicler, who frequently accompanied the shah.

11 Figueroa, *L'Ambassade de D. Garcias de Silva Figueroa en Perse*, p.321.

12 There were no permanent embassies in those days. An ambassador would stay until the ruler he was visiting summoned him to a farewell audience and gave him leave to depart. An ambassador might be detained at a foreign court for as long as four years before being allowed to depart, which was what happened to the first ambassador Abbas sent to the Moghul court in 1591, much to the annoyance of Abbas.

13 There was a separate entrance to the harem – the shah's private quarters – on the west side of the Royal Square to the south of the Ali Qapu palace building, which was the main entrance to the whole palace complex.

14 *A Chronicle of the Carmelites*, Vol. 1, p.243.

15 Foster, William, *English Factories in India 1618–21* (Oxford, 1906), p.xxviii.

16 *A Chronicle of the Carmelites*, Vol. 1, p.258.

17 *TAAA*, trans. Savory, Vol 2, pp.1203–4.

18 Figueroa, *L'Ambassade de D. Garcias de Silva Figueroa en Perse*, p.461.

19 Wilson, Arnold, *The Persian Gulf: An Historical Sketch from the Earliest Times to the Beginning of the Twentieth Century* (Oxford, 1928), p.148.
20 Foster, *English Factories in India 1622–23* (Oxford, 1908), p.xiv.

Chapter 11

1 Roemer, Claudia, 'Die Osmanische Belagerung Bagdads 1034–35/1625–26', *Der Islam* (1989), p.124.
2 Roemer, 'Die Osmanische Belagerung Bagdads'.

Chapter 12

1 Vermeulen, U., 'L'Ambassade Persane de Musa Beg aux Provinces-Unies (1625–1628)', *Persica*, 7, 1978.
2 Vermeulen, 'L'Ambassade Persane de Musa Beg'.
3 Their portraits now hang in Petworth House in Sussex.
4 Penrose, *The Sherleian Odyssey*, p.207.
5 Ferrier, R.W., 'The European Diplomacy of Shah Abbas I and the first Persian embassy to England', *Iran*, XI (1973).
6 Penrose, *The Sherleian Odyssey*, p.215.
7 Penrose, *The Sherleian Odyssey*, p.216.
8 In May 1271, Prince Edward, the future King Edward I of England, landed at Acre with a small force of English crusaders and sent a three-man embassy to the Mongol ruler of Iran, Aqaba, to ask for help against the Mamluks of Egypt, who were threatening the last Crusader strongholds in the Holy land.
9 Steensgaard, *Carracks, Caravans and Companies*, p.363.
10 Penrose, *The Sherleian Odyssey*, p.223.
11 Herbert, *Travels in Persia*, p.xxiv.

Chapter 13

1 Herbert, *Travels in Persia*, p.42.
2 Herbert, *Travels in Persia*, p.54.
3 Herbert, *Travels in Persia*, p.76.
4 Herbert, *Travels in Persia*, p.80.
5 Herbert, *Travels in Persia*, p.155.
6 Herbert, *Travels in Persia*, p.156.
7 Penrose, *The Sherleian Odyssey*, p.237.
8 Stevens, Sir Roger, 'Robert Sherley: The Unanswered Questions', *Iran* (1979).
9 Calmard, Jean, 'Franco-Persian Relations to 1789', *Encyclopaedia Iranica*.
10 *TAAA*, trans. Savory, Vol. 2, p.1288.
11 *TAAA*, trans. Savory, Vol. 2, p.1303.

Chapter 14

1 Di Gouvea, *Relation des Grandes Guerres et Victoires Obtenues par Le Roy de Perse Chah Abbas*, p.115.
2 *A Chronicle of the Carmelites*, Vol. 1, p.285.
3 According to Safavid tradition, Shah Ismail I's father, Sheikh Haidar, designed the bonnet for his followers.
4 Pinkerton, 'Extracts from the Travels of Pietro Della Valle in Persia', p.32.
5 Di Gouvea, *Relation des Grandes Guerres et Victoires Obtenues par Le Roy de Perse Chah Abbas*, p.112.
6 Bull, *Travels of Pietro Della Valle*, p.156.
7 Pinkerton, 'Extracts from the Travels of Pietro Della Valle in Persia', p.93.
8 *TAAA*, trans. Savory, Vol. 2, p.300.
9 Penrose, *The Sherleian Odyssey*, p.69.
10 *A Chronicle of the Carmelites*, Vol. 1, p.159.
11 *TAAA*, trans. Savory, Vol. 1, p.525.
12 *TAAA*, trans. Savory, Vol. 1, p.529.
13 Manwaring, George, 'A True Discourse of Sir Anthony Sherley's Travel into Persia', in Sir E. Denison Ross, *Sir Anthony Sherley and His Persian Adventure* (London, 1933), p.214.
14 Pietro Della Valle's wife was a Nestorian Catholic whom he met and married in Baghdad on his way to Iran.
15 Pinkerton, 'Extracts from the Travels of Pietro Della Valle in Persia', p.66.
16 The title 'khan' was given to governors of large provinces.
17 *A Chronicle of the Carmelites*, Vol. 1, pp.249-54.
18 *A Chronicle of the Carmelites*, Vol. 1, p.158.
19 Figueroa, *L'Ambassade de D. Garcias de Silva Figueroa en Perse*, p.290.
20 Ross, *Sir Anthony Sherley and His Persian Adventure*, p.161.
21 Darke, Hubert, *The Book of Government or Rules for Kings*, translated from the Persian (London, 1960), p.78.
22 *TAAA*, trans. Savory, Vol. 1, p.533.
23 Amanat, Abbas, *Pivot of the Universe: Nasir al-Din Shah and the Iranian Monarchy, 1831-1896* (I.B.Tauris, 1997), pp.71-3. I have used Professor Amanat's summary of 'The Book of the Covenant'.

Chapter 15

1 Figueroa, *L'Ambassade de D. Garcias de Silva Figueroa en Perse*, p.293.
2 Tavernier, Jean-Baptiste, *Voyages en Perse* (Les Librairies Associés, Paris, 1964), p.244.
3 Herbert, *Travels in Persia*, p.230.
4 Herbert, *Travels in Persia*, p.232.
5 Pinkerton, *Travels of Pietro Della Valle*, p.64.
6 On the festival of *Abpashan*, see Chapter 9, Note 1. *Mehregan* is a harvest festival associated with the ancient Iranian god Mithra and is celebrated on 2 October. *Chaharshanbe Suri* is a festival of fire celebrated at the end of the Iranian calendar year, just before *Noruz*, and celebrates the triumph of light over darkness and the coming of Spring.

7   Herbert, *Travels in Persia*, p.215.

8   The name Chehel Sutun or 'Forty Columns' was used for somewhat similar palace buildings where there was an open verandah with a wooden roof supported by columns, a feature known as a *talar*. The most famous surviving example is the Chehel Sutun palace in Isfahan, built by Shah Abbas II in 1647. The number forty is not meant to be precise; it simply indicates that there were many columns.

9   Pinkerton, 'Extracts from the Travels of Pietro Della Valle in Persia', p.26.

10 Di Gouvea, *Relation des Grandes Guerres et Victoires Obtenues par Le Roy de Perse Chah Abbas*, p.115.

11 Figueroa, *L'Ambassade de D. Garcias de Silva Figueroa en Perse*, p.293.

12 Pinkerton, 'Extracts from the Travels of Pietro Della Valle in Persia', p.69.

13 Pinkerton, 'Extracts from the Travels of Pietro Della Valle in Persia', p.70.

14 *A Chronicle of the Carmelites*, Vol. 1, p.168.

15 Pinkerton, 'Extracts from the Travels of Pietro Della Valle in Persia', p.172.

16 Di Gouvea, *Relation des Grandes Guerres et Victoires Obtenues par Le Roy de Perse Chah Abbas*, p.114.

17 On the confinement of the princes to the harem, see Chapter 3, p.38 and Chapter 9, p.105.

18 *A Chronicle of the Carmelites*, Vol. 1, p.286.

19 Babaie et al., *Slaves of the Shah*, p.91.

20 Pinkerton, 'Extracts from the Travels of Pietro Della Valle in Persia', p.54.

21 The degree of royal hospitality may be judged from the provisions that Shah Abbas allotted to Pietro Della Valle for a month. The weights are given in patmans which were equivalent to 9.5 lb or 4.3 kg: '250 patmans of flour, 150 of rice, 36 of butter, 80 fowls, 19 capons, 17 lambs, 600 eggs, 15 patmans of chick-peas, 12 of salt, 3 of spices, 10 of dried pomegranate seed, 27 of onions, 27 of wine [they knew Della Valle drank little], 50 thick and long wax candles, 12 patmans of tallow candles, 5 of raisons without stones, 5 of dry apricots, 5 of vinegar, 10 of cheese in small white pieces without rind (more like thick cream), 3 of sugar, 5 large decanters of rose water, 5 patmans of honey, 1,000 oranges, 100 patmans of barley for the cattle, beside 15 chiles of land to grow barley [each chile generally yielding 10 horse loads] and 45 loads of wood for firing.' (Pinkerton, 'Extracts from the Travels of Pietro Della Valle in Persia', p.57.)

22 *TAAA*, trans. Savory, Vol. 2, p.764.

23 See Chapter 9.

24 Babaie et al., *Slaves of the Shah*, p.98.

25 The silkworm is fed on the leaves of the mulberry tree. See Matthee, Rudi, *The Politics of Trade in Safavid Iran: Silk for Silver, 1600–1730* (CUP, 1999), pp.33-45 for a full explanation of silk production under the Safavids.

26 According to the *Shorter Oxford Dictionary*, a league was usually equivalent to 5 kilometres or 3 miles. It is unlikely that the streets were as long as that, or indeed that the circumference of the city was as great as Della Valle says. Both, however, were obviously impressive.

27 Pinkerton, 'Extracts from the Travels of Pietro Della Valle in Persia', p.53.

28 Herbert, *Travels in Persia*, p.174.

29 Curzon, George, *Persia and the Persian Question* (London, 1892), Vol. 1, p.77.

Chapter 16

1 Pinkerton, 'Extracts from the Travels of Pietro Della Valle in Persia', p.85.
2 Blair, Sheila, 'The Ardabil Carpets in Context', in Andrew Newman (ed.), *Society and Culture in the early Modern Middle East: Studies on Iran in the Safavid Period* (Leiden/Boston, 2003).
3 *A Chronicle of the Carmelites*, Vol. 1, p.164.
4 Di Gouvea, *Relation des Grandes Guerres et Victoires Obtenues par Le Roy de Perse Chah Abbas*, p.100.
5 Father Paul Simon, the first superior of the Carmelites in Isfahan, wrote in a report to Rome in 1608: 'On the 21 December the Shah went outside Isfahan because his "Lent", in which Muhammadans do not eat during the daytime, had begun: and since the Shah, who did not observe [the fast], did not wish to scandalise his subjects, he went off hunting.' *A Chronicle of the Carmelites*, Vol. 1, p.122.
6 Pinkerton, 'Extracts from the Travels of Pietro Della Valle in Persia', p.61. The official was the vizier of Mazandaran, Saru Taqi, who became grand vizier under Abbas's grandson and successor, Shah Safi I.
7 Halm, Heinz, *Shi'ism* (Edinburgh University Press, 1991), p.90.
8 Momen, Moojan, *An Introduction to Shi'i Islam: The history and doctrines of Twelver Shi'ism* (Yale, 1985), Vol. 1, pp.111–12.
9 Pinkerton, 'Extracts from the Travels of Pietro Della Valle in Persia', pp.33–8.
10 Calmard, J., 'Shi'i Rituals and Power II. The Consolidation of Safavid Shi'ism: Folklore and Popular Religion', in C. Melville (ed.), *Safavid Persia: The History and Politics of an Islamic Society*, I.B.Tauris, London, 1996.
11 Falsafi, Nasrullah, *Zendegani*, Vol. 3, p.883, quoting the Safavid chronicle *Nuqavat ul-Asar*.
12 Langlès, L., *Voyages du Chevalier Chardin en Perse et autres Lieux de l'Orient* (Paris, 1811), Vol. 9, pp.38–9.
13 Uthman, the third Caliph of Islam, who reigned CE 644–656.
14 Sherley, 'A brief Compendium of the History of Sir Anthony Sherley's Travels into Persia', p.1399.
15 It is also known as the Illuminationist (*Ishraqi*) School of philosophy.
16 Newman, Andrew, 'Mir Damad', *Encyclopaedia Iranica*.
17 Nasr, Seyyed Hossein, 'Spiritual Movements, Philosophy and Theology in the Safavid Period', *Cambridge History of Iran*, Vol. 6.
18 Moin, Baqer, *Khomeini: Life of the Ayatollah* (I.B.Tauris, 1999), p.48.

Chapter 17

1 *A Chronicle of the Carmelites*, Vol. 1, p.189.
2 McChesney, 'Four Sources on Shah Abbas's Building of Isfahan', pp.103–34.
3 McChesney, 'Four Sources on Shah Abbas's Building of Isfahan', pp.103–34.
4 Babaie et al., *Slaves of the Shah*, pp.80–113. The work explores and highlights the prominent role of the *ghulams* in carrying out an imperial building programme.
5 Herbert, *Travels in Persia*, p.127.
6 Herbert, *Travels in Persia*, p.129.
7 Fryer, John, *A New Account of East India and Persia being Nine Years' Travels 1672–1681*

(The Hakluyt Society, London, 1912), p.240.

8 A *Chronicle of the Carmelites*, Vol. 1, p.189.

9 Langlès, *Voyages du Chevalier Chardin en Perse*, Vol. 7, p.389.

10 Langlès, *Voyages du Chevalier Chardin en Perse*, Vol. 8, p.19.

11 Junabadi, Mirza Beg b. Hasan, *Rawzat al-Safaviyah*, quoted in McChesney, 'Four Sources on Shah Abbas's Building of Isfahan', pp.103-34.

12 Curzon, *Persia and the Persian Question*, Vol. 2, p.45.

13 Bull, *Travels of Pietro Della Valle*, p.125.

14 See Lambton, Ann, *Landlord and Peasant in Persia* (OUP, 1953), pp.405-7. The author says that at the time she wrote the book, in the early 1950s, the size of a *jarib* varied between some 400 sq. metres and 1,450 sq. metres.

15 Figueroa, *L'Ambassade de D. Garcias de Silva Figueroa en Perse*, p.285.

16 Langlès, *Voyages du Chevalier Chardin en Perse*, Vol. 7, p.273.

17 On the origins of the Nimatis and the Haidaris, see Keyvani, Mehdi, *Artisans and Guild Life in the later Safavid Period* (Klaus Schwarz Verlag, Berlin, 1982), pp.209-11.

18 Later both the Capuchins and the Jesuits set up missions in Isfahan, the Capuchins early in the reign of Shah Safi I (1629-42) and the Jesuits in 1653 under Shah Abbas II (1642-66).

19 Herbert, *Travels in Persia*, p.131.

20 'Coffee', *Encyclopaedia Iranica*.

21 Herbert, *Travels in Persia*, p.45.

22 Langlès, *Voyages du Chevalier Chardin en Perse*, Vol. 4, p.69.

23 Herbert, *Travels in Persia*, p.202.

24 Langlès, *Voyages du Chevalier Chardin en Perse*, Vol. 4, p.224.

25 On this project and Sheikh Bahai's role in it, see Chapter 16.

26 Figueroa, *L'Ambassade de D. Garcias de Silva Figueroa en Perse*, p.199.

27 A *Chronicle of the Carmelites*, Vol. 1, p.104.

28 Floor, Willem, 'The Talar-i Tavila or Hall of Stables, a Forgotten Safavid Palace', *Muqarnas*, 19 (2002).

Chapter 18

1 Keyvani, Mehdi, *Artisans and Guild Life in the later Safavid period*, p.72, quoting Lippomano, the Spanish ambassador in Iran 1585-6.

2 These measures are described in Chapter 3.

3 Floor, *The Economy of Safavid Persia*, p.33.

4 Pinkerton, 'Extracts from the Travels of Pietro Della Valle in Persia, p.116.

5 On the design of caravanserais, see Hillenbrand, R., 'Safavid Architecture', in Jackson, Peter, and Lockhart, Laurence (eds), *The Cambridge History of Iran*, Vol. 6.

6 Matthee, *The Politics of Trade in Safavid Iran*, p.78.

7 Figueroa, *L'Ambassade de D. Garcias de Silva Figueroa en Perse*, p.306.

8 See Chapter 15, including footnote 25 on mulberry trees.

9 Floor, *The Economy of Safavid Persia*, p.30.

10 Thévenot, *The Travels of Monsieur Jean de Thévenot*, Part II, p.77.

11 Matthee, *The Politics of Trade in Safavid Iran*, p.25.

12 Tavernier, *Voyages en Perse*, p.79.

13 Matthee, *The Politics of Trade in Safavid Iran*, p.88.

14 Matthee, *The Politics of Trade in Safavid Iran*, pp.99–105.
15 Babaie et al., *Slaves of the Shah*, p.62.
16 Langlès, *Voyages du Chevalier Chardin en Perse*, Vol. 8, p.125.

Chapter 19

1 Welch, Anthony, *Artists for the Shah: Late Sixteenth-Century Painting at the Imperial Court of Iran* (Yale University Press, 1976), p.185.
2 Canby, Sheila, *The Rebellious Reformer: The Drawings and Paintings of Riza-yi Abbasi of Isfahan* (London, 1996), p.17.
3 Welch, *Artists for the Shah*, pp.68–9.
4 Blair, Sheila, *Islamic Calligraphy* (Edinburgh University Press, 2006), p.xxii.
5 Blair, *Islamic Calligraphy*, p.423.
6 Falsafi, *Zendegani-ye Shah Abbas-e Avval*, Vol. 2, p.323.
7 Floor, Willem, 'Dutch Painters in Iran during the First Half of the 17th Century', in *Persica*, VIII (1979).
8 Figueroa, *L'Ambassade de D. Garcias de Silva Figueroa en Perse*, p.205.
9 Langlès, *Voyages du Chevalier Chardin en Perse*, Vol. 7, p.329.
10 Skelton, Robert, 'Ghiyath al-Din 'Ali-yi Naqshband and an episode in the Life of Sadiqi Beg', in Hillenbrand, Robert (ed.), *Persian Painting from the Mongols to the Qajars* (I.B.Tauris, London, 1997).
11 Blunt, Wilfred, *Isfahan, Pearl of Persia* (Elek Books, London, 1966), p.72.
12 Welch, Anthony, *Shah Abbas and the Arts of Isfahan* (New York, 1973); Hillenbrand, Robert, 'Safavid Architecture', in Jackson and Lockhart (eds), *The Cambridge History of Iran*, Vol. 6.
13 Hillenbrand, *Safavid Architecture*.
14 Babaie et al., *Slaves of the Shah*, p.89.
15 Rypka, Jan, *History of Iranian Literature* (D. Reidel Publishing Company, Dordrecht, Holland, 1968), p.300.
16 Falsafi, *Zendegani*, Vol. 2, pp.336–61.
17 *TAAA*, trans. Savory, Vol. 2, p.692.

Chapter 20

1 'Dès que ce grand et bon prince eut cessé de vivre, la Perse cessa de prospérer.' Langlès *Voyages du Chevalier Chardin en Perse*, Vol. 3, p.291.
2 Newman, *Safavid Iran*, pp.7, 92, 114–15.
3 Tapper, Richard, *Frontier Nomads of Iran: a political and social history of the Shahsevan* (Cambridge University Press, 1997), p.55.
4 Langlès, *Voyages du Chevalier Chardin en Perse*, Vol. 5, p.252.
5 Rettelbach, Gerhard, *Khulasat As-Siyar. Der Iran Unter Schah Safi (1629–1642) Nach Der Chronik des Muhammad Ma'sūm Khuājagī Isfahānī* (Munich, 1978), p.18.
6 Babayan, Kathryn, *The Waning of the Qizilbash*, pp.90–104.
7 Under Shah Abbas I and Shah Safi, the blinding was done by passing a red-hot blade in front of the eyes. However, as in the case of Prince Imam Quli, this was found not to guarantee complete blindness, so from the reign of Shah Abbas II the pupils of the eyes were extracted with the point of a dagger and brought to the shah in a

handkerchief. Cruel though this was, the Iranians argued that it was more humane than the Ottoman practice of killing the new sultan's brothers.

8 Newman, *Safavid Iran*, pp.84, 97.
9 Although homosexual relationships were common between men and youths, even boys, and are frequently alluded to in Persian poetry, nonetheless sodomy was a serious offence in Shi'i law. If a complaint was made, as in this case, then the law was liable to be enforced.
10 Lang, D.M., *The Last Years of the Georgian Monarchy* (New York, 1957), pp.12–17.
11 *A Chronicle of the Carmelites*, Vol. 1, p.316.
12 Newman, *Safavid Iran*, pp.89–99.
13 Langlès, *Voyages du Chevalier Chardin en Perse*, Vol. 9, p.515.
14 Langlès, *Voyages du Chevalier Chardin en Perse*, Vol. 5, p.215.
15 Although the elder son had the advantage when it came to deciding the succession, there was no rule of primogeniture.
16 Newman, *Safavid Iran*, p.99.
17 'La richesse et l'abondance se trouvèrent diminuées dans un grand excès.' Chardin added that the wealth of Iran appeared to him to have diminished by half between his first visit under Abbas II in 1665 and his final departure under Sulaiman in 1677. Langlès, *Voyages du Chevalier Chardin en Perse*, Vol. 3, pp.292–3.
18 *A Chronicle of the Carmelites*, p.471.
19 Krusinski, *The History of the Late Revolutions of Persia*, pp.83–90.

Conclusion

1 Savory, Roger, 'The Safavid State and Polity', in R. Holod (ed.), *Studies on Isfahan, Proceedings of the Isfahan Colloquium, 1974, Part I, Iranian Studies VII* (Chestnut Hill, MA, 1974).
2 Tapper, *Frontier Nomads of Iran*, pp.54–5.
3 Fryer, *A New Account of East India and Persia*, p.244.
4 Malcolm, Sir John, *The History of Persia* (John Murray, London, 1829), Vol I, p.359.
5 Langlès, *Voyages du Chevalier Chardin en Perse*, Vol. 3, p.291.
6 Malcolm, Sir John, *Sketches of Persia* (London, 1827), p.120.
7 One is a popular history by Panahi Simnani entitled 'Shah Abbas the Great: the Man of a Thousand Faces' (*Shah Abbas-e Kabir: Mard-e hezar Chehreh*). The other is a historical novel by Bahram Afrasiabi called 'The Sun of the Ali Qapu' (*Khorshid-e Ali Qapu*). I am grateful to John Gurney for this information.

Select Bibliography

Readers wishing to consult a fuller bibliography should consult Andrew Newman's *Safavid Iran: Rebirth of a Persian Empire* (I.B.Tauris, 2006).

General Histories of Iran

Axworthy, Michael, *Empire of the Mind*, Hurst and Company, London, 2007.

Bausani, Alessandro, *The Persians*, Elek Books, 1971.

Blow, David, *Persia Through Writers' Eyes*, Eland, 2007.

Brown, E.G., *A Literary History of Persia*, 4 vols, CUP, 1959-64.

Rypka, J., *History of Iranian Literature*, D. Reidel Publishing Company, Dordrecht, Holland, 1968.

Garthwaite, Gene, *The Persians*, Blackwell, Oxford, 2005.

Morgan, David, *Medieval Persia 1040-1797*, Longman, 1988.

Malcolm, Sir John, *The History of Persia*, John Murray, London, 1829.

Sykes, Sir Percy, *A History of Persia*, 2 vols, 3rd edition, Macmillan, 1963.

General Works on Religion

Arjomand, Said Amir, *The Shadow of God and the Hidden Imam*, University of Chicago Press, 1984.

Halm, Heinz, *Shi'ism*, Edinburgh University Press, 1991.

Madelung, Wilfred, 'Al-Mahdi' and 'Shi'a', *Encyclopaedia of Islam*, 2nd edition.

Momen, Moojan, *An Introduction to Shi'i Islam: The history and doctrines of Twelver Shi'ism*, Yale, 1985.

Newman, Andrew, *The Formative Period of Twelver Shi'ism*, Curzon, 2000.

Waterfield, Robin, *Christians in Persia*, London, 1973.

Works on the Reign of Shah Abbas and the Safavid Period

Abisaab, Rula Jurdi, *Converting Persia: Religion and Power in the Safavid Empire*, I.B.Tauris, 2004.

Algar, Hamid, 'Nuktawiyya', *Encyclopaedia of Islam*.

Allouche, Adel, The *Origins and Development of the Ottoman-Safavid Conflict*, Klaus Schwarz Verlag, Berlin, 1983.

Aubin, Jean, 'Révolution chi'ite et conservatisme: Les Soufis de Lahejan, 1500–1514', *Études Safavides II, Moyen Orient et Océan Indien*, 1, 1984.

Aubin, Jean, 'Chiffres de Population Urbaine en Iran Occidental autour de 1500', *Moyen Orient et Océan Indien*, 1986.

Aubin, Jean, 'L'Avenement des Safavides Reconsidéré', *Moyen Orient et Océan Indien*, 5, 1988.

Aubin, Jean, 'Les Ambassades Portugaises à la Cour de Shah Isma'il', *Journal of Azerbaijan Studies*, 1998.

Babaie, Sussan, Babayan, Kathryn, Baghdiantz-MacCabe, Ina, and Farhad, Massumeh, *Slaves of the Shah: New Elites of Safavid Iran*, I.B.Tauris, London, 2004.

Babayan, Kathryn, *The Waning of the Qizilbash: The Spiritual and the Temporal in Seventeenth-Century Iran*, PhD thesis, Princeton, 1993.

Babayan, Kathryn, 'Sufis, Dervishes and Mullas: the Controversy over Spiritual and Temporal Dominion in Seventeenth-Century Iran', in C. Melville (ed.), *Safavid Persia: The History and Politics of an Islamic Society*, I.B.Tauris, London, 1996.

Bacqué-Grammont, Jean-Louis, and Adle, Chahryar, *Les Ottomans, Les Safavides et La Géorgie 1514–1524*, Istanbul, 1991.

Bellan, Lucien-Louis, *Shah Abbas I*, Paris, 1932.

Blair, Sheila, 'The Ardabil Carpets in Context', in Andrew Newman (ed.), *Society and Culture in the early Modern Middle East: Studies on Iran in the Safavid Period*, Leiden/Boston, 2003.

Blair, Sheila, *Islamic Calligraphy*, Edinburgh University Press, 2006.

Blunt, Wilfred, *Pietro's Pilgrimage*, James Barrie, London, 1953.

Blunt, Wilfred, *Isfahan: Pearl of Persia*, Elek Books, 1966.

Bomati, Yves and Nahavandi, Houchang, *Shah Abbas: Empereur de Perse 1587–1629*, Paris, 1998.

Boxer, C.R., *The Portuguese Seaborne Empire 1415–1825*, London, 1969.

Burton, Audrey, *The Bukharans: A Dynasty, Diplomatic and Commercial History 1550–1702*, London, 1997.

Calmard, Jean, 'Shi'i Rituals and Power II. The Consolidation of Safavid Shi'ism: Folklore and Popular Religion', in C. Melville (ed.), *Safavid Persia:*

The History and Politics of an Islamic Society, I.B.Tauris, London, 1996.

Calmard, Jean, 'Franco-Persian Relations to 1789', *Encyclopaedia Iranica*.

Canby, Sheila, *Persian Painting*, The British Museum Press, 1993.

Canby, Sheila, *The Rebellious Reformer: The Drawings and Paintings of Riza-yi Abbasi of Isfahan*, London, 1996.

Canby, Sheila, *The Golden Age of Persian Art, 1501–1722*, The British Museum Press, 1999.

'Coffee' and 'Coffeehouse' in *Encyclopaedia Iranica*.

Davies, D.W., *Elizabethans Errant. The Strange Fortunes of Sir Thomas Sherley and His Three Sons as well in the Dutch Wars as in Muscovy, Morocco, Persia, Spain, and the Indies*, New York, 1967.

Dickson, Martin, *Shah Tahmasp and the Uzbeks: The Duel for Khurasan with Ubayd Khan, 930–946/1524–1540*, PhD thesis, Princeton, 1958.

Efendi, Dourry, *Relation de Dourry Efendy, Ambassadeur de la Porte Othomane auprès du Roi de Perse*, Paris, 1810.

Emerson, John and Floor, Willem, 'Rahdars and their Tolls in Safavid and Afsharid Iran', *Journal of the Economic and Social History of the Orient*, Vol. 30, 1987.

Falsafi, Nasrullah, *Zendegani-ye Shah Abbas-e Avval*, 3 vols, Tehran, 1974 (1st edn, 1953).

Ferrier, R.W., 'The European Diplomacy of Shah Abbas I and the first Persian Embassy to England', *Iran*, XI, 1973.

Ferrier, R.W., 'An English View of Persian Trade in 1618', *Journal of the Economic and Social History of the Orient*, Vol. XIX, Part II, 1976.

Ferrier, R.W., *A Journey to Persia: Jean Chardin's Portrait of a Seventeenth-century Empire*, I.B.Tauris, London, 1996.

Ferrier, R.W., 'East India Company', *Encyclopaedia Iranica*.

Fischel, Walter J., *The Story of a Jewish Community in Persia*, The Joshua Starr Memorial Volume, New York, 1953.

Floor, Willem, 'Dutch Painters in Iran during the First Half of the 17th Century', in *Persica*, VIII, 1979.

Floor, Willem, 'The Dutch and the Persian Silk Trade', in Charles Melville (ed.), *Safavid Persia: The History and Politics of an Islamic Society*, I.B.Tauris, London, 1996.

Floor, Willem, 'The Rise and Fall of Mirza Taqi, the Eunuch Grand Vizier (1633–45) Makhdum al-Omara va Khadem al-Foqara', *Studia Iranica*, 26, 1997.

Floor, Willem, *A Fiscal History of Iran in the Safavid and Qajar Periods 1500–1925*, Bibliotheca Persica Press, New York, 1998.

Floor, Willem, *The Economy of Safavid Persia*, Wiesbaden, 2000.

Floor, Willem, *Safavid Government Institutions*, California, 2001.

Floor, Willem, 'Dutch-Persian Relations', *Encyclopaedia Iranica*.

Foster, William, *English Factories in India 1618–21*, Oxford, 1906.

Foster, William, *English Factories in India 1622–23*, Oxford, 1908.

Gascoigne, Bamber, *The Great Moghuls*, London, 1971.

Glassen, Erika, 'Die frühen Safawiden nach Qazi Ahmad Qumi's Khulasat-at-Tawarikh, *Islamkundliche Untersuchungen*, 5, Klaus Schwarz Verlag, Freiburg, 1970.

Grey, Charles (ed.), *A Narrative of Italian Travels in Persia in the 15th and 16th centuries*, Hakluyt Society, 1873.

Gurney, J.D., 'Pietro Della Valle: the limits of Perception', in *Bulletin of the School of Oriental and African Studies*, XLIX/1, 1986.

Hammer, Joseph von, *Geschichte des Osmanischen Reiches*, Pest, 1828.

Haneda, M., 'Army', *Encyclopaedia Iranica*.

Herzig, Edmund, ' The Deportation of the Aremenians in 1604–1605 and Europés Myth of Shah Abbas I', *Pembroke Papers*, 1, 1990.

Herzig, Edmund, 'The Rise of the Julfa Merchants in the Late Sixteenth Century', in C. Melville (ed.), *Safavid Persia: The History and Politics of an Islamic Society*, Pembroke Persian Papers 4, London, 1996.

Hillenbrand, R., 'Architecture', *Encyclopaedia Iranica*.

Hourani, Albert, 'From Jabal 'Amil to Persia', *Bulletin of the School of Oriental and African Studies*, XLIX/1, 1986.

Hunarfar, L., *Ganjinah-i Asar-i Tarikhi-yi Isfahan*, Isfahan, 1965–6.

Imber, Colin, *The Ottoman Empire, 1300–1650: the structure of power*, London, 2002.

'Isfahan', *Encyclopaedia Iranica*.

Islam, Raizul, *Indo-Persian Relations*, Tehran, 1970.

Jackson, Peter and Lockhart, Laurence (eds), *The Cambridge History of Iran, Vol. 6: The Timurid and Safavid Periods*, Cambridge University Press, 1986.

Jafariyan, R., *Din va Siyasat dar Dawrah-yi Safavi*, Qum, 1991.

Jafariyan, R., *Ilal-i bar Uftadan-i Safaviyyan*, Tehran, 1994.

Keyvani, Mehdi, *Artisans and Guild Life in the later Safavid period*, Klaus Schwarz Verlag, Berlin, 1982.

Lambton, Ann, Landlord and Peasant in Persia, OUP, 1953.

Lambton, Ann, 'Quis Custodict Custodes', *Studia Islamica*, VI, 1956.

Lang, D.M., *The Last Years of the Georgian Monarchy*, New York, 1957.

Lockhart, Laurence, *The Fall of the Safavi Dynasty and the Afghan Occupation of Persia*, Cambridge University Press, 1958.

Lockhart, Laurence, 'The Persian Army in the Safavi Period', in *Der Islam*, 1959.

Luft, Paul, *Iran unter Schah Abbas II (1642–1666)*, PhD thesis, Göttingen, 1968.

Mahdavi, Shiren, 'Muhammad Baqir Majlisi, Family values and the Safavids', in Michel Mazzaoui (ed.), *Safavid Iran and her Neighbours*, University of Utah Press, 2003.

Matthee, Rudi, *The Politics of Trade in Safavid Iran: Silk for Silver, 1600–1730*, Cambridge University Press, 1999.

Matthee, Rudi, 'Anti-Ottoman Concerns and Caucasian Interests: Diplomatic Relations between Iran and Russia, 1587–1639', in Michel Mazzaoui (ed.), *Safavid Iran and her Neighbours*, University of Utah Press, 2003.

Matthee, Rudi, 'Unwalled Cities and Restless Nomads: Firearms and Artillery in Safavid Iran', in C. Melville (ed.), *Safavid Persia: The History and Politics of an Islamic Society*, I.B.Tauris, London, 1996.

McChesney, R.D., 'Four Sources on Shah Abbas's Building of Isfahan', *Muqarnas*, 5, 1988.

McChesney, R.D., 'Barrier of Heterodoxy? Rethinking the Ties Between Iran and Central Asia in the 17th Century', in C. Melville (ed.), *Safavid Persia: The History and Politics of an Islamic Society*, I.B.Tauris, London, 1996.

Melikoff, Irène, 'Le Problème Kizilbas', *Turkica*, 1975.

Melville, Charles, 'From Qars to Qandahar: the itineraries of Shah Abbas I (993–1038/1587–1629)', in *Études Safavides*, ed. Jean Calmard, Paris/Tehran, 1993.

Melville, Charles, 'Shah Abbas: the Pilgrimage to Mashhad', in C. Melville (ed.), *Safavid Persia: The History and Politics of an Islamic Society*, I.B.Tauris, London, 1996.

Moreen, Vera B., 'The Persecution of Iranian Jews during the Reign of Shah Abbas II (1642–1666)', *Hebrew Union College Annual*, Vol. LII, Cincinnati, 1981.

Morton, A.H., 'The Ardabil Shrine in the Reign of Shah Tahmasp I', in *Iran, Journal of the British Institute of Persian Studies*, 12, 1974; 13, 1975.

Morton, A.H., 'The clūb-i tarīq and Qizilbash ritual in Safavid Persia', in Jean Calmard (ed.), *Études Safavides*, Paris/Tehran, 1993.

Morton, A.H., 'The Early Years of Shah Isma'il in the Afzal al-Tavarikh and Elsewhere', in C. Melville (ed.), *Safavid Persia: The History and Politics of an Islamic Society*, I.B.Tauris, London, 1996.

Nasr, Seyyed Hossein, 'Spiritual Movements, Philosophy and Theology in the Safavid Period', *Cambridge History of Iran*, Vol. 6.

Newman, Andrew, 'Towards a Reconsideration of the Esfahan School of Philosophy, Shaikh Baha'i and the Role of the Safawid Ulama', *Studia Iranica*, 15/2, 1986.

Newman, Andrew, 'The nature of the Akhbari/Usuli dispute in late Safavid Iran', in *Bulletin of the School of Oriental and African Studies*, LV/I, 1992.

Newman, Andrew, J., 'The Myth of the Clerical Migration to Safavid Iran', *Die Welt des Islams*, 33, 1993.

Newman, Andrew, *Safavid Iran: Rebirth of a Persian Empire*, I.B.Tauris, 2006.

Newman, Andrew, 'Mir Damad', *Encyclopaedia Iranica*.

Oberling, P., 'Georgians and Circassians in Iran', *Studia Caucasica*, I, 1963.

Palombini, Barbara von, *Buendniswerben Abendländischer Mächte um Persien 1453–1600*, Freiburger Islamstudien, Wiesbaden, 1968.

Papazian, H., 'Armenia and Iran. vi. Armeno-Iranian Relations in the Islamic Period', *Encyclopaedia Iranica*.

Parizi, Muhammad Ibrahim, *Siyasat va Iqtisad-e Asr-e Safavi*, Tehran, 1969.

Penrose, Boies, *The Sherleian Odyssey*, Taunton, 1938.

Perry, John, 'Forced Migration in Iran during the Seventeenth and Eighteenth Centuries', *Iranian Studies*, Vol. 8, 1975.

Quinn, Sholeh, *Historical Writing during the Reign of Shah Abbas: Ideology. Imitation and Legitimacy in Safavid Chronicles*, University of Utah Press, 2000.

Rabino di Borgomale, H.L., 'Les Dynasties Locales du Gilan et du Daylam', *Journal Asiatique*, 1949.

Rahman, F., *The Philosophy of Mulla Sadra*, Albany, 1975.

Reid, James, 'The Qajar Uymaq in the Safavid Period, 1500–1722', *Iranian Studies*, Vol. 11, 1978.

Roemer, Claudia, 'Die Osmanische Belagerung Bagdads 1034–35/1625–26', *Der Islam*, 1989.

Roemer, Hans Robert, 'Die Türkmenischen Qïzïlbaš, Gründer und Opfer der Safawidischen Theokratie', in *Zeitschrift der Deutschen Morgenländischen Gesellschaft*, 2, 1985.

Roemer, Hans Robert, *Persien auf dem Weg in die Neuzeit. Iranische Geschichte von 1350–1750*, Beirut, 1989.

Röhrborn, Klaus Michael, *Provinzen und Zentralgewalt Persiens im 16 und 17 Jahrhundert*, Berlin, 1966.

Ross, E. Denison, 'The Early Years of Shah Isma'il, Founder of the Safavi Dynasty', *Journal of the Royal Asiatic Society*, 1896.

Ross, Sir E. Denison, *Sir Anthony Sherley and His Persian Adventure*, London, 1933.

'Safavids', *Encyclopaedia of Islam*, 2nd edition.

Sarwar, Ghulam, *History of Shah Isma'il Safavi*, Muslim University, Aligarh, 1939.

Savory, Roger, 'The Principal Offices of the Safavid State during the Reign of Ismail I (907–30/1501–24)', *Bulletin of the School of Oriental and African Studies*, XXIII, London, 1960.

Savory, Roger, 'The Sherley Myth', *Iran, Journal of the British Institute of Persian Studies*, V, London, 1967.

Savory, Roger, *Iran under the Safavids*, Cambridge University Press, 1980.

Savory, Roger, 'Qizilbash', *Encyclopaedia of Islam*, 2nd edition.

Skelton, Robert, 'Ghiyath al-Din 'Ali-yi Naqshband and an episode in the Life of Sadiqi Beg', in Steensgaard, Niels, *Carracks, Caravans and Companies: The Structural Crisis in the European-Asian Trade in the early 17th Century*, Scandinavian Institute of Asian Studies, Monograph Series No. 17, 1973.

Sohrweide, Hanna, 'Der Sieg der Safawiden in Persien und seine Rückwirkingen auf die Shi'iten Anatoliens in 16 Jahrhundert', *Der Islam*, 1965.

Spicehandler, Ezra, 'The Persecution of the Jews of Isfahan under Shah Abbas II (1642–1666)', *Hebrew Union College Annual*, 1975.

Steensgaard, Niels, *Carracks, Caravans and Companies: The Structural Crisis in the European-Asian Trade in the early 17th Century*, Scandinavian Institute of Asian Studies, Monograph Series No. 17, 1973.

Stevens, Sir Roger, 'Robert Sherley: The Unanswered Questions', in *Iran*, 1979.

Subrahmanyan, Sanjay, *The Portuguese Empire in Asia*, Longman, 1993.

Suny, Ronald Grigor, *The Making of the Georgian Nation*, I.B.Tauris, 1988.

Szuppe, Maria, 'La Participation des Femmes de la Famille Royale à l'Exercice du Pouvoir en Iran Safavide au XVIe Siècle', Part I: *Studia Iranica*, 1994; Part II: *Studia Iranica*, 1995.

Tapper, Richard, *Frontier Nomads of Iran: a political and social history of the Shahsevan*, Cambridge University Press, 1997.

Vermeulen, U., 'L'Ambassade Persane de Musa Beg aux Provinces-Unies (1625–1628)', *Persica*, 7, 1978.

Welch, Anthony, *Shah Abbas and the Arts of Isfahan*, New York, 1973.

Welch, Anthony, *Artists for the Shah: Late Sixteenth-Century Painting at the Imperial Court of Iran*, New Haven and London, Yale University Press, 1976.

Wilber, Donald, *Persian Gardens and Garden Pavilions*, Vermont, 1962.

Willan, T.S., *The Early History of the Russia Company 1553–1603*, Manchester, 1956.

Wilson, Arnold T., *The Persian Gulf: An Historical Sketch from the Earliest Times to the Beginning of the Twentieth Century* (Oxford, 1928).

Iranian Primary Sources

Afushtah'i Natanzi, Mahmud, *Nuqavat al-Asar fi Zikr al-Akhyar*, ed. Eshraqi, Tehran, 1971.

'Aqa'id al-Nisa, *The Customs and Manners of the Women of Persia*, translated by James Atkinson, London, 1832.

Don Juan of Persia: A Shi'ah Catholic 1560–1604, translated and edited with an introduction by G. Le Strange, The Broadway Travellers, Routledge, London, 1926.

Eskandar Beg Munshi, *Tarikh-e Alam-Ara-ye Abbasi*, translated by Roger M. Savory (*The History of Shah Abbas the Great*), Boulder, CO.

Fazlullah b. Ruzbihan Khunji Isfahani, *Tarikh-e Alam-Ara-ye Amini*, Persian text edited by John E. Woods with abridged English translation by Vladimir Minorsky, *Persia in AD 1478–1490*, Royal Asiatic Society, 1992.

Khwandamir, Ghiyas al-Din, *Habib al-Siyar*, J. Kumai (ed.), 4 vols, 3rd edition. Tehran, 1362AH. Tome Three, *The Reign of the Mongol and the Turk*, Part Two: *Shahrukh Mirza to Shah Isma'il*, translated and edited by W.M. Thackston, Harvard, 1994.

Qummi, Qazi Ahmad, *Khulasat al-Tavarikh*, Dr Ehsan Eshraqi (ed.), 2 vols, Tehran, 1984; translated and edited by Hans Müller as *Die Chronik Hulasat at-Tavarih des Qazi Ahmad Qumi: Der Abschnitt über Schah Abbas I*, Akademie der Wissenschaften under der Literatur Veröffentlichungen der orientalischen Kommission, Vol. 14, Franz Steiner, Wiesbaden, 1964.

Rettelbach, Gerhard, *Khulasat As-Siyar. Der Iran Unter Schah Safi (1629–1642) Nach Der Chronik des Muhammad Ma'sūm Khuājagī Isfahānī*, Munich, 1978.

Rumlu, Hasan, *Ahsanu't-Tavarikh*, translated by C.N. Seddon, Oriental Institute, Baroda, 1934.

Tadhkirat al-Muluk, *A manual of Safavid administration*, translated and explained by V. Minorsky (Luzac & Co., London, 1943).

Yazdi, Jalal al-Din Munajjim, *Tarikh-i Abbasi ya Ruzanamah-i Mulla Jalal*, Sayf Allah (ed.), Vahid Niya, Tehran, 1987.

European Primary Sources

The Book of Duarte Barbosa: An Account of the Countries Bordering on the Indian Ocean and their Inhabitants, written by Duarte Barbosa, and completed about AD 1518. Translated from the Portuguese by Mansel Longworth Dames, Vol. I, Hakluyt Society, 1918.

Bull, George, *Travels of Pietro Della Valle* (Hutchinson, London, 1989).

A Chronicle of the Carmelites in Persia, London, 1939.

Don Juan of Persia: a Shi'ah Catholic 1560–1604, translated and edited with an introduction by G. Le Strange, The Broadway Travellers, Routledge, London, 1926.

Cartwright, John, *The Preachers Travels*, London, 1611.

Figueroa, Don Garcia, *L'Ambassade de D. Garcias de Silva Figueroa en Perse*, Paris, 1667.

Fryer, John, *A New Account of East India and Persia being Nine Years' Travels 1672–1681*, The Hakluyt Society, London, 1912.

Gouvea, Anthoine Di (Antonio De Gouvea), *Relation des Grandes Guerres et Victoires Obtenues par Le Roy de Perse Chah Abbas contre Les Empereurs de Turquie Mahomet Et Achmet son Fils En Suite du Voyage de Quelques Religieux de l'Ordre des Hermites de S. Augustin envoyez en Perse par le Roy Catholique Dom Philippe Second Roy de Portugal*, Rouen, 1646.

Grey, Charles (ed.), *A Narrative of Italian Travels in Persia in the 15th and 16th centuries*, Hakluyt Society, 1873.

Herbert, Thomas, *Travels in Persia 1627–29*, London, 1928.

Kaempfer, Engelbert, *Am Hofe des Persischen Grosskönigs*, ed. Walther Hinz, Horst Erdmann Verlag, 1977.

Krusinski, Judas Thaddaeus, *The History of the Late Revolutions of Persia*, London, 1733.

Langlès, L., *Voyages du Chevalier Chardin en Perse et autres Lieux de l'Orient*, Nouvelle Édition, 10 vols, Paris, 1811.

Le Bruyn, Cornelius, *Travels into Muscovy, Persia and part of the East Indies*, translated from the original Dutch, London, 1737.

Membré, Michele, *Mission to the Lord Sophy of Persia (1539–1542)*, translated with an introduction and notes by A.H. Morton, SOAS, 1993.

Minadoi, Giovanni, *The History of the Wars between the Turks and the Persians*, translated into English by Abraham Hartwell, London, 1595.

Morgan, E. Delmar and Coote, C.H. (eds), *Early Voyages and Travels to Russia and Persia by Anthony Jenkinson and other Englishmen*, New York, 1963.

Olearius, Adam, *Moskowitische und Persische Reise*, Rütten & Loening, Berlin, 1959.

Pinkerton, John, 'Extracts from the Travels of Pietro Della Valle in Persia', in *A General Collection of the best and most interesting Voyages and Travels in all parts of the World*, Vol. IX, London, 1811.

Raphaël du Mans, *Estat de la Perse en 1660*, L'Harmattan, Paris, 1995.

Sanson, Nicolas, *The Present State of Persia*, London, 1695.

Sherley, Anthony, 'A brief Compendium of the History of Sir Anthony Sherley's Travels into Persia: And employed thence Ambassador to the Christian Princes; penned by himself, and recommended to his brother Sir Robert Sherley, since that sent on like Ambassage by the King of Persia', in *Purchas His Pilgrimes, The Second Part*, London, 1625.

Stanley of Alderley, Lord, *Travels to Tana and Persia by Josafa Barbaro and Ambrogio Contarini*, Hakluyt Society, 1873.

Tavernier, Jean-Baptiste, *Voyages en Perse*, Club des Librairies de France, 1964.

Tectander, Georg, *Eine Abenteuerliche Reise Durch Russland Nach Persien 1602–1604*, Herausgegeben von Dorothea Mueller-Ott, Tulln, 1978.

Thévenot, Jean de, *The Travels of Monsieur Jean de Thévenot, Newly done out of the French*, London, 1687.

Index

1. Engraving of the first Safavid ruler, Shah Ismail I. German school, 1557.

Massagetæ Cyro nocuere, Scythæque Dareio:
Turca tibi nocuit, sed Scytha cessit ABAS.

ANTONI Orator Persæ, Angliæ, regis, ad illud

2. Above left: Engraving by Domenicus Custos of Shah Abbas I, praising him for his victories over the Ottomans and comparing him to Cyrus the Great. Augsburg, 1602.

3. Above right: Engraving of Anthony Sherley, possibly by Domenicus Custos, early seventeenth century.

4. Below: The Chahar Bagh Avenue in Isfahan. Engraving by the Dutch artist and traveller, Cornelis de Bruin, who was in Isfahan from 1703 to 1704.

5. Above: The shrine of Imam Riza in Mashhad. The dome over the tomb chamber in the centre was decorated with gold tiles by Shah Abbas.

6. Right: The Italian traveller, Pietro Della Valle, taken from 'Viaggi', his account of his stay in Iran (1617–22).

7. Ceremonial departure from Isfahan of Shah Sulaiman I (H) and his grand vizier (i) for the Festival of Sacrifice (*Eid-e Qurban*) outside the city. Engraving by Engelbert Kaempfer, who spent over four years in Iran (1683–88) during the reign of Shah Sulaiman.

8. The interior of the dome of the Sheikh Lutfallah Mosque in Isfahan.

9. The Ali Qapu ('Lofty Gate'), which was the main entrance to the palace complex in Isfahan.

10. Shah Sultan Husain, the last ruler of Safavid Iran. Engraving by the Dutch artist and traveller, Cornelis de Bruin.

11. Tradesmen's tents in the Royal Square in Isfahan. Engraving by Cornelis de Bruin.

1. Shah Abbas (centre with purple hat) receiving the Moghul ambassador, Khan Alam. Painting by the Moghul artist Bishan Das, c.1619.

3. Shah Abbas with a gun.
Contemporary Safavid painting from
an eighteenth-century Moghul Album.

2. Fritware tile panel, which originally covered the lower part of a wall, probably in a palace in Isfahan. Period of Shah Abbas.

4. Drawing of a calligrapher by Riza Abbasi, Isfahan, c.1600. The shah's royal seal is at the bottom right-hand corner.

5. Above: Meidan-e Shah (the Royal Square) in Isfahan, now renamed Meidan-e Imam. The dome of the Sheikh Lutfallah Mosque is on the left and the portal and minarets of the Royal Mosque, the Masjid-e Shah, now renamed the Masjid-e Imam, can be seen at the far end of the square.

6. Below: The Interior of the Royal Mosque in Isfahan.

7. A sample of nastaliq script for collection in an album by the Iranian calligrapher, Abd al-Rashid Daylami (d.1670). He emigrated to India, where he held high office at the Moghul court, after his uncle, the calligrapher Mir Imad Qazvini, was murdered on the orders of Shah Abbas.

8. **Above left:** Portrait of a European, probably by Riza Abbasi. Gouache heightened with gold on paper.

9. **Above right:** A falconer by Riza Abbasi, late sixteenth century.

10. **Right:** Sir Robert Sherley (1581–1628) in Persian costume by Sir Anthony van Dyck (1599–1641), Petworth House, The Egremont Collection (acquired in lieu of tax by H.M.Treasury in 1957 and subsequently transferred to The National Trust).

11. **Above:** The Allahvirdi Khan Bridge over the Zayandeh River in Isfahan. The river is virtually dry in the summer.

12. **Below:** One of the pigeon towers outside Isfahan. The pigeon dung was used as fertiliser. There were more than 3,500 such towers around the city in Safavid times.

13. Shah Abbas portrayed on a late nineteenth-century 'Mohtashem' rug from Kashan in central Iran.

CPSIA information can be obtained
at www.ICGtesting.com
Printed in the USA
LVHW080958291220
675315LV00012B/232